Elephant Baseball is an exploration of the universal trials of adolescence, experienced in a most unique and formative setting—one that also shaped my own life. Paul Heusinkveld's vivid recollections of life at the Kodaikanal School remind us that the world is big and diverse, but that making a difference in it is as easy as guiding one person down a path of service.

Chris Van Hollen,
United States Senator and former Kodaikanal School student

Missionary literature is replete with the record of service and sacrifice. Seldom mentioned are the associated experiences of the children of these dedicated Christians. Heusinkveld records with remarkable sensitivity the fears and triumphs of a child separated from parents for nine months each year. While the locale is exotic, and the time past, the reader will resonate with many of those emotions. As the author approaches adulthood, tremendous loss is experienced. The eventual transcendence of that loss brings the account without self-pity, self-congratulation, or moralizing, to a deeply satisfying and even triumphant conclusion.

Dennis Voskuil,
Western Theological Seminary President Emeriitus

Elephant Baseball takes you on a journey to a small village high in the Palni Hills, into the world of a group of young boys coping with life in a strict Christian boarding school, far away from their families. Paul Heusinkveld has opened that world for us, providing a fascinating glimpse and an empathetic tale of their tribulations and triumphs, their pleasures and their pains. As a boy who went to Kodai myself at roughly the same time, I was carried back as I read the stories, as if I were experiencing them again. Heusinkveld has an amazing ability to evoke the essence of the place, the sounds and smells and sights, as well as the thoughts and feelings of the boys. His memory of the people and events, his gift for story-telling, and the heart-rending experiences he and the boys were going through give the narrative a texture and flow that makes it difficult to put the book down.

Thomas Staal,
United States Agency for International Development

More commendations or

ELEPHANT BASEBALL

THE HISTORICAL SERIES OF THE REFORMED CHURCH IN AMERICA
NO. 88

ELEPHANT BASEBALL
A Missionary Kid's Tale

Paul Heusinkveld

Artwork by Bruce Peck

WILLIAM B. EERDMANS PUBLISHING COMPANY
Grand Rapids, Michigan / Cambridge, UK

Wm. B. Eerdmans Publishing Co.
2140 Oak Industrial Drive SE, Grand Rapids, Michigan 49505

Cambridge CB3 9PU UK
www.eerdmans.com

Printed in the United States of America
Second printing, 2017

Library of Congress Cataloging-in-Publication Data

Names: Heusinkveld, Paul, 1950- author.
Title: Elephant baseball : a missionary kid's tale / Paul Heusinkveld ;
    artwork by Bruce Peck.
Description: Grand Rapids : Eerdmans Publishing Co., 2017. | Series:
The historical series of the Reformed Church in America ; no. 88 |
Includes index.
Identifiers: LCCN 2016053090 | ISBN 9780802875501 (pbk. : alk.
paper)
Subjects: LCSH: Heusinkveld, Paul, 1950- | Children of
    missionaries--India--Kodaikanal--Biography.
Classification: LCC BV2094.5.H48 A3 2017 | DDC 266/.57092 [B]
--dc23 LC record available at https://lccn.loc.gov/2016053090

For Holly "Tegan" Heusinkveld,
my daughter,
who more than anyone
needs to know.

The Historical Series of the Reformed Church in America

The series was inaugurated in 1968 by the General Synod of the Reformed Church in America acting through the Commission on History to communicate the church's heritage and collective memory and to reflect on our identity and mission, encouraging historical scholarship which informs both church and academy.

www.rca.org/series

General Editor
> Rev. Donald J. Bruggink, PhD, DD
> Western Theological Seminary
> Van Raalte Institute, Hope College

Associate Editor
> James Hart Brumm, MDiv
> Blooming Grove, New York
> New Brunswick Theological Seminary

Copy Editor
> Laurie Baron
> Holland, Michigan

Production Editor
> Russell L. Gasero
> Archives, Reformed Church in America

Commission on History
> James Hart Brumm, MDiv, Blooming Grove, New York
> Lynn Japinga, PhD, Hope College
> David M. Tripold, PhD, Monmouth University
> Douglas Van Aartsen, MDiv, Ireton, IA
> Matthew Van Maastricht, MDiv, Milwaukee, Wisconsin
> Linda Walvoord, PhD, University of Cincinnati

Contents

Acknowledgments

The continuous encouragement and editing from my dear friend, Donald Luidens, professor emeritus of sociology at Hope College in Holland, Michigan, made this book possible. Like me, Don grew up as a missionary child in Arabia and attended Kodai School in southern India. This familiarity, as well as his gift with the written word, his insights into the life of adolescents, and his understanding of foreign cultures are priceless contributions for which I am deeply thankful.

I also deeply appreciate that fellow Kodai School classmate, Bruce Peck, has graciously permitted me to use his etchings, which evoke the adventurous, mysterious, romantic, exotic India we knew.

Bruce, the son of missionaries to India, is an award winning print maker specializing in etchings of India and New England. As part of the Cultural Exchange Through the Visual Arts Program of the Department of State, his artwork is on display at U.S. Embassies. His portfolio can be seen on www.brucepecketchings. com. He and his wife Ann split their years between Topsham, Vermont, and Kodaikanal, India. Bruce and Ann are committed to bettering the lives of Indian children through the work of Kids Health India, whose work can be seen on KidshealthIndia.org.

Foreword

Donald A. Luidens

As its unorthodox title would suggest, *Elephant Baseball* is not a typical offering of the Reformed Church Historical Series. It has few footnotes. It is rife with dialogue and embedded short stories. It luxuriates in narrative fluidity. It conjures up a time and place more akin to Rudyard Kipling's *Kim* than to modern "objective" or "historic" tomes. Its tales are true in the deepest sense of touching something at the core of our humanity; and, to the best of the author's recollection, they happened as they are described.

Since the heyday of world missions in the mid-nineteenth century, the Reformed Church has been a significant player in outreach to non-Christians around the world. Beginning in China, India, and the Arabian Gulf, RCA missionaries have scattered across the globe. That is a rich and lasting story which has justly demanded academic recording and faithful promoting.

The RCA Historical Series has been at the heart of that enterprise. It has published a score of memoirs and scholarly accounts of individual and collective missionaries' work throughout the world.

Yet, there is a hidden side to mission work that has received scant attention. When one considers that most RCA missionaries have been family units, and when one considers that most RCA missionary families include several children, one can begin to comprehend the extent of the hidden component of mission life. The work and lives of the adult missionaries are due and have received careful scrutiny. Yet, the lives of the other – the unwitting, often unwilling – members of the mission community, have been virtually ignored. What of the children of missionary parents? What is life in the mission world like for this underreported constituency? How do they cope with their ambiguous positions between starkly contrasting worlds? How do they relate to parents who are thoroughly absorbed in "the Lord's work," often to the neglect of their own progeny? How does forced and prolonged removal from hearth and home echo in the depths of their lives?

Enter *Elephant Baseball*.

Author Paul Heusinkveld, along with countless other offspring of missionary families, was plucked from the loving, embracing arms of his missionary parents and thrust pell-mell into the midst of a youthful subculture teeming with Harry Potter-esque tangles and twists. At the tender age of ten, he followed his older brothers to boarding school. But this was no mere bus ride away from home. In January, 1961, Paul left the familiarity of his home in Bahrain, trekked 2,500 miles over the Indian Ocean and across the Indian subcontinent to Kodaikanal in southern India. Car, boat, plane, train, and bus each took him farther from home and all that he knew and loved.

In "Kodai" he enrolled at Highclerc School, a boarding academy for missionary children ("mish kids," as they were fond of calling themselves) from as far away as Iraq, Burma, East and West Pakistan, and Ceylon. He soon learned that he was an "Arab," a member of a subgroup who could converse in Arabic together, just as the "Burmese" and "Pakistanis" could converse among themselves in their own dialects. Language affinities were just one of several dividing lines which ran through the campus. Boys and girls were judiciously housed on different sides of the campus; elementary, middle, and high school youth were rigidly stratified; and as an incoming fifth grader, Paul found himself on the lowest rung of the ladder. Despite these divisions, almost all the students were Americans and were encouraged to celebrate their "native" land. Fire crackers on the Fourth of July, Thanksgiving turkey on the appointed day, and the ritual raising of the American and Indian flags each morning all served as dissonant harmonies for these "Arabs," "Burmese," and "Indians."

Elephant Baseball is a story of one boy's struggle to comprehend who he was becoming in this world between worlds. Neither fully American nor fully Arab or Indian, he grew to selectively identify with what he found most appealing from his rich tapestry of experiences. In this poignant retelling of his youthful years, Paul is alternatingly funny, heart-warming, and heart-rending. His remarkable memory for details and for the people who crossed his path makes them come vividly to life in his compelling narrative.

Elephant Baseball is one person's recollection, yet it is emblematic of the lives which countless mish kids – the present commentator included – shared in the shadow of our missionary parents. While our parents' stories are unquestionably powerful and noteworthy legacies, the hidden story of their children has too often been forgotten. With *Elephant Baseball*, this hidden story is reclaimed and comes vibrantly back to life.

Kodai Lake with Perumal Mountain in background

Prologue

I wake well before sunrise, so early that even the loud-mouthed, insomniac rooster is still asleep. With my teacher, Mr. Reimer, and my seventeen-year-old classmates Peck, Fletch, and Zorn, I catch a ride on a passing lorry. I don't ask what a lorry is doing on these roads this early in the morning; I'm just grateful for the lift as we head off on our hiking adventure. We ride in the truck as it struggles over twisting, high mountain roads, heading to the top of a craggy escarpment which overlooks Manjampatti—a huge game reserve lying deep in the valley below.

Crammed in the flatbed of the truck, we huddle together against the frigid morning air that rips through our clothes, extracting degrees from our body heat. The world is pitch black except for the shifting patch of winding pavement that the headlights illuminate. Only the noise of the engine breaks the utter stillness.

Slowly, a widening red band breaks through the darkness on the eastern horizon. At Manamanure we jump off the truck and wave our good-byes to the driver. As if mimicking its name, the air of this place smells of horse droppings. We're on the outskirts of a small, dusty village part way down a South Indian mountainside. Electricity hasn't made it this far into the hinterlands in the late 1960s, so the town is still wrapped in slumber.

As the sun rises, it seems I can see forever in the clear mountain air, and there is no other sign of humanity besides the sleeping village. By the time we finish stretching our legs and relieving ourselves on the side of the road, there's enough light to make out our intended path. We're heading down to Manjampatti, Elephant Valley, which lies in a shadowy void below us, surrounded on three sides by thrusting mountain slopes. Humans rarely visit the secluded valley and nature reserve of Manjampatti; our small group will be the only people in the valley. It's a hiking adventure of a lifetime.

As dawn breaks we begin the five-thousand-foot descent on foot, plunging down the mountainside in great bursts of energy. We can feel the temperature rise and the humidity grow clammy during our descent. The climate contrasts sharply and unfavorably with the clear, cool air higher up. Following paths that grow smaller and smaller, dwindling to almost nothing, we find ourselves wading through vast expanses of waist-high grass. Gusts of wind sweep across the blades, making the grasslands look like the ocean's surface being tossed about. Copses of higher shrubs, scattered here and there, are little islands floating in this wind-swept sea.

We stumble across a yard-wide path of matted grass, so flat and level that I imagine a steamroller has passed through here.

"What could have made this?" I ask Peck.

"Oh, that's the trail of a large python," he replies nonchalantly.

The back of my neck tingles as I imagine beady eyes peering through the meadow at me. I picture a serpent waiting to wrap itself around my waist and swallow me whole. Spooked, I step more cautiously. But I'm excited at the same time. We're heading into a remote valley where wild elephants still roam. From time to time we pass signs of elephants—including gross piles of dried dung—but we haven't spotted any of the behemoths by the time we reach the valley floor.

Here, the ground is parched and the plants look emaciated compared to the lushness of higher altitudes. We are so tired from the early rising and the exhausting descent that we agree to nap for a while before setting out again. Gratefully, we all stretch out on a rocky outcropping in the shade of a huge tree growing next to a fast-moving stream. The rhythm of the babbling brook is soothing, and I'm out like a light.

I'm awakened by Fletch yelling, "Let's play elephant baseball!"

I'd never heard of elephant baseball, but it doesn't take me long to figure out what's involved. Fletch is waving a large stick, and Peck has a greenish, softball-sized orb in his hands. It's elephant scat, the tightly knit dropping of a passing beast. When hit, the "ball" shatters into an odorous cloud of grass, leaves, and twigs. Peck pitches and Fletch happily swings away, scattering scat all over the place. I can hardly contain myself I'm laughing so loudly.

The novelty of the game is intoxicating. I tremble with excitement as we play with utter abandonment, oblivious to its impact on the clothes we're wearing—all we have for the next three days. My hair, my clothes, and my nose are permeated by elephant dung dust. It's exhilarating!

Afterwards, when most of our adrenaline has been used up, we dive into the frigid stream to wash the dung from our bodies. The cool, mountain water works its magic on us. Before long, we are renewed enough to resume our elephant hunt, tracing larger and larger circles around our improvised campsite. Despite searching all afternoon, we fail to see even one elephant.

Returning to camp at dusk, we cook supper over wood gathered from the forest ringing our search area. In the glow of the campfire, watching its embers flicker and spark, we tell stories late into the night. It becomes so dark that the stars stand out like sparkling crystal. Their constant flickering, like that of our campfire, keeps me mesmerized. I pick out occasional satellites, one of which does a U-turn. I don't know how this is possible, but that is what I see. Perhaps it's an airplane. I can't imagine why a plane would be flying over this remote area of India in the middle of the night.

Something happens as I lie there, gazing into the heavens. I feel something deep, metaphysical, soul-touching. I'm convinced that what I'm sensing is integral to human experience. It's what my ancestors must have felt as they looked into the clear, starry host for thousands of years. I sense some kind of spiritual awakening going on in me, something far bigger than I am and yet something that is part of me. Whatever is happening, it touches all the way from heaven to the core of my being. I feel incredible elation. I'm part of all this and it is part of me.

I wake in the middle of the night, roused by the sound of the whistling wind. The sun stopped heating the plains hours ago, and now the cold air from the mountains is tumbling down the mountainsides, rushing through the open expanses of tall, wild grass and playing an entrancing tune. It lulls me back to sleep.

When morning comes, I can hardly get up because my feet hurt from yesterday's hiking. But I resolve to ignore the pain, bolt down breakfast, and set out with my companions to catch a sleeping elephant. We are excited because just twenty feet from our campsite there is fresh, steaming elephant spoor. The steam indicates that the elephant had been there within the last fifteen minutes. We are amazed that a two-ton elephant could have crept up on us and checked us out without our being aware of its presence.

Despite our enthusiastic efforts, we return in late morning without having sighted the pachyderm. After lunch and another swim, we again rest by the stream. Exhausted, I pull my sore feet out of my boots, take off my socks, and lie down under a tree. I sleep so soundly I don't notice the changing angle of the sun. With its movement across the sky, my feet emerge from the shade. After two hours, I awake to discover the tops of my feet are baked a deep scarlet. Nevertheless, we resume our elephant hunt.

In the late afternoon we ascend a hill to get a commanding view of the area, but even from that lofty perch we fail to see any elephants. Disappointed once again, we decide to head back toward camp, with Mr. Reimer well in the lead. Rounding a clump of tall bamboo, Mr. Reimer sees a huge tusker right in front of him. Warily he backtracks to find us, cautioning us to be quiet and watch our steps. We can hear a herd of elephants bellowing back and forth, crashing through the undergrowth. They sound as though they are right in our intended path, so we proceed with care. Although sighting elephants is the very reason we launched this three-day expedition, I hold back, praying for safety: "Dear Lord, please don't let us be stomped to death." We inch forward, mindful that a whole herd of elephants would likely include young ones, always a dangerous situation for intruders.

My heart is pounding, and I don't know if I'm more scared or more thrilled with the excitement of our precarious situation. Either way, this is where I'm meant to be, and this is where I want to be. We wait until it's quiet, by which time the elephants have left the area. Once again, we have failed to see them, but we were close. By the dim light of the stars we thread our way back to camp. For our safety, Mr. Reimer moves our camp to an abandoned ranger's hut that has a trench around it to keep elephants from getting too close.

It's Saturday evening, so Mr. Reimer conducts a short worship service. We won't have time for one tomorrow, and he feels obliged to ensure our spiritual needs are not forgotten, even on a camping trip. I welcome the service, since the near life-threatening encounter with the elephant herd has left me scared and in need of calming down.

After prayers, we sit around the campfire and reflect on our day.

"Well, maybe tomorrow you will see an elephant too," Mr. Reimer consoles us, reminding us that he was the only one who actually spotted our quarry. Under the circumstances, I'm not sure I want to see any elephants. But Mr. Reimer isn't done with his reassuring comments. "In any case, we've seen bison, tiger prints in mud, shed skins of snakes—including that of a king cobra—and gliding lizards. Maybe tomorrow you'll get to see one of the elusive jungle people who live in the valley. They have had virtually no contact with modern man." This startling prediction gets our attention. We spend the rest of the evening speculating about this primitive human species that supposedly live in trees and are unrelated to the local Tamil population.

I sleep well, but in the morning, wake to find the tops of my feet are covered with huge, bright red blisters. The pain is almost unbearable.

"Hey, I've got second degree burns on the top of my feet."

"That's the dumbest thing I've ever heard!"

I limp around showing off my bizarre feet, begging for sympathy. I don't get any.

"Guys, I gotta do something about my feet, they really hurt."

Finally, Mr. Reimer takes pity on me and cracks a coconut. "Here's some coconut oil to put on them. We don't have anything else." I slather thick gobs of coconut oil over my feet. I know that coconut oil is viewed as a universal cure-all in India, so hopefully it'll do some good for me.

By the time we break camp at mid-morning, the tops of my feet hurt so much I can't lace my boots. Nevertheless, I manfully hike back up the five-thousand-foot mountain trail, gripped by sheer agony. Helpfully, my buddies respond with laughter at all my pitiful complaints. In fact, as they retell each other the story of my stupidly falling asleep in the sun, even I begin to laugh. It helps to relieve the pain. A slimy mixture of blood and coconut oil oozes out from my shoes; it's enough to turn one's stomach and set off another round of belly laughs.

Other than the pain and the laughter, the trip back to school is a blur. There are no words to describe how happy I am to see my dormitory bed. After taking a shower and getting in bed, I refuse to hobble out for the rest of the day. People come to look at the carcass of my mangled feet, pointing and jeering.

"How could anyone hurt the tops of their feet on a hike?" I'm asked with incredulity. I know I'm a spectacle, so I laugh, too.

"Was the hike worth the pain?" Bugs asks.

"Yeah, I'd do it again tomorrow."

"But, you didn't see any elephants," Bugs protests.

"True, but I felt their presence and that's better than nothing. Besides, I played elephant baseball!" Bugs thinks the sun has affected my head, too.

But I know better.

Typical tea shop along an Indian road

CHAPTER 1

Getting There

My Mom and Dad are missionaries, and that makes all the difference.

Autumn's chill has just filled the air and made the lawn glisten with a covering of ice. It's late afternoon, and Mom is putting the finishing touches on our Thanksgiving feast. As I sit on the window seat, waiting for the arrival of our guests, the biting cold seeps through the misted windowpanes and chills my nose and ears. I can feel it wrapping my face as I peer out into the gloom.

"Do you see anyone coming?" Mom calls from the kitchen.

"Not yet!" I reply, wiping the window one more time.

I have grown comfortable with the happy pace of life in America. But I know all that is coming to an end. In the last couple of weeks, as we sat around the dinner table, Dad and Mom have dropped hints that we will soon leave Michigan and return to "the field." "The field" is what we call our overseas missionary assignment in Arabia, where we lived until a year ago. I know that when we return to "the field," I will be sent to boarding school in South India. Then my life will change forever!

Before we came to Michigan we lived in Iraq and Oman, where my parents were medical missionaries. Along with my older brothers, David and Terr, we came to the States in the summer of 1959 on furlough. "Furlough" is what we call not being on "the field." Because I had only lived in Arabia, coming to America was tough for me. There was much that was very new. I went to a formal school for the first time, spoke nothing but English (except to my brothers; we used Arabic so that no one else could understand us), and wore shoes all the time. I ate processed food, adjusted to cold winters and snow, watched television, and lived in the modern world. All of that was new to me, but I gradually grew to like the comforts of America. Now, I am not sure I want to return to Arabia.

Mom spent weeks getting things ready for Thanksgiving dinner. She invited a bunch of "mish kids"–that's what we call sons and daughters of missionary families–who are students in a nearby college. I know many of them, and of course Dave and Terr know all of them. Like me, they grew up in Arabia and India, and they went to the same boarding school that Dave and Terr attended. I am excited because I will soon be following in their footsteps. I am also a bit scared, because attending the boarding school means leaving home for nine months at a time and living with hundreds of strangers.

"They're here, Mom!" I cry out as the college students trudge up our footpath. There are hugs all around as my parents greet each one. "Hi, Uncle Maurie" and "Hi, Aunt Ellie," they respond. Of course Dad and Mom aren't really their uncle and aunt, but in the mission world, all adults are uncles and aunts for other mish kids. We're like an over-grown family with branches in many countries. I've always loved that.

"My goodness, Paulie, you've grown up since I saw you last!" Marilyn is a senior in college, and I haven't seen her for many years.

"I'm nine," I reply proudly and glare at Terr who still thinks of me as a little shrimp. "D'ja hear that, Terr? Marilyn thinks I've grown up!" Terr just stares back at me with a grin on his face. If I was bigger, I'd make him wipe that grin off.

Outside, the sun sets early on the November evening, trapping the glowing lights and cozy warmth inside. I'm eager to get started with supper. Mom's gigantic buffet includes platters of turkey, steaming mashed potatoes, and vegetables, all of which I am going to smother in gravy. Then I'll have rolls, cranberry sauce, and a piece of the fresh pie which I see on the sideboard.

After we've gathered around the table, we remain standing in a solemn circle as Dad gives the blessing.

We mish kids have come to expect that prayers will be long; we know that a long prayer is a good prayer, a sort of mini-sermon. And Dad delivers a lo-o-ong prayer. He covers major current news stories, comments on the need for Christians to provide service to the poor and needy, and praises the work of all missionaries, especially the parents of our guests. As he drones on, I peek through slit eyelids at the generous feast and silently pray that all the steam won't escape before we sit down. As much as I find Dad's prayers tedious, their familiarity warms my heart.

"Well, have you started to pack your suitcases yet?" someone asks. The words fall heavily on the lighthearted chatting, causing everyone to pause for a moment. We are all used to packing our suitcases and moving. That's a regular part of our lives. But that doesn't make it easier. I have become used to life in the States, and leaving it feels like something that should remain far in the future.

"Not yet, but we need to go soon," Dad replies in a manner that cuts short any further conversation along these lines. "Paul, please pass the peas for everyone."

After an awkward pause, we all return to eating good food and discussing other topics. Soon everyone is pleasantly full and tired enough to sit in overstuffed chairs and couches and mellow out. Some of the college boys watch a football game on the television or play board games. Mom plays the piano and accordion while a couple of girls sing along, to everyone's delight. There is a lot of casual talk about previous adventures and happy times in Arabia and India. I soak it all in, relishing every minute of it.

Chatter lasts until late into the dark autumn night. I try to pay attention as the mish kids describe their experiences in Arabia, India, and the mission field.

"But it can be lonely. Especially when we're in Kodai School," says Marilyn. Others mutter agreement, and all talk stops for a while. I can tell that each is thinking about being lonely, although I can't imagine Marilyn ever being lonely.

Then, to change the topic, someone points out how important Christian mission work is. A couple say they are thinking of becoming missionaries themselves. Dad talks for a long time with Lew, a college junior, who is wondering what to do with his life. Dad says he can relate to Lew's dilemma.

"I had some of the same questions about my future," I hear Dad admit. "Fourteen years ago I was given the book, *Whither Arabia?*, by an Arabian mission doctor. It changed my life and persuaded me to become a medical missionary. It's not an easy decision to make. I know your parents struggled with that choice, too." Dad rises and walks to a bookshelf, returning with a book for Lew. "Here's a volume which may be of interest to you, Lew. It may give you a sense of your vocation. Here, it's yours." I glance over Lew's shoulder and see that the title is *History of the Arabs*.

"Thanks," Lew responds. "I'll be sure to read it."

Two weeks later I wake up to hear that Dad has left for New York City.

"Your father has things to take care of," Mom explains off-handedly.

"What things?" I ask.

"Work things, preparations for our trip. It's complicated. Someday you'll understand."

I don't like the line, "Someday you'll understand." It usually means that I won't understand at all, and that I just have to accept it. It also means that no one is going to explain anything to me. Ever. But I suspect that this has something to do with returning to the field.

I suspect correctly. Soon, we follow Dad to New York City. The trip begins with bad weather, reminding me how miserable Michigan winters can be. I look forward to the heat of the desert, where snow never shows its bitter face. In the next week we fly to Europe and then to Kuwait, where we stay for Christmas with mission friends.

Even though it is winter, it is good to feel the familiar, mid-day warmth of the Arabian Desert. All the fun activities of Christmas—parties, colorful church services, festive meals, gifts—make for as good a Christmas as I can hope for. By the time Christmas is over, I have become close friends with Teddy, who will be in my grade in boarding school. He and his dog, Nejim, show me all over the mission compound. Teddy and I vow to be friends for life.

Two days after Christmas, we fly from Kuwait to our new home in Bahrain. As is the custom, most of the mission family comes out to the airport to meet us. It's good to see friendly faces again. We move into the Yateem House, right across the street from the American Mission Hospital where Dad and Mom will work. Mom hires Abbas to be our cook. He's a gifted cook and always manages to put together delicious meals, no matter how limited his ingredients may be. His only shortcoming is that he often shows up late, or some days not at all. Needless to say, this makes Mom unhappy and upsets her usual calm demeanor. Any interruption to the strict schedule our medical family follows can put her in a sour mood. I don't like it when Mom's upset!

Our next-door neighbors are Uncle Gerry and Aunt Rose Nykerk and their three children, David (whom we call just "Nykerk"), Nancy, and Laila. During the first week we are in Bahrain, Dave and Terr arrange to play tennis with Nykerk and Nancy. I eagerly volunteer to be the ball boy, chasing stray balls and avoiding being hit by fast shots. After the games are completed, Nykerk chugs down five bottles of Coke in a row. I can hardly believe it. This is an incredible gastronomic feat. More amazingly, Nykerk shows no concern about the cost of the soda. Nykerk is my instant hero!

It is fun being back in Arabia and on the mission compound again. This is my world; I know its sounds and rhythms. Five times a day the *muezzin* calls believers to pray. We can hear the calls coming from minarets all over the city. Throughout the day, we hear donkeys braying and their bells clanging and masters yelling at them. In the evening, Arab music on dozens of radios blends softly in the night air. Mealtime discussions in our household include talks about medical curiosities and about breaking news of local political events. Through the church services and mission parties, we build bonds with the other missionary families. I love all of it.

However, I know this calmness isn't going to last. We are barely settled in Bahrain when I have to prepare for boarding school. Clothes for a whole year have to be bought, sorted, labeled with my name tags, and folded. Suitcases have to be packed. I am proud of my brand new suitcase, which we bought in Europe on our way here and which still smells like leather.

The boarding school is located in Kodaikanal (or Kodai), in the mountains of South India, and it will take us many days to get there from Bahrain. Since the school year begins in January, we have arrived just in time to join the other mish kids in their annual trek to Kodai. I'll finish the last half of fifth grade and the first half of sixth in the coming school year. Dave and Terr have been through this before, so they know what has to be done and are eager to share the details with me. Sometimes their help comforts me and sometimes it scares me to death.

Mish kids from the other compounds–Kuwait, Oman, and Iraq–arrive in Bahrain in early January. It is my first time traveling with just a bunch of kids, and I wonder how we are going to survive without adults to look out for us. Nykerk, my hero, is our leader. There are twenty of us, including four who will be my classmates. Teddy is one of them.

Late on the night of January eighth, six cars carry us and our luggage to the airport. The caravan snakes through the narrow, winding streets of old town Bahrain. The silent, dimly lit, mud-walled houses under darkened skies make me feel sadder as I leave home and all that is familiar.

Dave leans over to whisper in my ears.

"You're about to enter a whole new world."

"Aren't we going to fly to India?" I ask, confused.

"This is a world which is run by kids," he replies, scaring me once again. "If you do what Nykerk and I tell you to do, you'll be fine." This comforts me a little. Nykerk, the oldest one in our gang, is only seventeen. He's in charge of all our passports, tickets, and money. Since he's my hero, I'll have no trouble doing what he says. Or what my big brother, Dave, says.

My first nasty experience with this new world comes quickly. When we get to the airport, the other kids smell the fresh leather of my new suitcase and make fun of it.

"D'jou get that from your Mommy?" one of them teases. "Only a newbie would bring a new suitcase to Kodai." I'm embarrassed. I just want to be one of the guys and not stand out in any way, but already I'm being picked on as a rookie.

As we walk out to the airplane, Mom gives me a big hug and kiss. "You be good, now, Paul," she whispers. That only makes me feel even more like a rookie.

But Dad firmly grips my hand in an adult-like way that is supposed to tell me that I'm a man. "Have a good year," he says gruffly. I can barely look into his eyes.

"I will, Dad."

I board the plane and take a window seat so that I can wave to my parents. They stand on the tarmac in their thick winter coats waving silently at the airplane. I don't think they see me. It's hard for me to see them through my tears. I feel like a lamb being led off to the slaughter. Dave puts his arm around my shoulders. "You'll be all right," he reassures me.

"When will we see them again?"

"They'll come to visit in May," he responds. Hardly encouraging news. May seems like an eternity away. The plane's huge engines roar to life, shaking the whole aircraft and drowning out any further conversation. In midnight's pitch black, I gloomily watch out the window as the lights on the ground became smaller and smaller, and we are swallowed into darkness.

Our journey to Kodai is an adventure, and I try to enjoy it. From Bahrain we fly to Delhi and then take a rickety, World War II, surplus DC-4 to Madras. Dave tells me that this heap is left over from planes which flew "the Gap" between India and China during the war. "To survive that action, it must be a strong machine," he reassures me. It strikes me that the crate is a worn-out pile of junk, stained by dark oil slicks streaming from its four huge piston engines. Every rivet, loose object, and panel rattles all the time. In the dark hours of night, I can see white flames spurt from the engines, and when daylight comes, blue smoke belches out. Since the plane is not pressurized, we fly low, which means we can't fly above the turbulence. As a result, it's a rough, vomit-producing ride. At least I wasn't one of the goof-ups who puked.

Madras is a brief stop in our trip. We spend the day swimming at a local pool and generally killing time. At last we head to the station to catch our night train to South India. While we wait, we have supper in the station's open air cafeteria. The food is flavored with a light dusting of rail yard soot that floats in through the windows. The dining area is dimly lit by a cheerless light bulb strung high above our heads. In the growing darkness, I can see ratty, half-starved crows watching us with their glassy black eyes. It turns out they are waiting for a moment when we're not paying attention to our plates. Suddenly, one of them swoops down and scoops up a beakful of food from my plate. I'm so startled, I don't have time to scare him away.

"Rookie!" Humiliated again.

At the edge of the shadows, a scrawny dog lies motionless, pretending to be asleep. Thanks to the thieving crow, I know that the dog is also watching through squinted eyes for anything that we might drop from our plates. I've learned my lesson, and I wolf down my food to protect it from other birds and dogs. I notice that everyone else is eating quickly, too. Did they know they should do that before the crow flew in?

After a while, we gather our bags and board the "Pandian Express." I look around for pictures of pandas, but there aren't any. Apparently this train isn't named after pandas. That makes sense, because pandas don't even grow in India, anyway. The older kids are calm about the upcoming trip, but I can't imagine anything more exciting than an overnight train ride across the plains of India. I try to control my enthusiasm so that I won't annoy the older kids. I've already learned that they seem happier when I don't say anything.

After we settle into our compartments, Nykerk allows us to wander on the platform beside the train as long as we promise to be on board when the engine's bell signals time for departure. He tells us that there will be multiple stops along the way, each providing an opportunity for us to get off and stretch for a few minutes or buy snacks and comic books. We stroll around the platform looking at various vendors. Two or three of us put our allowances together so we can buy the latest edition of Superman comics.

In the minutes before we leave, I visit the steam locomotive with some of the other boys. We stand under the open cab of the engine, chatting with the engineer and admiring the fierce power of iron and steam. The engineer's assistant runs around with his greasy oil can, squeezing out small drops of oil on various fittings and then throwing shovelfuls of coal into the firebox. Each time he opens the firebox cover, I can feel the violent heat of its raging fire.

But the engine is not so violent. There's something calming to me about the slow rhythm of a steam engine. Its thump-thump keeps pace with the beating of my heart. I like it much more than the shrill whine of airplane engines or the shrieking gears of buses. The engineer wears only thin clothing and drips a lot with sweat from the heat of the glowing firebox.

A few short whistles from the engine horn and a pleasing call from the conductor signal that it is time to depart. We climb up to our compartments as the train pulls out. I realize that we'll be stuck here until the next stop, because there is no passageway between the compartments. To cool the air, we keep the windows wide open, something which I love. I quickly realize that I love to sit and watch the passing world, so I claim a bottom bunk next to an open window. The soot which flies in my face is a small price to pay for being able to watch the Indian countryside as it flies by.

We are riding in first-class compartments, all with green interiors. Ours is a sleeper carriage—Terr calls the railcars *"carriages"*—with four fold-down beds. Each compartment has a tiny bathroom with a soot-covered sink that pumps out awful water—greasy and undrinkable. The toilet is really gross. Its bowl opens to the tracks below. A sign on the wall tells us we aren't allowed to use the toilet when we're in the stations. Duh! That makes sense.

It is late evening when we pass through the outskirts of Madras. From my window perch I can peer into intimate worlds of dimly lit apartments and houses. In my mind, I imagine people sitting around low tables, eating supper with their hands, and quietly visiting together. They probably do this every night after a long day's work.

I watch for hours, thinking about the wonder and magic of this world of strangely shaped trees, rice paddies sparkling in the moonlight, children guiding water buffalos home through muddy ponds, women tending cooking fires, and old men balancing on their haunches outside their homes. It is a far cry from Michigan or Bahrain, that's for sure! Yellow cooking fires light the nighttime world, just enough for me to pick out some of what is happening. I imagine that beyond the edges of the light, gentle beasts and exhausted villagers move silently about in the darkness.

The train wends its leisurely way through rice paddies and sugarcane fields, over bridges spanning wide rivers, and along barren areas where life-giving streams do not reach. The overnight train ride is long and hot. Occasionally, small embers from the engine fly in through the open window and singe my skin. We play with the controls of the two metal fans mounted on the wall, pretending they are propellers on an airplane. Their highest speed is barely enough to move the air around and provide some relief from the heat. The lamplight in the compartments is so weak that we can't read, so we spend the evening talking and looking out at the passing countryside. It doesn't take long before we fall asleep, exhausted from our three-day journey. Tomorrow we'll arrive in Kodai.

I awake at daybreak and gaze out the window at the countryside rolling by and coming to life. It's mostly farmland, but we also pass through small towns and villages with their many colored houses and buildings. The whitewashed houses have grown tan under layers of dust. Houses that were once red are now salmon-colored after years of baking in the sun.

I'm bored. In fact, the other guys in our compartment are also bored, so we decide we have to do something about that. We decide that there must be more interesting things going on in the compartment next to ours. That's where the girls are. Since there's no connecting passageway, we have to take things into our own hands. Before too long I'm making my way out of the train door, trying not to look down at the speeding train wheels. I follow Teddy who has already inched along the outside of the carriage, making his way to the compartment behind ours. I feel a little like Spiderman and hope that some of his power sticks to my fingers. The passing wind is really gusty, and I have to hang on tightly. In the windows barely an inch from my nose, I can see the reflections of the telephone poles whizzing by behind me. After what seems like forever, I finally pull myself into the girls' compartment and flop down on the floor, panting and laughing next to Teddy. When he finds out about it, Nykerk is not happy with this little adventure, but we suspect that he has done the same thing a million times. It's also clear that the girls are super impressed that we are so brave. I feel like I'm back in good standing with everyone else. My rookie days are behind me!

When we finally have a rest stop, we all pile out of our compartments and visit the vendors on the platform. The other elementary boys and I hit the food stands. Although I've had "Indian" food before, this is the first time I get to eat real Indian food. Boy, is it spicy! My tongue is on fire, and my throat is scorched. Whatever it is made of, it is not long before my stomach is rumbling.

Fortunately, we arrive at Kodai Road Station, the end of the train trip, at nine in the morning. We haven't lost anyone to speeding trains, falling telephone poles, or food poisoning. In drizzling rain, we wait what seems like hours for a bus to take us on the last leg of our journey—a bumpy trip along the flat, dusty plains and then up the seven-thousand-foot climb to Kodaikanal.

When the bus finally arrives, our suitcases are loaded on a wooden platform on top and covered with a tarpaulin to protect them from the rain. The tarp bulges threateningly, looking like it will burst and spill our stuff all over the road. All this extra weight on the roof makes the bus sway from side to side as it cruises along the pothole-filled roadways. I can take the swaying as long as we're on the flat pavement of the plains, but once we hit the steep, winding mountain stretch, I am overcome by the jostling and heave some of my breakfast out the window. Streaks of puke stick to the side of the bus.

Terr tells me that this road from the plains up to Kodai is called "the *Ghat*." I think that's a good name, because my gut will never forget what it's going through!

The bus slowly meanders up the winding mountain passage, and I see fantastic sights when I look down toward the plains far below. When we pass a waterfall, Dave tells me it's called Rattail Falls. With great authority he announces, for the benefit of all the newcomers, that it is the fifth highest waterfall in the world.

I can't get over the amazing colors of the birds which fly past the bus. Some of them sound like humans singing, and others send a chill down my spine with their piercing and scary cries. Monkeys play along the side of the road, ignoring the risk of the passing bus. They provide great entertainment with their crazy antics as they beg for handouts. Snakes slither across the road and veer off into the underbrush as the bus rolls by. Steep cliffs jut up into the sky, and the mountain climber in me gets really excited. Despite the sharp angles and ridges, they look like great climbing peaks.

For three and a half hours, the bus inches up the mountainside. I can't believe we only go thirty-two miles in that amount of time. The bus is constantly changing speed, braking frequently and swerving around potholes, swaying back and forth, and maneuvering through sharp, hairpin turns. As the bus shifts between uphill climbing and downhill coasting, the engine's sounds and diesel smells make me feel lightheaded.

The air gets colder and colder as the bus gains altitude. Since the bus is open-sided, there is no protection from the cold air. As a result, I feel tired and chilled through. Holding my arms tightly to my chest, I rub my hands together to stay warm. It was wonderfully hot down in the plains, so I didn't think to take a sweater out of my suitcase. Now that my bag is tied tightly to the top of the bus, I can't get at it.

As I sit there in my chilly misery, watching the distant plains disappear behind the clouds, it suddenly hits me that I am far away from my parents and home. I can't help thinking about the journey that is coming to a close. We left the States four weeks ago. Four weeks of travel in cars, trains, airplanes, and buses had taken me halfway around the globe. It had been snowing in Michigan when we left, and it was incredibly cold in Europe. Kuwait and Bahrain were pleasantly mild. But now, with the cold, thin mountain air attacking my body, a sense of total tiredness overcomes me. I just want to crawl into a warm bed and go to sleep.

At long last, the bus pulls into Kodai. We trundle off the bus, bleary-eyed, tired, and dazed. One by one, we unload our luggage from the top of the bus and then drag our suitcases up the hill to our dormitories. I'm assigned to Phelps Hall, a somewhat newer dormitory on the other side of campus from the entrance. Tired as I am, I can barely make the hike. Dave helps me with my stuff and turns me over to Mrs. B., the white-haired old lady who will be my housemother, my "mom away from home," for the coming year. She looks very stern, and I don't know what to make of her.

"I've arranged for Teddy to be your roommate," she explains in a flat voice, and ushers me to my room. When we enter, she nods toward my life-long buddy from Kuwait. "You'll like him. Teddy's a good boy and will show you what to do and not do here at school. You will need to listen to his advice and live and study the way he does. He's a very good boy!" Teddy shifts on his feet, embarrassed by these compliments.

"Teddy, Paul's your new roommate. Please teach him how we behave properly here in Phelps Hall." Her tone is such that I have no doubt Teddy will comply. Teddy and I look at each other and mumble, "Hi." She doesn't know that we're already friends for life, and we're not going to let on, either.

I slowly look around. The room is as bare as a prison cell. Four plain, whitewashed walls, two simple wooden bed frames with musty-smelling mattresses folded on top, and two dressers. A single bare lightbulb at the end of a long cord hangs down from the high, pointed roof made of corrugated metal sheets. This is my new home! I have never been in a room that my mother hadn't made cozy for me, so this place gives me the creeps. It looks more like a storeroom than a bedroom.

I'm exhausted after the long day of bumping up the *Ghat*, so I throw sheets on the mattress and climb in. As Teddy and I settle into our beds that first night, I feel lonesome and tired beyond description. Fortunately, thanks to Teddy being in the bed next to mine, I'm more tired than lonely, so I immediately fall into a deep, baby-like slumber my first night at Kodai School.

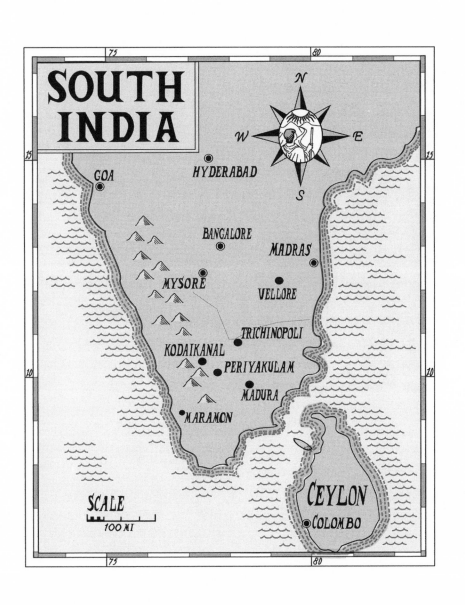

Kodai's bazaar, the "Budge"

CHAPTER 2

Settling In

When I wake up in the morning it takes me a few seconds to remember where I am and what I'm doing here. Then the ache begins again in my gut; I feel almost sick from the crushing homesickness. What has become of my life? I am so lonely that I wander around like a lost and confused puppy. When the morning mail comes and there is a letter from Mom and Dad, I can't even find the courage to open it. They must have mailed it before I even left Bahrain, knowing I'd want to hear from them. I find Terr to come to my dorm and read it to me, but even that doesn't help much. Thank goodness Teddy and my brothers are there, because they know the ropes and show me around. Terr takes me up to the dining hall for lunch, a damp and dreary walk. The monsoon season has barely ended, and everything feels wet, especially the walkways between the dorms and the other campus buildings.

Mrs. B. doesn't help much, either. On my way to the dorm bathroom that first morning, I pass her scolding one of the other kids, and I hear her mention "black marks." I quickly realize that she has very little patience with us; maybe she's been doing this housemother thing for too long. When I get back to the room, I tell Teddy about the scolding incident. Shaking his head, he responds, "She's not so bad." But something in the way he says it tells me it is a good idea to avoid Mrs. B. as much as possible. Then he explains about demerits. Mrs. B. can give out "black marks" for any disruption of the peace and calm of Phelps Hall. If you get too many of these demerits, Teddy says, you get stuck in your room over the weekend. From what I can tell, that's a fate worse than being spanked. I think about the cell-like enclosure that is my dorm room and shudder. On the spot, I decide to give Mrs. B. no cause to punish me.

Fortunately, Teddy and I share the room which is the farthest from Mrs. B.'s apartment. This is because Teddy is her special pet, and she knows she can trust him to obey the rules even if he's not being watched all the time. From my brief time of visiting Teddy in Kuwait, I know that he is a well-behaved kid, very conscious of his family's place in the mission world. He doesn't want to let down the family name. That's okay with me, because I don't want to let down my family name, either.

Miss Sawatski, our fifth grade teacher, is also stern and strict–a younger version of Mrs. B. As I sit in class, I realize that the other kids are more comfortable with the school work than I am. They understand the schedule–spelling first, then geography, then recess, then math, then lunch, then writing, then science, then recess, then music or art. Although I went to an American school for fourth grade, I had been home-schooled up to that point. Miss Sawatski senses my discomfort and sees it as a weakness to be poked at. A couple of times during this first day of school she chides me for not keeping up: "Paul, these are basic spelling words which you must know! Please work on them for the next class." "Paul, we're on page 2 of our workbooks, we're not using our textbooks anymore!" One time she accuses me of not focusing. I'm not sure what she means, because I'm so scared I might make a mistake that I stop to think before I say anything. If anything, I'm over-focusing!

The whole day is miserable, except at recess when I meet up with Teddy. He introduces me to some of the other kids, and they seem cool with me. They can't stand Miss Sawatski either, and tell me that the only good thing about her is that she gets sick a lot. When she's out, her replacement is Mrs. Root, and everyone agrees that Mrs. Root is wonderful. I begin to hope that Miss Sawatski gets sick very soon. Maybe not deathly sick, but just enough to keep her out of the classroom.

Thanks to Teddy, I now have a bunch of new friends. Before recess is over, we all arrange to meet after school in Teddy's and my room.

"The first thing you need to know, Paul, is you can't trust the grownups." This is the lesson that Bosch gives me when we're all seated crosslegged on our two beds. The room is full of fifth grade boys, and we're all glad to be done with the first day of school. I wasn't the only one to get reprimanded by Miss Sawatski, I know there are others in the room who are praying for sickness to hit her soon.

I've already had a couple of very unpleasant encounters with adults. First there was Mrs. B. scolding Bosch (that's who she was yelling at). Then there were the nasty comments from Miss

Sawatski. Bosch's advice sounds reasonable. Zero for two from the adults today.

"But you have to watch out so that they don't catch you," Bosch continues. That, too, sounds like good advice, although since he was caught by Mrs. B. it seems that Bosch doesn't always follow his own advice. "You have to be careful, like Teddy, so that Mrs. B. doesn't see you as a troublemaker. I got caught yelling in the dorm a couple of times last year, so she is *always* watching me. The littlest thing I do gets me in trouble. So be careful, Paul, you don't want to get on her black list, because ole Mrs. Battleaxe will never forget!" Everyone, including me, laughs at this little lecture. That's what they call Mrs. B.—Mrs. Battleaxe. I can tell that I'm going to get along well with these kids. The day is already looking up.

Just when I think it can't get any better, Teno holds up my pillow and calls out, "What's this?" He's mashing it roughly.

"Put it back," I shout, "it's only my pillow." I try to grab the pillow back.

"I know that, you idiot, but what's it made of?"

Without realizing it, I had brought something new into the life of the dorm. The pillow I brought from the States is filled with foam, not feathers. Rather than put it back, Teno passes it around the room, and each kid sticks his mucky face into it. Some of them moan with pleasure. I can't help laughing, though I know Mom wouldn't think this was very sanitary.

As if that isn't enough, Teno steps out into the corridor surrounding the dorm's inner courtyard and yells, "Paul's mom gave him a foam pillow! You gotta feel this thing to believe it!" In a minute there are twenty kids squeezing and mashing my pillow. Someone calls me "Paul the Pillow Kid." The one good thing is that people seem to think the pillow—and therefore Paul the Pillow Kid—is cool, so maybe the name will stick. I can't help smiling to myself, even while I'm trying to take the pillow back from all the squeezers and mashers.

And then it gets crazy. "Pillow fight!"

In no time at all, the room empties and kids are racing back to their rooms and returning with their pillows. I am so surprised, I can't move. Then the swinging begins. Someone smashes his pillow right, square in my face, bringing tears to my eyes. I grab my pillow from the floor to use as a shield, but someone else hits me on the back of the head. I am ready to bawl, but then I realize everyone is hitting everyone else, roaring with laughter. I know I have to get in there, or I'll be left out, so I weigh in with my foam pillow flying in all directions. I don't even think about Mrs. Battleaxe and what she might do to us.

I soon discover that the best pillows to be hit by are the feather ones. While they spit stray feathers all over the place, they are soft enough to do no damage. The ones you don't want to get hit by are the cotton-filled ones. They are hard as rocks. It's as if the cotton batting has turned into a clump of clay with all the moisture in the air, and they lose all of their softness. You do NOT want to get hit by one of them. My foam pillow is almost as ineffective as a feather one, but it does a little more damage. Then, as quickly as the fight began, it ends. I don't realize it at first, but someone has spotted old Battleaxe coming down the walkway to Phelps. A barely whispered warning has everyone scattering to their rooms. I get the message real fast, and scurry to mine. When I get there, I see that Teddy is calmly reading a textbook. I try to remember if he was out there during the pillow fight, but can't remember seeing him. He just smiles smugly when I ask if he participated.

Out in the corridor, all is eerily quiet. When I peek out the door, I see no one except Mrs. B. making her way around the courtyard, looking in all directions. Every once in a while she picks up a feather and nods her head as if she knows something bad is going on. Maybe she thinks it's too quiet, too, for a mid-afternoon. But there is nobody to reprimand, so she finally gives up and goes back to her apartment. Whew, that was close. The Foam Pillow Fight is one for the record books.

The second day of classes is a blur. Spelling, Indian geography, multiplication tables, essays, bugs and beetles, and painting creep by at a snail's pace. When the final bell rings, we're out of class in a second. Today we're going exploring. As he had done in Kuwait, Teddy announces that he is taking me for a sightsee around the campus. I know a few of the places already, but there's a lot that I haven't seen, so as soon as we're out of class we begin our tour, starting at the classroom building on top of the Kodai School hill. Like most campus buildings, it is built around an inner courtyard with covered corridors ringing it.

In front of the class building is a small green space with two flag poles, one which carries an American flag and the other, an Indian one with Gandhi's spinning wheel. I've already been out here during recess. Attached to the main building are the library, administrative offices, and—most importantly—the dining hall.

Spreading out from the classroom building on terraces which march down the hillside are a series of dormitories for boys and girls. I can't remember all their names, but one of them gets my immediate attention because I've walked through it several times already. This is Block Hall, which houses seventh and eighth grade boys. Whenever it's drizzly, Teddy tells me, we Phelps kids take a short-cut through Block to get to the dining hall and classrooms. That's because Phelps Hall is down the hillside from Block. I know that Wissahickon Hall is even further down than Phelps, because that's where Terr and Dave live.

Beyond Wissy is the outer wall, and across a small street is Kodai Lake, a starfish-shaped lake which looks wonderful—a place waiting for adventure—from the top of the hill. Teddy tells me about the fun of punting on the lake; I can't wait for the weather to warm up so I can go boating myself. The girls' dorms, Kennedy and Boyer Halls, are on the opposite side of the classroom building, and therefore far from boy's prying eyes. Teddy waves at them when we walk by. "We're not allowed near those places."

Phelps is where I live. It's a single story, rectangular building with an open courtyard surrounded by a verandah-like, covered walkway. All the rooms open onto this walkway. The tiled roof sits atop walls of hand-hewn granite stones. There are two ways to get out of the building, and both are locked at night to keep burglars out and us in; however, each room's window opens to the outside and we can easily jump out if we want to escape. However, other than the girls' dorms on the other side of the campus, there isn't much to escape to. But it's nice to know we can get out if we need to.

Eucalyptus trees are all over the campus, regularly shedding their bark along with their "eucy" nuts. The sharp odor of eucy-oil – something like Vicks VapoRub—is everywhere, making us feel like we live in a medical ward. When Teddy takes me down to Phelps, we pass through Block again and are greeted with a rain of eucy nuts from one of the rooms. The Block middle schoolers hate us kids. Maybe that's because they lived in Phelps a year or two before. From other rooms we hear a bunch of nasty remarks as we walk through:

"Be quiet, punks! Shut up and get out of here."

"Are those your school clothes or are you wearing a costume? Whoever dressed you pipsqueaks didn't know what they were doing!"

"You kids know why you're in boarding school? Cause your mother doesn't love you."

"You punks stink, have you had a bath recently?"

"You better get a haircut or you'll turn into a girl."

"Are you old enough to be away from your mommy?"

"Your shoes are on the wrong feet."

"Are you able to wipe yourself or does Mrs. B. have to do it for you?"

"We're going to tell Mrs. B. that we heard you cussing!" I already know that if there is anything to get Mrs. B.'s blood boiling, it's naughty words.

Walking through Block is like plowing through a shooting gallery. Everyone takes potshots at you. I can't wait until I am old enough to move here and take potshots at some future Phelps pipsqueak.

After supper I head back to my dorm room with Teddy to do a little homework. "It's bath night," Teddy announces, so I get my towel and soap and follow him to the bathing room. Much to my surprise, standing at the doorway are three Indian *ayahs*–local cleaning ladies–with rubber aprons covering their *saris* and with mean-looking sponges in their hands. I watch in horror as all the other fifth-grade boys strip to their birthday suits and shuffle in line, filing into the bathing room. I strip too, trying to retain some small piece of modesty by holding my towel in front of me.

"What'sa matter, Paulie, hiding something?" My face turns red, and I try not to look around.

All of a sudden, I feel a sharp whack on my butt. The pain is unbelievable, and I slip on the wet tiles and go down on my knees. Modesty flies out the window. This really hurts! Laughter and hoots echo around the large, tiled bathing room.

"Is that a hickey on your butt?"

"Don't worry; your growth spurt will come soon!" Now I'm blushing from head to toe and everyone can see it. My life must be over.

"Stop that," one of the *ayahs* calls out. "Bad boy!" At last, someone has come to my defense. Then I realize she's talking to me, and I was the victim. This is not a good situation.

Slowly getting back to my feet, I decide I have to keep an eye out for another flicking towel. Much to my relief, someone else is targeted, and he immediately retaliates. In a flash, there are twenty naked boys at war with each other, snapping their wet towels in all directions. I can't stand by when three kids go after Teddy, so I jump in to defend him.

"You, next!" demands the head *ayah*, pointing at me, and I turn from the towel fight and meekly move into the bathing area. I can see that there is a shower room next door, but someone— probably Mrs. Battleaxe–has decided that little boys don't deserve to take showers. We have to take "baths" using a large basin.

I'm immediately attacked by the *ayahs* who work together to scrub me down. The sponges feel more like coral, scratchy and dangerous. All my embarrassment disappears with the pain, as every inch of me is tortured. I can hardly keep my eyes open because of the soap dripping from my scalp, but I don't want to see what's happening to me and my friends. This is too humiliating and agonizing.

It is clear from the way the *ayahs* manhandle me that they have scrubbed thousands of naughty boys, and they have no patience for our shenanigans. When we laugh and tease each other, they remain focused and stern. Even my fall to the floor, which I'm sure has bruised my knee for life, gets no sympathy from them. They are like machines, getting us clean as quickly as possible so as not to waste the precious, limited supply of hot water.

As I towel myself off, I hear Bosch protest, "The water's cold! Lemme outta here!" But he's held fast by three hands while three other hands scrape him down with the coral. He begins to wail, but the machine-women keep scrubbing. There are still three fifth-graders standing in line, and I can see that they are petrified. They know that the water will only get colder, and the *ayahs'* sympathy has completely disappeared. I have no pity on them, because they are the ones who attacked me. But I promise myself that I'll always be one of the first boys in line when bath nights roll around. I don't want to miss the hot water.

All of our screaming and protesting has wakened the dead. As I wrap the wet towel around myself and trudge back to my dorm room, Mrs. B. shows up. She's not in a good mood. She has had enough of our yelling and wants to set things straight before they go too far. It is, after all, a brand new school year, and she wants to set clear limits.

While I watch, however, things really get out of hand. Back in the drying area, a couple of guys are goosing each other! As if towel flicking wasn't enough, now they're pinching each other's butts. Without seeing Mrs. B., they chase each other out into the veranda of the courtyard and stop dead in their tracks. Mrs. B. is livid, turns bright red. I'm afraid she'll explode. It's bad enough that naked missionary kids are running around in plain sight, but they're pinching and poking each other to boot! The demerits will fly tonight!

"You naughty boys are all going to get demerits!" she shouts. "I'm going to report you all for goosing!" In an instant, everyone stops dead still. Did she say "goosing"? We can't believe Mrs. B. even knows the word, much less that she will actually write "goosing" on a demerit report!

"I'm going to post our infraction report inside our door," whispers Teddy. "Can you imagine that? My first demerits of the year are for 'goosing'!" It's hard to keep from laughing. Everyone will remember our heroic parts in the Great Shower War!

At last it's the weekend, and I can't wait to let off some steam. All week long we've been cooped up in the classroom and dormitory. Mrs. Battleaxe reported our shower fight, and the whole of Phelps got in trouble. Even those who weren't there. We had to come right down to our rooms after class. We could only get out for meals. I'm stir-crazy and have to get out. Fortunately, we're going hiking, and I'm so excited I can hardly contain myself.

"Slow down, Paul," Teddy warns. "You'll need that energy for the climb up to the waterfall!"

With our knapsacks and canteens filled with lunch and water, we head out on a three-mile walk to the magical Fairy Falls. It runs down in filmy streams from mysterious, cloud-covered mountaintops. I don't know the adults who are supervising us fifth grader hikers, but they don't get in our way.

When we arrive at the base of the falls, we run to the pool and dive in. There, with tadpoles and frogs darting all over to keep out of our way, we splash with happy abandon. In a few minutes, we're chilled to the bone and covered with filthy, black mud. Life doesn't get better.

"Snake!" yells Paul B., and points to a slithery green creature that is making its way toward the water. "It's a banana viper!"

We all scramble to the shore and watch, scared and fascinated, as the viper slips into the pool. With only its head above the surface, it skims across the pool to the other side, from time to time disappearing into the depths. Finally, it doubles back to our shore, and we descend on it with sticks and rocks, smashing its head into the ground. Victory! Triumphantly, but cautiously, we head back to the water, keeping an eye out for any siblings that might be lurking in the forest.

It's not long before Teddy screams, "Snake!" and we all scatter again. Grinning, he hauls up a slender twig from the bottom of the pond, and we all yell at him, threatening to hold him underwater or worse if he does that again. By now we are imagining snakes everywhere, and Mr. B. doesn't help things.

"Do you smell that?" Mr. B. asks as we huddle on the shoreline, shivering. "Smell that smoke? That must be from a forest fire up the mountainside. The snakes are probably heading to water to get away from it." That explanation doesn't make things better. But it isn't long before we're back in the pool, alert to anything that breaks the surface.

Seeking more daring fun, we climb up to the naturally carved "water slides" that line the falls. These are grooves in the stone that have been carved by hundreds of years of water flow. Before long, we discover that sliding down the stone water slides wears out the bottoms of our swimsuits. But we're having too much fun to care about damaging our trunks or about exposing hunks of our butts. We boys don't stop. Our bottoms are quickly covered with blisters and scratches. I know that I'm going to have to sew a patch onto my suit, just like all those boys who have come here before. The patches are all kinds of colors and shapes, and they're all cool. I can't wait to get mine. The girls are more conscious of the delicate condition of their swimsuits and only go down the slide a couple of times so they don't tear anything. Such sissies.

When we've had enough of the water, we fashion little boats from twigs and small branches and race our "boats" downstream. I love taking in the variety of nature, and I find that learning about reptiles and plants is interesting. Thanks to this trip, I decide that there's no better classroom in the world than hiking and camping in the mountain jungles of South India. As soon as we head into the forest, I'm alert and engaged. This is heaven on earth for me. I want to do this again and again.

The next morning, I wander down to Wissahickon to visit Dave and Terr. I want to tell them about the Fairy Falls hike and see if they've heard anything from Mom and Dad. I know that we youngsters are not appreciated in Wissy, but since I have brothers to visit I will be tolerated for a short stay.

Dave and Terr are in the commons room—called the social room—with a bunch of older kids, lifting weights and talking big boy talk. While I stand, listening to them, I feel my ears grow red with embarrassment at the things they're saying. I suspect some of the topics are chosen to humiliate. Sensing my discomfort, Terr takes me back to his room and offers me a cookie and a glass of powdered milk. He and Dave have bigger allowances than I do, so they have more food to munch on. I'll have to remember this the next time I'm starving to death.

I notice Terr looking at my hands while I'm dipping my cookie into the milk. He doesn't look happy, and it suddenly dawns on me that I'm going to be in big trouble with Mom. "Paul, if you stop biting your finger nails, I promise that I will send you a care package every two weeks. Now, I want Terr to check and make sure you stop this awful habit." That was Mom's final warning when I left Bahrain, and sure enough, the care packages arrived right on schedule. For the first four weeks.

"Mom's going to be mad about this!" he warns as he makes me spread my fingers.

"I just forget. I don't even know when I'm doing it. I must be chewing my nails at night," I plead. But Terr isn't buying my explanation. In fact, he is prepared for my protests.

"You'll get tetanus if you keep chewing your nails! I just read an article that guarantees that's what will happen if you keep this up." His warning really scares me, so I chew my finger nails because I'm so anxious. "Paulie," he whines, calling me by my baby name. I'm really upset that he caught me, and I can feel myself on the verge of tears, once again.

Terr senses this, too, and decides to move on. "Well, other than the finger-nail business, it looks like you're getting along pretty well. How's the homesickness going?" I feel myself getting choked up at the very mention of "home," but then I realize he is complimenting me, so I swallow it back.

"Yup. Things are fine. Teddy's a great roommate, although he studies all the time. And I have a good time with my buddies. Can't stand spelling, but I like science."

"That's good to hear. I'll tell Mom. She'll be relieved." I have begun to realize that my life for years to come will be among the friends I have made the past few days. From now on, when I go "home," I'll be visiting my parents–much like Dave and Terr have done for years. It had been Mom, Dad, and my home that they had visited during school breaks. In the future, I will also be a visitor like them. While that is a strange thought, I'm not as concerned about it as I was just a week ago.

With that reassurance, we return to the weight room, and Terr challenges me to do a lift. He has to keep taking weights off the bar until he gets down to seventy pounds, which I struggle to hoist over my head. The rest of the room erupts in laughter, so I know it's time to return to the little kids' dorm.

When I get back to Phelps, I see a bunch of guys have gathered in the courtyard to play *mibs*, marbles. I race to my room and pick up my bag stuffed with steelies, pee-wees, tiger-eyes, *kabolies*, and clay marbles. I have been playing marbles since I was a little kid, and I believe I am ready to compete with my new friends. Kaz quickly sets the serious tone of the tournament.

"Keepsies," Kaz calls out, and we all nod in agreement. He draws a large circle in the middle of the yard and each of us throws a marble into the middle. I choose carefully, because I don't want to lose my best marbles. If they're already a little chipped, they give you a good grip, which can be an advantage. Clay marbles shatter easily, so no one really wants to use them. As a result, the whole "pot" in the middle of the circle is filled with clay marbles, castaways that no one minds losing.

Since he called the game, Kaz opens up play. He kneels down, holding his favorite shooter tightly in his fist. He positions the tiger-eye carefully so that a chipped section is up against his thumb. This gives him good control. With a quick flick of his thumb, he sends his marble into the "pot," scattering marbles in all directions. He's a good shot, and marbles scuttle toward the edge of the circle. One slips out, so Kaz grabs it up and gets another shot.

This time he fires from where his shooter had landed on the first round. His second shot goes awry, and Kaz groans because he left his shooter inside the ring. I'm next, and the first shot I take is at Kaz's shooter, a beautiful tiger-eye with orange stripes. I get down on the ground, lying on my stomach because I don't want to miss on this one. Ignoring the damp dirt, I draw my fingers together, my pointer draped over my middle finger. Taking careful aim, and using just the right amount of force so that my own shooter won't get trapped in the circle, I let it fly. Smack! Kaz's beauty flies out of the circle, and I grab it up. He'll have to find another shooter. My own shooter lands right next to a clay marble. I make short work of that and two others. I'm relieved that my shooter is safely outside the circle when I finally lose my turn.

An hour later, we're all shivering. The cold, damp air has seeped into our bodies, and we need to get out of the open courtyard. Back on the smooth cement floor of our courtyard veranda, Paul B. pulls out his top, winds the string around it, and gives it a jerk. Several others take tops out of their pockets and begin to spin them on the cement. I jog to my room for mine and join in. In the future, I'll be sure to carry my top with me in case I need it for pick-up matches like this. Like marbles, tops are cheap, so we all have a bunch of them. That's a good thing, because we're soon playing "keepsies" with the tops, and mine shatters when Kaz hits it square on the crown. He can keep that one!

Saturday night is movie night, and I tramp with my buddies up to the gym. In fact, when we get there, we have to fight for seats together because the place is packed. It seems as though all 240 students have come out for the evening's entertainment. We whistle and cheer when the first 16 mm. short begins. It's a Three Stooges classic, and the hall is filled with laughter. Life doesn't get any better than this.

Suddenly, right in the middle of the show, our piano teacher stands up and blocks the screen. In her distinctive English accent Mrs. G. yells out, "I cannot watch such worthless absurdity!" The room grows instantly silent except for the crazy shenanigans on the screen. Then Mrs. G. stomps out of the theater, and we all let out a sigh. Dumbfounded, I wonder what mental or emotional disorder Mrs. G. might be suffering from that keeps her from enjoying the ultimate in entertainment. Teddy just shrugs. "That's typical Mrs. G.," he explains.

Happily, I don't have to wait too long for our next trip into the mountains. Two weeks after our Fairy Falls hike, the adults—I have already begun to think they are "our keepers"—announce we're ready for another weekend camping trip and mountain climb. I heartily agree and am one of the first to arrive at the gathering point near the campus flag poles. The teachers loan me camping gear, which is definitely ancient stuff. The olive color tells me it comes from World War II surplus castoffs. The sleeping bag has been used for so long that it stinks with mildew. Even the canvass covering of the canteen smells funny. The knapsack and sleeping bag are heavy and musty, as though they've been sitting in a damp closet forever. As if that isn't enough, the tents and cots that are coming in a lorry are just as stinky. And heavy! I don't know how we'll drag them to the campsite. But Teddy and Bosch assure me that we'll make it.

We're going to climb Mount Perumal, the mysterious, picturesque peak that I see every day on Kodai's horizon. It looks like a volcano to me, but Teddy says that it's not. I'm not convinced. Its sides come together in a flat top, just like a volcano.

Perumal appears on all manner of Kodai School stuff, from icing on cakes to patches on clothes.

It takes us all morning to hike to the base camp where we set up camp with the overnight supplies that arrived by truck (brought by the Indian staff from the school). Then we begin to climb. The early coolness of the morning has given way to a comfortable day, warm and sunny. As long as we're on the sunny side of Perumal, it is easy climbing. We even take off our jackets and tie them around our waists. I double-knot my sleeves to make sure I don't lose it along the narrow paths. When we circle around to the shady side of the mountain, it is cool again, and some guys undo their jackets and put them on. I'm so excited that I don't bother with that.

There are a lot of trails up the mountain—most of them carved by cattle herders who drive their flocks to the high country for the scrub grass. We see cattle—and their droppings—everywhere. As we get to the upper levels of the climb, we each pick a different path, always circling higher and higher. At last we race the last yards to the top. By now, the sweat is pouring off of me, even when I'm in the shade. When I finally flop down on the peak, I'm excited to see that I'm the seventh person to get there.

When all the others arrive, we roll a huge, three-foot-square rock over the edge. I watch as it crashes down, skipping in twenty-foot bounces, smashing small trees and bushes as if they were paper. Because there is nothing to keep me from seeing it, I watch until it finally settles into a ledge hundreds of feet below. I breathe a sigh of relief that it didn't hit any humans, animals, or houses and wipe them out. I don't join in when another boulder is pushed off the peak.

Weekends are turning out to be worth the pain of the school week. On the Saturday after the great Perumal adventure, I go skating on the gym's wooden floor. Even though it is rippled and warped, it is the only wooden floor in all Kodai, so it's ideal for skating. The only real drawback is the stone walls around the gym. I learn the hard way that they don't move if I run into them! After a particularly unpleasant crash, I hold back my tears. Blinking, I look around and realize that everyone is watching me. I swallow my tears.

"Way to tackle the wall," Kaz yells. Others laugh, but it is not mean laughing. It's almost as if Kaz was saying, "Way to take your lumps." I realize that my "courage" is well appreciated by my peers. After that, I brush off every painful encounter with the walls and other skaters. I even point out the black and blue marks which spot my carcass, something which is really admired by all. I might even create a sling the next time I "injure" my arm.

Crashing is not infrequent for me. Since I don't have skates of my own, I have to use one of the school's old, bent, clip-on pairs. Someone must have discarded them years ago. Their chipped, out-of-line wheels make me the wobbliest and slowest skater on the floor, so I lose every race. More painfully, the worn out clips regularly slip off my shoes, sending me bashing into the wall. At least I'm not like one of the boys who can't skate and has to pull others around the gym. Disappointed that I have to use these junkers, I decide I'll write home and beg Mom to send me money for a decent pair of skates.

In celebration of Washington's birthday, the whole school gathers in the gym for a skit contest. Shouting, laughter, jibes, wise cracks, and yelling fill the gym. It's the perfect place to have fun. With Bosch, Paul B., and Teno, I star in a hilarious "Doctor's Office" skit. Bosch is the doctor, and we're the patients. It is so funny that we win the first prize. The prize is a worthless piece of junk, but we love the reputation we get. Even the Wissy kids are laughing at us. Maybe they'll forget my eighty-pound lift.

It's Sunday night, and I'm sick again. Vomited all afternoon. I'm getting tired of this routine because it makes for a terrible way to start the week. I'm sick of being sick every Monday morning, puking my guts out. It makes me moody, and I can't pay attention in school. By Monday afternoon I am usually feeling better again.

When I tell him about it, Dave decides it must be something I eat every Sunday. It doesn't take him long before he narrows it down to the fried eggs that are only cooked on Sunday morning and that are cooked in thick butter-oil called *ghee*. *Ghee* has the consistency of motor oil. I guess I'll have to stop eating fried eggs for now.

But food is a big part of my life, as it is for all of my friends. Any talk about limiting what I eat makes me unhappy. We talk about food all the time. Everyone agrees Kodai School food is pretty bad; that's probably because the school has a five dollar a month food budget for each child. They can't afford steaks or anything like that. This makes sense to me; after all, mish kids are supposed to live without luxuries. We also suspect that the school likes us to focus on food to keep us from thinking about other things that might get us into trouble.

In spite of all the complaining about food, we eat a lot of it, and sometimes it's tasty and probably even healthy. However, I am always famished! The big problem with the food is that there is never enough of it.

Although I'm still a bit queasy, I am ready to chow down on Monday night. As usual, we line up outside the dining room waiting for the bell. My buddies and I get there twenty minutes early in order to get fed first. We excitedly watch the dishes being carried to the teachers' dining room next to the main hall. The smells build our appetites. Basing our guesses on the size and shape of the platters being carried and on the smells that float our way, we try guessing what the dishes might be. Tonight, someone suggests that it will be white rice and *muragh chaney*. Smells good.

As soon as the bell rings and the door flies open, we charge to our table. Our mouths are already watering. "First," calls out Teddy as he slaps the head chair. I yell "second!" The four other kids each call out a number as soon as they arrive at the table and touch their chairs. This ritual is an important moment, because it sets the order of how we are served.

When we all find seats and settle down, my brother Dave stands up. He has volunteered to give the prayer tonight, and I know it's going to be a good, short one. "Lord, bless this food to our bodies so that we may serve you. Amen." Nice and sweet. Not all prayers are like that.

Last week we had two very different prayers. One came from a "holy roller" who gave a long prayer-sermon about ending world poverty, bringing peace to the world, and helping us lead good and moral lives. By the time she was done, our food was cold and we were all yawning. The next night things got better. A senior volunteered to pray, and he said, "Rub-a-dub-dub, Lord bless this grub, because it really needs it." Our jaws dropped as we watched the kid being removed from the dining room by Mr. Root, the principal. He won't be allowed to pray again, that's for sure. But he is my new hero.

Dave says his prayer with real meaning—that's important if a short prayer is going to be good enough for the teachers who generally believe a good prayer is a long prayer. After Dave's prayer, food is brought to the table and Teno, who was the "sixth" person to reach our table, cuts the good dishes into six pieces. This is where the order really counts. The first kid—Teddy—gets to choose the first piece. Then, as the second kid, I take my piece, and so on. This means that everyone gets their rightful share of the good food. Kid Six is highly motivated to divide the food as equally as possible, so that he gets a fair share too.

As I look around at the other tables, I realize that all the boys' tables use the same routine. However, the girls don't do this, which amazes me. They just take a helping of the food and then pass the platters to the next girl. I can't figure out their lack of need to get the best and most food. That's just one thing that confuses me about girls.

Something I miss at dinner is that we have no ketchup, no real butter, no sugar, no grated cheese, no salad dressings, no oil or vinegar, no mayonnaise or relish or pickles or anything of that sort, nothing to make the meals tastier. The only flavor additions we have are salt and pepper, and at breakfast we get jam and a tasteless, slimy, lard-like substance the cooks call "butter." You could fool me.

Hot porridge, in two varieties, is served almost every breakfast because it is cheap. The cooks tell us it is healthy. Most of us can't stand it. Thank God I like the two varieties it comes in, one a sticky, white, congealed goo we called "library paste." The other has a brown, grainy appearance and looks like sea silt, so we call it "beach sand." At least after breakfast, I can leave the dining hall feeling full, whether I eat library paste or beach sand!

Saturday breakfasts are special because pancakes are served. They are meant to be a treat and are not bad in themselves, but the problem with pancakes is that there is nothing to put on them: no real butter and no syrup. There is a gooey substance called *jaggery* which is placed on the tables with the pancakes and is intended as a substitute for syrup. *Jaggery* is unrefined brown sugar made from the sap of Palmyra palms; it is an awful sludge that tastes something like cough medicine. I never heard of *jaggery* when I lived in America, and it's no wonder why.

Most Indians, being Hindus, are strict vegetarians. Even the thought of eating meat makes most of them uncomfortable.

Thus meat is hard to come by. It's almost treated like an illegal substance, bought on the sly. In fact, it comes in strange pieces and looks strange to anyone used to eating meat in the States. Its eye-appeal is zero because it usually contains things that look like gizzards, and we pick around them trying to find edible morsels somewhere.

On the other hand, the fruit is excellent. That's the one really good food at school. While apples and oranges are not available, we get delicious mangos, tangerines, guavas, passion fruit, plums, custard apples, jackfruit, papaya, finger-sized bananas, and watermelons. We eat a lot of it, knowing that this is a healthy side of school food. Even though we love fruit, given the choice we would quickly trade our exotic fruits for some good bread or meat, dessert or junk food. But since no one gives us that choice, we enjoy the fresh fruits as much as possible.

There are also a bunch of bizarre vegetables that are prepared for us. We don't get the usual American vegetables like corn, sweet potatoes, celery, lettuce, kidney beans, or cucumbers. Instead, we get lentils, something that looks like okra, various tuber- and squash-like vegetables, and others with no American equivalent. They all have long, hard-to-pronounce Indian names and strong, bitter tastes that take getting used to.

After we finish our food, we sit back contentedly and chat, waiting for the fruit desert. Putting aside our troubles, homework, and school stresses, we talk about what we're going to do next weekend. Teno wants to go on another hike; Teddy is into skating; others have other ideas. We speculate about the Friday night movie, and then we wonder why girls are so complicated. I mention the fact that they just dish out their food without measuring it, and everyone says they can't figure that out, either.

"Will you boys please hold it down!" shouts Miss Slifer. It's not enough that she has to be on our case in class; she's also one of the dinner monitors. For a couple of minutes we whisper nasty things about her, but then someone bursts out laughing, and the quiet spell is broken. Soon we're back to our noisy jabbering. We have to talk loudly in order to be heard over the other noisy tables. We can't figure out why this bugs the staff. It is especially odd; they don't use our dining hall and can sit in the quiet solitude of their own dining room. Besides, they always get the good food.

As if to soften Miss Slifer's harsh words, Mrs. Root approaches us and explains: "Ladies and gentlemen and proper boys and girls don't behave in this manner. This is most immature." She is trying to appeal to our sense of responsibility, but that doesn't work. We continue to jabber at high decibel levels.

But this isn't the end of it. A week later we arrive in the dining room. Large rectangular mats hang from the high ceiling. The mats have been hoisted into the rafters and attached so they dangle there.

"They are made from reeds found in the nearby jungle swamps," Miss Slifer announces before tonight's prayer. "They are filled with pitch. We hope they will absorb your racket. Since you have no clue what 'quiet' means, we have to take this extreme measure. Now, Steve, please offer grace."

Steve gives a long prayer and asks God to bless the hangings so that we kids won't keep disturbing the real, serious students. As soon as he says "amen," we test the noise hangings. We quickly learn that they don't make a lick of difference in the noise level. The only effect they have is to hang threateningly over our heads. We guess that, if the ropes come loose, the heavy mats will crash down on our heads. That would really shut us up. At Teddy's suggestion, we decide that we'll always pick tables by the walls because they don't have noise hangings over them. We think we've won the noise wars. But we're wrong.

A week later, the teachers try something different.

This time, when we walk into the dining hall, we are told that even the high school students have complained. We're told that elementary kids are so noisy that nobody else can hear themselves think. "This isn't going to end well," Fletch whispers to me. I nod in response. And we're right.

It's Miss Slifer, again, who makes the announcement: "It has been decided that, in order for everyone to have a relaxing and peaceful dining experience, all students in the elementary grades will not be permitted to speak during meals. The only exception is that you may ask, politely, for others to pass you food. We are hoping that this rule will help us all learn to be considerate of each other during mealtimes. Thank you." I know that by "us all" she really means "the elementary boys."

Wow, is that a downer! We look around at each other wondering how we'll get through the meal without talking. But Teno, always ready to find a way to get what he wants, sees a loophole and charges right through it. "Bobby, please pass the potatoes to Hannes right away, 'cause he needs the energy in order to play Response right after supper."

"Hey, pass the potatoes to me first," Kaz pipes in. "I need to eat quickly so that I can leave right away and get the Response from my room before we all meet in front of the gym."

By now, we've all caught on to the pattern. "Just pass the potatoes to everyone so we all can play ten minutes after supper."

"With all the people who have to be passed food, don't you think it would be better if we waited fifteen minutes before we begin to play?"

Turning to the table next to us I politely ask, "Do you have any leftover potatoes, please? We'd like to have more potatoes before we have to begin our world-championship Response game at six o'clock in front of the gym. We have some extra peas, if you'd like them, so that you can have the energy to join our game."

Like an infection, all the elementary tables are soon buzzing with polite conversations about serving the food and whatever else is on our minds. It won't be long before the staff gets rid of this silly rule, too. In the meantime, I bet, there will be a lot of loud, polite, protracted conversation about passing the food.

One other consequence of the relative silence is just as hated by the teachers—and enjoyed by us. In the moments of silence, we can hear each other pass gas. Before we head out to play Response, one of us can't hold one in, so he tries to cover himself in this awkward situation. "That was a delightful curry, but I'm afraid it made someone pass baby's wind." He is very careful not to be vulgar in his comments.

"No, rather than the curry, I suspect that the *jaggery* is the source of someone's distended stomach," Kaz responds, equally careful not to step over the properness line. By now everyone else at the table is holding his breath, stifling a gutful of laughter.

"Miss Slifer, he just let one," Paul B. shouts out, pointing to the culprit.

"I never!" comes the protest.

"He did!" "He didn't!" others join in. We never would have known about the gas passing if it hadn't been quiet for a few seconds. By now, the noise level has returned to normal, and no one can hear anyone passing gas. Or asking for food to be passed.

It goes around and around in a circle. No noise means we can pinpoint who is passing gas; flatulent people are quickly singled out; singled out people feel the need to deny, as loudly as they possibly can get away with, that they are the source of the fart. We all quickly realize that the whole thing would go away if we didn't have to keep silent. Since Kodai food is well known for its ability to create gas, this will be an on-going issue until the silence rule goes away.

That night, instead of playing Response, we decide to form a new, secret society called the Blue Flame Club, and its members will be very carefully chosen for their abilities. We decide that all of us deserve to be charter members, and that we will invite skilled gas passers to join us. We talk eagerly of the day when our club will be the most notorious secret club on campus. We decide that dry-curry days will be our national holidays that will require special gas-club celebrations.

"Teddeeee, I'm dying," I moan.

"Mmmph."

"Really, I'm dying. Ya gotta help me."

"It's probably just gas. Let it out, you'll feel better."

"No, man, I'm really hurting, here."

"It's 2 AM, Paul, just go back to sleep."

"I can't, the bed is soaked from my sweat, and my stomach is bloated and gurgling."

"Just go to the bathroom, it's probably diarrhea."

I've been through that before. Bouts of diarrhea are common; they last a few days and make you run to the toilet often. Everybody knows when you're sick. With one bathroom for the whole dorm, there's no hiding such personal troubles. The ghastly smells permeate the dorm; the gross sounds that accompany tummyaches, especially the explosive ones, echo around the tiled walls of the bathroom for all to hear and respond to. Some sounds are shocking, some bring words of sympathy, others cause laughter.

"I think I'm gonna puke!"

He mumbles something in an effort to calm me.

Nauseated, light-headed and wishing my Mom was at my side, I'm afraid of vomiting in bed so I crawl out of its warmth, open our door to the open courtyard outside and lean over the small wall hoping to upchuck whatever is sending spasms through my body. Of all the rooms, ours is the furthest from Mrs. B.'s apartment, thanks to Teddy's good-boy image.

Strong winds blow bone-chilling rain at me, making my pajamas even more uncomfortable. Eucy trees sway in the driving thunderstorm, like scary ghost riders against the backdrop of violent clouds. Lightning bursts across the sky, lighting up the shadowy courtyard, awakening even more ghosts.

I stumble back to my door.

"Teddy, I think I'm gonna die!"

"Put your finger down your throat, that always works," he yells from bed.

I try to follow his advice, but I choke instead of puke.

"Let's go see Mrs. B.," he says, falling out of bed. He grabs my arm and holds me up like a big brother.

"Thanks, Teddy," I choke out.

"C'mon," Teddy begs. "Hurry up."

I hang onto Teddy, well aware there is no one else to give me comfort, "I'm OK." Then I stop to try to retch again. Barefoot on the wet cement that is stone cold and slippery, we stumble down the dark passageway, tripping over shoes, baseball bats, and toy cars left strewn about from the previous night's play. In the midst of my agony, I realize how soggy my PJs are. I have no clean, replacement pair, so I'll have to sleep in them no matter how wet they get.

The winds pound on us as we reel down the open verandah, looking for Mrs. B.'s window. A faint, yellow glow from the last ashes of her nightly fire means she is probably asleep. Everything else is totally black, broken by bright gray with each bolt of lightning that flashes across the sky and slams into a hillside tree. The freezing rain splatters us, and I realize that we're going to confront Mrs. Battleaxe in her own den. Certain that she will bark at me for getting sick, I drag my feet even more.

The thought of waking Mrs. B. puts the fear of God in me. Teddy promises me it'll be OK and assures me that Mrs. B. won't get mad if I tell her "this is Teddy's idea." I put on my sorrowful, wounded puppy look, hoping that will soften up Mrs. B. I know she's from the old school where men were men and boys were told to "be a man." Boys are supposed to be manly, unemotional, independent, and not bother adults with our problems, especially something as minor as a "touch of nausea."

Teddy knocks on the door. After what seems like an eternity, it opens silently and a large, black figure appears, looming a foot taller than us. By the dim light of a dying fire behind it, the figure fills the darkened doorway. Brief flashes of lightning in the sky behind us light her up long enough to let us recognize the dark shadow as Mrs. B.

I'm living in a nightmare.

"Pauly's sick," Teddy says in a pleading voice.

"What's the matter?"

I can feel her unseen eyes penetrating right through me, and I'm not sure now if I'm more sick or more scared.

But, then Mrs. B. amazes me. With a surprising amount of kindness, she says, "Come with me." She gently leads me into her bathroom and asks me to sit down on the toilet seat. Maybe she can be nice, after all. Bleary-eyed, I watch her mix up a fuming concoction that looks like a bad chemistry experiment. Fear is back in me.

"Drink this as quickly as you can," she orders.

The threat is back in her voice, so I cringe and suck down the brew. The bitter mixture has a flavor I've never even imagined in nightmares. It tastes like metal, mud, and food gone bad. She's really killed me this time!

Almost immediately I barf my guts out, spraying gooey brown chunks of supper all over her bathroom's whitewashed walls. Vomiting is not a skill I've learned yet, and I do a rather poor job of it. Mrs. B.'s eyes widen in horror and anger. In a brief moment of insight, I wonder if Mrs. B. has ever seen anything so disgusting in all her years as a nurse and housemother. She's too shocked to say anything. I retch repeatedly, finally gasping dry-heaves that bring nothing up. Out of the corner of my eyes I can see Teddy cringing in the doorway. I've even grossed him out. I now know what it feels like to turn myself inside out. I don't want to do that ever again.

For a moment, the nurse in Mrs. B. takes an academic interest in the explosive power of my barfing, but the brief interest is quickly replaced by rage at the realization that I've transformed her once spotless bathroom into a ghoulish mess. Her jaw moves like a robot, but what comes out is barely audible.

"You can go back to your room now," Mrs. B. wheezes, pointing to the door with an angry expression.

I'm exhausted and dazed as we pass through her doorway, heading to our room. I've never been through such an awful experience, and never even imagined my body could do such a thing.

The drizzle hasn't stopped. I shuffle slowly with Teddy's support, shivering the whole way in my sopping PJs, wondering if I will live to see another day–or at least long enough to make it to breakfast and have my two pieces of toast and some hot tea. Dripping wet and totally exhausted, I flop into my bed and fall into a dreamless sleep.

In the morning I'm utterly washed out. Mrs. B. stops by to see me and declares me well. I'm not allowed to stay in bed. Since I have no fever and am not vomiting any more, I am officially no longer sick and can't be sent to the dispensary–what we call the "Dishpan." I stumble around campus in a stupor. But no one notices, since no one takes much note of a fifth grade punk, unless of course you do something truly outrageous.

March comes, bringing with it the most pleasant weather I've ever known, and also the annual school Field Day. This is my first ever Field Day, so I'm excited about everything. All of us have been divided into two teams–a blue team and an orange team. I'm on the blue team. Throughout the year we compete for points. Even punk nine-year-olds can win points for the team. Field Day is the biggest point day of the year, and I'm eager to win points for the ole' blue side.

"Hey, I got an idea," Bosch announces the week before Field Day. We're sitting in our room, and Paul B.'s sixth grade brother is visiting from Block Hall. "You'll love this one! We'll buy a bunch of watermelons, slice 'em up, and sell 'em on Field Day. If we pool our money to buy enough watermelons, we'll all be millionaires. Everyone will be so famished and hot from the sun and tired from all the excitement, they're gonna forget their missionary stinginess and buy all that we can sell!" Bosch's plan sounds good to me. I give him a couple of my remaining rupees, and he heads off to buy supplies.

The money-making plan is foolproof, and with frenzied excitement we talk it up in the days before Field Day. All our friends are sure they'll buy slices from us.

On the morning of the Field Day activities, Bosch and the rest of us salesboys are on Bendy Field right after breakfast. We carry our stock of melons down to the field and set up shop. As the morning wears on, we aren't selling much. By late morning we start walking around, carrying slices and making our sales pitch. Still, few sales. It finally dawns on us that most students aren't carrying cash in their sweat clothes, so they can't make the purchases.

At noon we report back to Bosch and he thinks about it for a while.

"We'll have to try something different," Bosch decides when we're munching on sandwiches from our school-supplied bag lunch. "We'll sell on credit. No one has cash, so we'll keep track of who has bought from us, and we'll collect later." Bosch is a genius in business, so naturally we all agree.

While we take turns selling slices, we also take turns participating in Field Day events. Much to my surprise, I come in fourth in the fifty-yard dash. After my second race, I wander over to the shot put field. Teddy has signed up to compete in shot put and discus. With his bulk, he's not one for running or jumping, so he winds up in the heft-based events.

"What if I step over the line after I've released the cannon ball?" I hear him ask the judge as I walk up. Teddy loves to make a big show of sports, but not being very athletic, he doesn't take it too seriously. He waves at me, smiling. Then he returns his focus to the pit, walking around it to get the feel of the circle. Once that's done, he crouches down and springs up. Five times. Each time, he holds back and doesn't fling the shot.

"C'mon, Teddy!" yell some angry opponents. I'm already rolling on the ground.

"Judge, how much more time do I have on this turn?" He's enjoying this.

"Just get going. We haven't got all day!"

Teddy crouches one more time, sees that his sneakers are untied, and stoops to retie them. Picking up the shot, he carefully brushes the grass from it, polishing it against his tee shirt. Eying the distance in front of him, he sets again, spins violently, and lets the shot dribble out of his hands about five feet from the pit.

"Oh, oh." He smiles broadly at the judges who are doing all they can not to burst out laughing. Hitching up his shorts, Teddy bows to an imaginary audience, wipes his forehead, and saunters over to sit on the grass with me. "Must have hit a gust of wind," he explains, raising a wetted finger to test for air currents. I love it. I wish I had his ability to take things so lightly.

Field Day activities are concluded with a delicious Indian feast eaten on the field. For plates, we use broad, green, banana leaves into which the rice and curry are spooned. Now Teddy can enjoy his favorite Field Day sport: eating. He does it with gusto.

As we eat, the winners are called up to the platform one by one to get their ribbons. My brother, Dave, wins the K Award for being one of the top athletes of the day. I'm proud to join him on the platform when they hand out my ribbon, too.

On the business front, the afternoon is a great success. We unload all of our remaining melons, keeping careful track in a book who has bought what, and how much they owe us. I see dollar signs and candy bars dancing in my mind as we walk back to Phelps Hall.

"Okay," Bosch says, "where's the record book?" He looks around at a half-dozen blank faces.

"Don't you have it?"

"No, I was watching the stock while you guys wandered around making the sales and writing them down. Don't you know where it is?"

No one knows where the book is. Without the book, we don't know who owes us, or how much they owe. The day has been a disaster! I try to remember how many slices I sold to my friends in Phelps, but I can't recall exactly.

I ask a couple of Phelps kids to pay, and they ask me how much they owe. When they discover that I don't have a record of the sales, they pay me for one and then walk away smirking— and spreading the news that we don't have a record of our sales. Within an hour, no one else agrees to pay us; everyone claims that they didn't buy any watermelons. We have lost all our savings. I'll never be a salesman. But Bosch gets us to admit that we had a great time. Maybe I'll invest in him again next year, after all.

A few nights later, the junior class puts on an ice-cream social. The whole school is invited to this annual event. This time, the juniors have added hamburgers to the usual ice-cream menu, and that's enough to bring every student to the event. My brother Dave is one of the salespersons at the stand, so I pester him to buy me hamburgers. After shelling out for four, he's had enough of me and tells me to skedaddle. I skedaddle.

Dave is a good older brother who looks after me and tries to make sure that I stay out of trouble. If anyone bullies me, I threaten to have Dave beat him up, and that usually works. Fortunately, I haven't had to ask Dave to actually beat up any of my classmates. I don't know if he'd really do it, but the others don't know that, so they always lay off.

At the beginning of the year, Dave gave me permission to charge food to his account at school activities. That didn't work out very well. When I bought too much stuff, he cut me off. He wrote home about it, and I got a stern warning from Dad about being a good little brother.

Dave also wrote, "Paul usually combs his hair in the morning, but since he doesn't use hair oil, his hair hangs all over his face by the end of the day." Mom wrote and told me to carry a comb in my pocket, but I know I'd lose it in no time. It seems like an awful waste of money, so I decide I won't carry a comb and just let my hair hang in my face. Maybe when I'm certain I won't lose the comb, then I'll begin to carry one. Even though Dave got me in trouble for my hair and won't let me use his credit, I still think he's a great brother.

To make up for the poor quality of the food dished out in the dining hall, Paul B.'s parents come up with a brilliant plan. They mail him a large package with a semester's supply of chocolate covered vitamins. They don't look like vitamins at all; they look like chocolate candy bars. In spite of the slightly metallic taste, we all enjoy Paul's candy. In fact, we polish off the whole package in a couple of days. After scarfing them down, we all come down with diarrhea that lasts a whole week. But no one complains or thinks it wasn't worth it. We'd do it all over again. We're not likely to get another chance; however, Paul's parents say they won't send him any more vitamin candy.

It's seven o'clock, the sun has set, and the mountain's chill makes us shiver in our thin pajamas. With the soothing pitter-patter of the rain on the roof, we settle down in the social room for our nightly dorm meeting. To share body heat, we huddle close together on the floor in front of the fireplace. I sit as close to the fire as I can in order to catch some of its heat. If you sit any further from the fireplace, the chill grabs you and freezes you to the bone. We're crowded on a hemp mat, as coarse and prickly as a hunk of rope. Even though it scratches our butts, it is much more comfortable than the icy-cold stone floor underneath it. A few of the sixth graders, wrapped in their blankets, are snuggled in the scruffy easy chairs that ring the room. We each own a pair of cheap rubber sandals to protect our feet from the cold floors, but none of us actually wears them. You can't run in them, and besides, anyone wearing them is a wimp.

It is a relaxed, calm time. Mrs. B. sits beside the fire in the only comfortable chair, and we clump around her like chicks swarming a mother hen. I love the routine. Mrs. B. looks at us all with her best caring look, which is still a bit scary.

"Have you boys all finished your homework? Paul? Teddy? Bobby? The rest of you?" We all nod solemnly. Even if we didn't finish our homework, we sure wouldn't admit it to Mrs. B. There's no telling what she might do. Then she asks if we've written our weekly letter to our parents. Again, we nod.

"Now, I just want to remind you that laundry will be due for the *dhobi* on Friday at 3 PM. Also, we'll have a special speaker in chapel on Sunday, so I want you all to be on your best behavior."

Mrs. B. pauses a minute for effect, and then continues. "Boys, I want to tell you that your prayers have been answered today." We look around at each other, wondering which of our prayers God decided to answer. Then she nods at Sam, who is bundled in a blanket with the rest of us, trying to keep warm and not stand out. Our eyes follow her nod, and Sam droops his head, embarrassed.

"Because you all prayed for him, Sam has been restored to us in good health. The pit has been removed." That's when I remember that Sam was in the Dishpan because he swallowed a plum pit. Two nights ago Mrs. B. called a special dorm meeting. In grave tones she told us that Sam might die if the pit wasn't removed because it had lodged in his lung.

Death was not a subject we knew or talked about very much, and by the time Mrs. B. was done, we were all frightened and nestled even closer to each other, wondering what the world was coming to. We prayed fervently for Sam's full recovery, a recovery that was now credited to us and to our prayers. Frankly, we hadn't noticed that Sam was gone, and we hadn't noticed when he returned. I look smugly over at the cowering Sam and pray that he's learned his lesson and will never swallow another plum pit into his lungs.

Mrs. B. is moving on to the next topic of the evening. "Now, let me see what I have on my demerit list. Johnny, I want to warn you once again, there will be NO running in the hall. You almost bumped into Mr. B. when you raced around the corner. I won't give you a demerit this time, but I don't want it to happen again. Do you hear me?" Johnny grimaces. "And I want this to be a warning to the rest of you. NO running." Johnny dutifully looks at the ground, but the rest of us know he's smiling inside. The main message we all hear is, "I won't give you a demerit." We know he got away with it again.

"You must be good little boys so your parents can be proud of you!" I feel like I have met two of the three points: I'm little and a boy. That's a pretty good batting average.

After Johnny has been sacrificed for all of us, Mrs. B. begins devotions. Being very religious, she has a real gift for prayer. Hers are long, but so full of feeling and so well worded that I actually enjoy prayer time. Tonight is no different. In the middle, she prays for Johnny to be well behaved and for Sam to be thankful. We all respond, "Amen!"

"Tonight's going to be a really exciting evening. I'm going to read one of my favorite Bible stories," she announces when the prayer is over. She reads the passage about the Good Samaritan and tells us how important it is for us to lend a hand to those in need, even if they're poor foreigners. This is a message that we mish kids know well.

Then she brings out *Pilgrim's Progress*, which we all love to hear, and takes up reading where she had left off last night. The section for tonight is about Pilgrim getting pulled out of deep, sinful quicksand by Help. I can just imagine Pilgrim struggling to free himself, to no avail. He's screaming and yelling helplessly, until finally Help arrives. Mrs. B. shows us the pictures which go with the passage. Then and there I resolve to pull anyone I meet out of the bogs of life. We head off to bed feeling contented. I decide that Mrs. B. must not be so bad after all.

That feeling doesn't last long.

The next afternoon, after school is done, my buddies and I head for the wall behind Phelps Hall. Like all the dorms, Phelps is built on a giant chunk of flat land that has been carved out of the side of the mountain. Behind the dorm is a steep cliff, about thirty feet high, which is one of our special places to play.

While "mountain climbing" is always a favorite thing to do, today we play with our miniature toys. These are Matchbox and Dinky toys, tiny metal cars and trucks which are the ideal size for the roads and mountain passes we have carved into the softer sections of the cliff wall. The roads, hairpin turns, and tunnels are very realistic. It has taken us weeks to build, and we're all proud of ourselves. We are experts at imagining what hairpin turns should look like, and we often find that our Dinky cars wind up with the same fate as real cars coming up the *Ghat*. They fall off the edge of the roads, tumbling into the valley far below.

While we're zooming our cars along twisting mountain ledges, Mrs. B. comes out to see what we're doing. We are eager to show her how tricky our construction has been, complete with rivers and little bridges, with "villages" and parking spots. The more we talk, the more her brows furrow. Standing back from the cliff face, she runs her eyes over the whole network of roads. She is not pleased.

"If you carve out any more of those roadways, the entire cliff will fall down on us!" she yells, nervously pointing a quivering finger at our tracks. "You have to stop right now and come down from there!"

We're stunned. We can't believe that Mrs. B. really thinks our mountain, which has stood for millions of years, is now ready to collapse on Phelps Hall. But she does believe it. She works herself into a stew, barely containing her rage. Finally, she stomps back to her apartment. But that isn't the end of it. She orders Mr. B., a gentle soul who we all like, to spank us for possibly bringing the mountain down on top of Phelps Hall!

Mr. B. reluctantly approaches us, muttering something about being disappointed by our naughty behavior. He orders us to our bedrooms and to prepare for a paddling.

When he gets to my room, he tells me to bend over. Then he administers a number of whacks to my butt with a ping-pong paddle. With the third whack, the paddle snaps clean off at the handle, and Mr. B. is left with only the stump of the racket in his hand. His arm is raised, ready for the next blow, but there is nothing to hit with. Briefly, I wonder about answered prayers and say a silent, "Thank you, God. I knew I wasn't doing anything wrong."

I look back at Mr. B. and realize there are many things going through his head. Not only does he not have a paddle to finish spanking me, but now he has to replace a perfectly good ping-pong paddle from the dorm's small budget. Turning red with anger and shame, Mr. B. tramps out of my room and doesn't finish spanking several other kids. I know now that the Mrs. B. of the social room is not like the Mrs. B. of the rest of the day.

Mrs. B. does not like us to play Response. The day after the paddling, we decide we will play Response, whatever the consequences. Kind of a grudge match.

Response is our favorite game. It's like tag, only we don't tag each other, we throw a "Response" at each other. The Response is made from the bed frame webbing that is used to hold up our mattresses. We strip the webbing from someone's bed and then roll it into a tube about two inches long and an inch around, and tie it tightly. Once a Response has been made, it isn't long before we're hiding, dodging, laughing, and making a general ruckus.

Soon we are running all over the campus. When Teno hits me with the Response, I grab it and take off after Teddy who runs across the flag pole green. I throw with all my might, and just miss him. But the Response rolls down the hill toward Boyer, and I have to hurry to pick it up so it doesn't bounce down to the girls' dorm.

"You boys are so silly," says Becky, a classmate who is on her way to her room in Boyer. Girls don't understand Response and why we love it. In my way of thinking, that's one more reason that girls are strange.

As the evening settles around us, our game is still going strong. In fact, another group is also playing Response, and we have to avoid getting hit by their Response. Only the group that you start with can play with your Response. The game will only stop when everyone gets exhausted and wants to quit for a few days. I've been in games that dragged on for weeks, only ending when the Response was finally lost.

I walk cautiously, because I know that someone may be lurking behind a tree or in the hallway or in the dark, ready to pelt me with the Response. Then, as I race down to Phelps Hall and the safety of my dorm room, a Response sails overhead and hits a roof tile, missing me by inches. The tile comes off and clatters to the ground, shattering into a million pieces. I'm really running now, doing all I can to avoid being hit by flying tiles and flying Responses.

Suddenly, a dark object sails past my head and slams up against a Phelps Hall window. The glass breaks right in front of me, splattering bits of glass everywhere. We're in trouble now, so I don't stop running until I'm in my room with the door shut. If Mrs. B. finds us, we'll have so many demerits they'll never let us out of our rooms again. There won't be any ping-pong paddles left!

"D'ja hear about Uncle Gerry and Aunt Rose Nykerk?!" shouts Teddy. Uncle Gerry and Aunt Rose were our neighbors when we settled into our house in Bahrain at Christmas time, and their son Nykerk is my soda-guzzling hero.

"No, what happened to them?"

"Their boat was bombed! The *Dara* went down!"

"When? Where? How do you know? Are they okay?" The questions come tumbling out. I know about the *Dara*. It is one of the British-India passenger boats that travel around the Gulf, to and from India.

"They're here in Kodai, and all the Arab kids are going to have supper with them tonight, so they must be okay." Although almost all the students at Kodai are American, we identify ourselves by our mission field. Those of us whose parents are missionaries in Arabia are "Arabs." Mish kids from Burma are "Burmese"; from Ceylon, "Ceylonese"; and so on. The majority of Kodai students are mish kids, although there are a few whose parents work in embassies or businesses. We Arabs stick together, kind of like cousins; so it is not unusual for us to get together when an Uncle or Aunt comes to town.

I can hardly wait for the time for us to gather with Uncle Gerry and Aunt Rose, and I spend the afternoon trying to find out what really happened to them. Nobody really knows, although there are rumors about passengers panicking, of ships colliding, of bombs, of sharks, and of stormy seas. By the time we arrive at *Dar es Salaam*, the cottage where Arab parents usually stay when they are visiting Kodai, we're bubbling over with excitement.

After hugging everyone, Aunt Rose sits us down, and we form a wide-eyed circle around the couch on which she and Uncle Gerry plant themselves. There are about fifteen Arab mish kids in the room, eager to get on with the story. Uncle Gerry begins.

"First, we want to thank God that we are here." There are murmurs of assent all around the room. "Aunt Rose and I are especially thankful that we can be with all of you tonight. We also want to tell each of you that your parents love you and send their love along. Teddy, your parents wanted to be sure we said 'hi' to you." Along with everyone else in the semi-circle, I'm fidgeting nervously by this time. Let's get on with the story!

"Well," resumes Uncle Gerry, "let me get this straight. Aunt Rose and I left Kuwait on the BI ship, *Dara*, almost two weeks ago, on the afternoon of April 5. Things were going well at first, but on the morning of the seventh, as we were about to set sail from Dubai, the steward told us that there was a large storm approaching and we would have to wait it out in the Gulf, rather than in port.

"As we were making our way out of Dubai, the Dara was struck by another ship, but the damage seemed to be slight, and we wanted to be away from the port when the storm hit, so we kept on sailing. Later, in the middle of the night of April seventh and eighth, a powerful bomb exploded on the ship, knocking out all electrical power and the PA system. As a result, it was impossible to announce what was happening."

Ships colliding. Storms coming. A bomb exploding. This was better than Mrs. B.'s stories in the social room.

At this point, Aunt Rose takes up the narrative. Her version of what happened, accompanied by cliffhanging details and lots of hand waving, is even more exciting than Uncle Gerry's. His logical style of storytelling is like Dad's; they're both doctors, after all.

"In the darkness, with no idea about what was going on," Aunt Rose continues, "we didn't know what to do. Uncle Gerry spotted our steward and grabbed him and asked 'What should we do?' 'Stay in your cabins. Everything is okay. We'll get things fixed very soon.' But the steward looked dazed and scared, so I didn't take his word for it. 'Gerry,' I said, 'we've got to get out of here!'"

By now, if you had dropped a pin, the whole room of mish kids would have hit the ceiling. We all want them to get out of there. Pronto!

"So we made our way down the corridor, using our hands to feel the walls because everything was pitch-black. Despite the stewards' orders for us to remain in our cabins, many people were struggling along with us, trying to get topside. When we found a staircase, we went up and up, until finally we stumbled onto the upper deck. There, all was in chaos, with crew trying to use hoses to put out fires that were spurting out of windows. Other crew members were marshaling people toward the lifeboats. Some lifeboats were already in the water, and the only way down was by rope ladder.

"A crewman shoved us toward one of these rope ladders, telling us to move quickly to get into the lifeboat. You have to remember, we were in the middle of the storm and the wind was fierce, beating us with a driving rain. Everything was confusing with people screaming and running all over the place, bumping into each other and slipping on the wet deck. The ship was rocking back and forth. It was awful. I tumbled a couple of times, scraping my knees." We all glance at her modestly covered knees and see a slight bulge under her dress which is probably a medical wrapping. We can imagine the pain of the scraped knees and feel the wind and rain pelting us as she continues her narrative.

"We looked around frantically for Mr. and Mrs. Singh, our dear colleagues from our mission hospital. They were a few cabins away from us, but we just couldn't find them. They probably stayed in their cabins, doing what the stewards told them to do. We never saw them again." I look around the room and realize that death has been mentioned again; everyone is silent, and a few of the girls have tears in their eyes.

"In any case, we didn't have much time to look around and think, because the crewmen pushed us to the railing and told us to climb down. Uncle Gerry went first, which was a good thing. I saw how he did it and tried to follow. I grabbed hold of the railing and climbed over, making my way down. I couldn't believe how slippery the rope ladder was, or how far down it was to the lifeboat.

"The little craft just tossed and turned in the turbulent waters, and I didn't think I'd ever get down there. At one point I yelled out, 'I can't hold on any longer,' and was ready to let go. Fortunately, Uncle Gerry called back that he was there to help. He held on to the rope and tried to steady it for me so that I wouldn't keep banging against the ship.

"At last, when I couldn't hang on any longer, I felt Uncle Gerry's hands on my feet, guiding them onto the ladder rungs. But the trouble was that the lifeboat was rising and falling with the waves, and as soon as I was reassured, his hand left my foot and the boat fell into a trough. Finally, he grabbed my foot again and hung on, guiding me to the bed of the boat, where I collapsed in exhaustion. We didn't even have time to hug each other, because Uncle Gerry was back up helping other people down the ladders.

"After what seemed like an eternity, the lifeboat cast off, filled with sobbing, frightened folks. As we floated away from the *Dara*, we could hear passengers shouting and crying, and others pleading to be rescued. The entire deck was lit by flames. It was awful. By the time we got back to Dubai, the storm had slowed down a bit, but we could still see the *Dara* burning in the distance."

She stops, and we all inhale. It is as if we hadn't breathed from the time she began to talk. Some kids sniffle, others dab at their eyes. I feel my throat tightening.

"No one knows who placed the bomb on the *Dara* or why they did it," Uncle Gerry says. "But they told us that over two hundred people died that night. There were eight hundred of us among the passengers and crew, and it could have been a lot worse; especially if more people had stayed in their cabins like the stewards told us to."

The room is tense and quiet. No one wants to break the mood, so not much more is said until we are walking back to the dorm.

"Hey Paul," Teddy says to me. "There goes your sleeping bag!"

I hadn't thought about my sleeping bag all evening. But it must be somewhere at the bottom of the Arabian Gulf having gone down with the *Dara*. I had been so excited when Mom ordered it from the Sears catalogue, but I couldn't carry it on the airplane with me from Bahrain. Uncle Gerry and Aunt Rose agreed to bring it with them, and I was looking forward to having it so that

I wouldn't have to be one of the wimps who had to borrow one of the smelly, old, World War II sleeping bags. Never mind. I can get over the loss of the sleeping bag, especially when I think of the two hundred dead people lying on the sea floor with it.

"Have you guys ever heard about Virginia Boyer?" Terr asks Teddy and me as we walk home from *Dar Es Salaam* in the darkness. I shake my head, so Terr continues. "She was a teacher here in the 1920s and was coming back from furlough in the US. When her boat was going past Gibraltar, a French boat rammed into it."

"On purpose?!"

"No, it was an accident. Anyway, when her boat began to sink, she got in one of the lifeboats. As she settled down, she heard the pitiful pleas of a woman and her two young kids. Her husband was still on deck because the lifeboat didn't have room for him. So Virginia got out of the lifeboat and gave up her seat for the kid's father. She went down with the ship!"

On top of all that we've heard from Uncle Gerry and Aunt Rose, this story of Virginia Boyer's sacrifice sends shivers down my spine. I imagine her standing at the railing, waving at the family as they float away and as she sinks with her ship into the Atlantic.

"That's where we get the name for Boyer Hall," Terr concludes. After hearing that story and all the other things tonight, I'm glad that Boyer Hall is far away from me.

"All nine planets are going to line up," Mr. Shaw announces in science class one day. "The solar observatory folks have told me that this is a rare astronomical event, so we're going to study it." He then draws a chart on the blackboard of the solar system, complete with the nine planets all in a row. It looks cool. He then talks about how the solar observatory was placed on a mountain nearby because of our clear, cloudless nights, and how the astronomers there are always sharing with Kodai teachers news of eclipses and other astronomical events. By the time the class is done, I am really impressed and eager to learn more about astronomy.

But not everyone is as interested in the astronomy part of the news as I am.

The planets lining up means something very different to Sammy. Sammy is a mish kid from Burma, and the Burmese are known for their piousness and strict reading of the Bible.

"When all those planets line up, it will cause their orbits to collapse, and then bring about the end of the entire solar system," Sammy announces to a group of us after class. This seems a bit far-fetched, but it does sound possible. Who knows what will happen when all the planets line up?

But Sammy is only getting started. "Because the solar system will begin to wobble, there will be huge fire storms on the sun which will warp the earth's atmosphere and cause dangerous weather patterns, storms, weird temperatures, droughts, famines, earthquakes, and even changes in the earth's rotation. All of this might even cause California to fall off the map and disappear under the sea." While few of us have ever been to California, this doesn't sound like a happy prospect.

Then Sammy adds a biblical zinger: "This is what the book of Revelation is all about. The end of time is coming!" We are mish kids, and we know stories about God's wrath for a sinful world. This sounds serious, and some of Sammy's listeners become convinced he's onto something. I'm still not sure.

The next morning more students have heard about Sammy's predictions, and fear begins to spread across campus. When I arrive in science class, Mr. Shaw is very upset. He assures us that nothing dangerous is going to happen when the planets line up and that the world is not going to come to an end. His words don't stop our imaginations from running wild. In fact, the very worried look on his face seems to confirm that something evil is happening in the heavens.

When someone asks him, "When *will* the world come to an end?" he answers that he doesn't know, that it is in God's hands. His response only adds fuel to the fire, and students panic even more. "So it *could* happen soon?"

"Of course, it could happen any time. But the planets being lined up won't make it happen. It will happen when God is ready to have it happen."

Given all that I've heard, I have difficulty sleeping that night, waiting for the planets to line up and the solar system to collapse and for time to end.

When morning comes and the world is still spinning along happily, we all breathe a sigh of relief. Mr. Shaw is especially relieved. We don't talk about the planets in his class that day. Maybe we won't talk about them ever again.

Once the planets have returned to their orbits and it is possible to laugh again, I join Bosch and Paul B. for an afternoon of after-hour boating. Phelps Hall is separated from Kodai Lake by a four-foot high stone wall and a small street. Late in the afternoon we make our escape over the wall and head to the closed boathouse on the edge of the lake. There we untie a punt and silently push off into the water. It is a beautiful afternoon, with the sun setting over the tops of the trees making for a great view. We are out of sight of the campus in a few strokes and head to the middle of the lake.

Once we're several hundred yards from the shore, Bosch takes a small length of lead pipe out of his pocket. Bosch is always hiding things in his pocket, so I'm not surprised. I'm a bit alarmed when he also takes out a firecracker and a marble. Ramming the firecracker into the pipe, with its fuse sticking out of the bottom end, Bosch adds the marble on the front end. He then produces a match and sparks it up. In an instant, the firecracker is burning, and Dave aims the "cannon" into the water.

I watch the arc of the flame as the cracker explodes, sending the marble fifty feet away from us, plopping into the lake. Water lilies are tossed high into the air amidst a waterspout. The "CRACK" carries all across the lake, echoing off the nearby mountain peaks. I duck into the punt, hoping no one sees us. But Bosch and Paul B. are rocking the boat they're laughing so hard, reviewing in loud terms how the cracker flew and blew. Just to see what will happen, Bosch throws a second firecracker into the lake. I watch in horror as a few fish begin to float to the surface, dead as doornails. With them come a couple of frogs. Bosch makes a comment about roasted frog legs, but I want to puke.

I settle back into the punt and just stare at the darkening sky, trying to ignore the floating corpses. Before long, I conclude that this whole experience has been a grand adventure, after all. We've broken a few school rules—which will surely gain us approval from our friends—and we've roasted some frog legs. Besides, who could forget such a glorious sunset?

As we walk back to school, Bosch spots a huge, fresh cowpie in the road.

"Hey I got an idea," Bosch says. "Let's put a firecracker in that Kodai Rose."

"What's a 'Kodai Rose'?" I ask suspiciously.

"That's what missionaries call 'cowpies,' you jerk. Haven't you heard that before?"

"'Course I have," I lie.

Without further discussion, he pulls out his largest firecracker, the "A-bomb," and carefully sticks it in the middle of the steaming, wet Kodai Rose. We can hardly move; we're riveted on Bosch. He lights the cracker which turns out to have an instant fuse. Before we can run away, it blows up with a huge explosion, sending bits of sticky, fresh, wet manure all over the place, splattering us from head to foot. Grinning with the excitement of the moment, we look at each other and roar with laughter. Life is good on this side of the campus wall.

On the walk back to school, we realize that the hot water will all be gone by the time we have our showers. I shiver to think of the cold water in this weather. We'll also have put on new sets of clothes. The old, manure-filled clothes will go into our laundry bags where they can be smelt by all our classmates. It will make them question where we got these strange odors. Like the manure, tales of our escapade will be spread far and wide, and we will be heroes.

As we climb the wall, however, our luck runs out. There, on the other side of the wall, stands the Gurkha. The Gurkha has no name, or at least none that we know. He is the campus law enforcer, a retired member of the British Imperial military who comes from Nepal. Like all Gurkhas, he is tall, in great physical shape, and looks very different from South Indians. We are all scared silly of him. Our Gurkha relishes the role of being a guard, appearing when we least expect—or want—to see him. Like now. He seemingly appears out of thin air, confirming our suspicions that he has a sixth sense for smelling trouble when it is brewing.

"Bad boys!" he pronounces. "In trouble now!" I can see him sniffing the air, recognizing the distinctive odor of manure.

"Us?" Bosch asks sheepishly. "We're just out for a walk around the campus." Guilt is written all over my face, but Bosch seems totally relaxed.

"Hey, show us your knife," Bosch boldly requests. I stare at him wondering what he has in mind. Maybe he's trying to distract our Gurkha.

As is customary for Gurkhas, ours carries a large, curved knife which he keeps hidden in a scabbard hanging from his belt. Although none of us have ever seen it out of the black sheath, it isn't hard to imagine what it looks like. It's big. Maybe a foot long, and probably well-polished, for our Gurkha is a stickler for neatness.

"If I take it out, I must make blood," he replies, scowling at us. "Must cut my finger." A part of the Gurkha tradition is that he should never take his knife out unless he is provoked. When he is provoked, he must respond with violence. If he takes it out unprovoked, he must cut his own finger to remind him that it should never be taken out unless there is a good reason.

His words put the sense of fear in me. "I promise I'll never go boating again. Just let us go back up to the dining hall for supper," I plead. I try to keep the note of whining out of my voice, but it's hard to do. His self-confident smirk doesn't help.

Then, mercifully, he nods his head and says, "Go!" We go, and quickly. I know that I'm on his watch list for sure. I fear that I'll never get away with anything ever again. But that fear doesn't last long. By the time we bathe and hit the supper line, our retelling of the adventure includes the eating of a hundred firecracker-cooked frog legs.

By mid-April, Phelps Hall is almost empty. Many parents have arrived in Kodai to avoid the summer heat in the plains of India and in the Arabian Gulf. This means that their kids leave campus for a month or more, staying in the "cottages" that were built around Kodai Lake by missionaries and British government officials. When Teddy moves out, Mrs. B. moves me into a room with Bosch, Kaz's older brother, and Tim. They are all sixth graders and known troublemakers. It seems to be Mrs. B.'s plan that I, as the "good boy" roommate of Teddy, transform the others into good boys.

Mrs. B. should have known better. I am only a fifth grader and know I can't tell sixth graders what to do. I have learned my place in Kodai life, and I have no intention of trying to break out of that place. Instead, I am delighted that I am rooming with a fun-loving, danger-seeking, wild bunch that is out to have a good time. They take me under their wing, teaching me a basic rule: if fun is done right, we can enjoy ourselves and avoid being caught. The only bad fun is the fun that we're caught doing.

I am an eager learner. The first night we are all together, Bosch tells me that I am going to be a lookout. He's heard rumors that there is a tunnel under Boyer Hall, where the elementary girls live, and he wants to investigate. What he needs is someone to cover for him in case Mrs. B. begins to prowl around the corridors. It is my job to distract Mrs. B. if that happens. I begin to rehearse how I will be sick and ask to be taken to her apartment. My stomach is turning summersaults, so pretending to be sick won't be a big problem.

When it is thoroughly dark and there is no one roaming the hall, Bosch eases out the window, careful not to be seen by the Gurkha as he clambers out. I watch him make his way cautiously up the hill, past Block Hall and around the corner. Then he is swallowed up in the darkness. I'm scared and excited. This is more fun than I've had since we blew up the frogs and fish.

Turning away from the window, I make my way back across the room to the door and crack it open. Silence. No one is out and about, so I relax a bit. Before too long, I begin to grow a bit weary and haul the edge of my bed closer to the door so that I can sit on it while staring out into the corridor. Bosch is taking forever, and I'm growing more and more sleepy. Soon, I nod off.

"Why is this door open?!" demands an angry voice.

I jump up with a start. It's Mr. B. making his nightly rounds.

"Sorry, sir. I was just letting some fresh air into the room. I'll close it."

"Well, do it and go back to sleep. Is everyone else asleep in there?"

"Yessir," I lie, praying that Bosch is asleep somewhere so the lie is only about the place he's sleeping, not whether or not he's asleep.

"Okay, then. Go back to sleep. It's late."

When he leaves, I sit up wide awake. When will Bosch return? Now it's not so exciting, and I begin to worry. I know that there are panthers and snakes out there, and I begin to fantasize about Bosch being attacked by one or the other. I wonder which would be worse, to be chewed to death by a panther or poisoned to death by a cobra. Just when I'm about to doze off again, Bosch taps lightly on the window.

"Why did you take so long?" I demand. "You had me scared to death. I lied to Mr. B." Then I noticed the mud clinging to his clothes. "You're a dirty mess. Where were you?"

Bosch ignores all my questions as he scrambles back into the room and brushes off the caked mud. "You won't believe the spiders under there!" he began. "Cobwebs everywhere."

"Under Boyer Hall?" I ask in amazement.

"Yup."

I ponder that for a minute. "What about the girls? Did you see any of them?"

"Well, I know where to look now. They were all asleep, of course, so I didn't see anyone in particular," he explains smugly. "But I know where to look now." There is a light in his eyes that tells me that this is important information.

I decide on the spot that Bosch is my new hero. He has successfully completed a night-time investigation and was not caught. While I can't imagine why he would want to go to Boyer Hall, his satisfaction is infectious. It does not matter to me that I had to lie to Mr. B.; it had to be done for the good of the expedition. We've pulled it off!

Later that night, as I review the evening's excitement, I realize that I have really made it. I am no longer just an outside punk kid trying to learn the ropes. I am now one of the guys—a "Kodai Kid"—ready for all the adventures which will come my way. I can hardly wait.

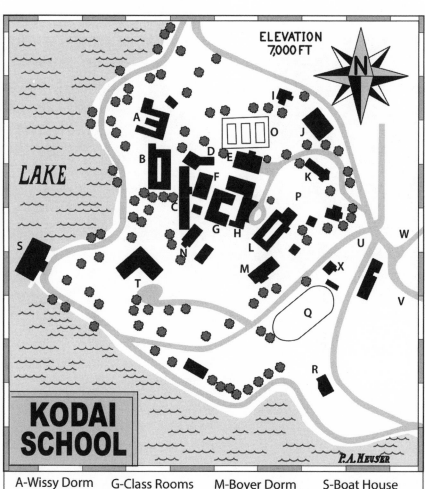

ELEVATION
7,000 FT

N

LAKE

A

B

C

D E

F

G H

I

J

K

L

M

N

O

P

Q

R

S

T

U

V

W

X

P.A. HEUSER

KODAI SCHOOL

A-Wissy Dorm	G-Class Rooms	M-Boyer Dorm	S-Boat House
B-Phelps Hall	H-Dining Hall	N-Science Classes	T-Carlton Hotel
C-Block Dorm	I-Dish Pan	O-Tennis Courts	U-Seven Corners
D-Airalee Dorm	J-KMU	P-Play Ground	V-to Coakers
E-Gym	K-Church	Q-Bendy Field	W-to Budge
F-Library	L-Kennedy Dorm	R-Benderloch	X-Pererra's

Typical town street in India

CHAPTER 3

Getting Involved

Warm weather finally arrives, and all of us are excited. It means that fifth grade will soon be over, and we will have a month's break from school before sixth grade starts. More importantly, it is "Hill Season," when missionary parents come up to the mountains for summer vacation. Dave and Terr have been talking about Hill Season for a long time. They promise me it will be the best time of the year, with parties, picnics, dances, carnivals, movies, plays, concerts, sporting events, boat regattas, and hikes. It sounds like heaven.

When Mom and Dad arrive at the end of April, Dave, Terr, and I move into *Dar es Salaam* with them. We hire a *coolie* to carry our belongings from the dorms. The *coolie* weighs about a hundred and ten pounds. He wraps a cloth around his head as a round platform, and then stoops down while other men balance the trunk on his head. The metal trunk must weigh as much as

81

the *coolie*, and I can't believe that he doesn't tip over or break his neck.

As he staggers off alone for the two-mile, one-hour journey up and down steep terrain to *Dar es Salaam*, I wince in pain imagining how his head and neck must hurt. Once he is on his way, we take a shortcut which is too steep for him, and are waiting when he arrives. We help him take the trunk off his head. I still can't figure out how he hasn't broken his neck.

With our clothing stowed away for the month, Mom, Dad, and we three boys settle down for the evening, sitting on folding chairs in our front garden. It is not easy reconnecting, being a family again. I've never been away for so long, and it feels odd to be back together again. I'm not quite sure what to talk about. I remember the old days when I lived at home and could say whatever I wanted to. Mom hugged a lot. Family life had a natural flow back then.

But as we sit staring at our feet in the gathering darkness, I don't know what to say. I can hardly tell them about Response, the after-hour punting, the pillow fights, or puking my guts out after eating all the vitamin candies. They don't want to hear about Mrs. Battleaxe or Miss Slifer.

I just want to be held close by my mother again, but I know that I'm not a little kid any more, and that's not what big kids are supposed to do. Dave and Terr don't seem to want to be hugged. To break the silence, I say, "I had a great time on the Perumal hike. I climbed right to the top." Even as I talk, I feel like what I'm saying has been "cleaned" for an adult audience. I realize that I have a whole new life that I can't share with Mom and Dad. Although I'm excited that they are here, I can't help feeling sad and out of place, too.

While we are getting used to each other again, I still have another week of fifth grade. The next morning, Dave and Terr walk me back to the campus so I'll be in class on time.

"I don't know what I can say to Mom and Dad," I complain to Dave and Terr. "There's so much I've been doing that I can't talk about."

"Yeah, you'll get used to that," Dave assures me. But, I'm not sure I ever will.

At noon, Mom and Dad show up to have lunch with me. We sit on the lawn in front of the gym and open the *tiffins* which carry our lunch. *Tiffins* are stacking metal pans which Indians use to keep food hot. Each pan holds a different dish, and I love opening them and discovering the goodies inside. As we sit in the sun, I point out some of the buildings on campus and tell Mom about some of the things that have happened there. Slowly I begin to relax with her again.

I'm happy when I walk back to *Dar es Salaam* after school. I feel like the ice has been broken and things will be back to normal. As I descend the hill from school, I can see smoke rising from the kitchen chimney. Swirls of grey smoke curl up to the low hanging clouds, where they mix and disappear into each other. I can smell wonderful smells, a sure sign that Sousai, our Indian cook, is preparing something delicious for supper.

Sousai comes with *Dar es Salaam*. Because the bungalow is shared by all Arabian mission folk, we all know Sousai. Besides caring for the house, he is a gifted cook, story teller, mission historian, house cleaner, gardener, laundryman, and general handyman. Thanks to his green thumb, the house is surrounded by flowers of every sort, brilliant in the sun, adding even more color to our lives. Sousai even keeps an orchid garden in the shadows of the cliff overhanging the house. Sousai's greatest gift, and we consider it heaven-inspired, is his cooking. He is a legend, a genius. After months of cafeteria food, we feel like we have moved to paradise.

From the most basic food ingredients, he turns out fabulous meals in his small, soot-filled kitchen with its ancient, black, cast-iron stove. He is really good at baking pastries and cakes decorated with icing pictures depicting Kodai scenes. Mount Perumal is one of his favorite scenes because we can see it from the campus and from *Dar es Salaam.*

His pastries greet us as we arrive from school just in time for late afternoon tea. Sousai is in his usual good spirits. He is always happy, and his mood makes me feel happy, too. We all dig in to the pastries he has baked for today, dipping them in our sweet, milky tea.

After tea, I spend some time with Dad showing him my homework assignments. Then he and I go out to the front lawn and take some golf putts, waiting for supper. Just when my stomach can't take the wonderful odors any more, Sousai rings a small hand-bell, announcing that supper is ready. Like magic, Dave and Terr appear out of their room, and with Mom and Dad we gather around the dinner table. Sousai waits silently in the nearby hall for Dad's prayer. Thankfully, it's not a long one tonight, but it is good to hear him pray again.

When the family says "Amen," Sousai begins to serve the soup. Not only is the soup delicious, but it is also a treat in itself since soup is never served at school. Thin toasted rusks come with the soup, and afterwards the main course arrives. It is a meat dish with steaming potatoes and fresh vegetables taken from the garden that day. I'm thankful that it isn't liver, which I can't stand. Since there is no refrigerator in the bungalow, I don't know how Sousai manages to keep food from spoiling. Everything tastes fresh. Finally, homemade pastry desserts are served. Sousai sets the dishes down with grand, sweeping arm motions. We all gasp in appreciation, and he smiles happily in response.

With supper comfortably behind us, we retreat to the living room where Sousai has started a fire to burn off the evening's chill. Sousai understands fire like no one I've ever known. He can turn a pile of wood into a glowing fire in minutes! We sit around the cozy glow of the fire. The wood gives off the soothing smell of eucalyptus, putting us all at ease. After a few minutes Sousai appears with a tray bearing a fresh pot of tea. I feel like our contented family has been restored after the awkwardness of yesterday.

As the evening comes to a close, we talk easily about the day. While Dave and Terr are reporting on their classwork, I snuggle close to Mom and read comics under the weak light bulbs. The general darkness of the room highlights the shifting light patterns of the fire. I can think of no better way to spend an evening and prepare for sleep. I don't remember going to bed, but I wake up in my room with the sun shining in.

As much as I like moving into a home with Mom and Dad and being a family and having good food, some aspects of being off campus are not so pleasant. When I wake up in the morning, I head to the "bathroom." Shivering, I look grimly at the "thunder bucket" which serves as a toilet. It is a pot, eight inches deep and a foot around, placed in a special chair with a hole in its seat. Using a thunder bucket is awkward, messy and embarrassing! I take off the cover and almost fall over from the stink.

Since *Dar es Salaam* has only cold water, bathing is a miserable business.

While I'm washing my hands, Sousai knocks on the door. He is carrying two large pots of hot water which he has heated in the kitchen. He then pours the hot water into the "bathtub," which is a round metal basin three feet around and ten inches deep. I dribble a little tap water into the tub to cool the steaming water, and carefully climb in.

As I settle cross-legged in the tub, the water rises deliciously up to the edge, hugging me in friendly warmth. But that doesn't last long. The cold tub, sitting on the cold floor, and chilled by the cool morning air doesn't take long to lose its warmth. Doing my best to skim off the soap suds, I quickly rise and reach for a towel. The brief moment of warmth is now past, and I have to work quickly to dry myself and get dressed.

When I get back from school that afternoon, the new routine begins again. Sometimes Teddy comes over to spend the afternoon. Tea time is followed by a short walk into the trees and down to the stream which flows behind *Dar es Salaam*. There, Teddy and I float sticks and tiny boats, racing them through the ripples and boulders. From time to time we spot a tadpole or frog and rush to catch it. Frogs do everything they can to escape our clutches. Their legs are amazingly strong and push against our fists as we hold them tight. I'm curious about the ribbing on their backs and the ways they croak with their mouths closed and their necks stretched out.

When it gets too dark to see much in the forest, we head home. The golf equipment is on the porch, so we grab it and do some practice putting. It is a lazy time of the day, and we are feeling the call of summer break. It's only a few more days before the school year is done. Before the supper bell rings, Teddy says good-bye and heads back to his parents' summer lodging down the road.

Because winter coolness is much more pleasant than summer heat in the plains of India and the deserts of Arabia, we have our long break from October to January. As a result, "summer vacation" is only a few weeks long, but it is the time that parents come to Kodai to get away from the heat. When the weekend arrives, fifth grade is officially over, and I run home like a boy released from prison. Now the fun can begin.

After a quick tea, the whole family heads back to the campus for an evening play. Because we have no television and very few movies, Kodai School puts on several plays during the summer break. A stream of us head through the gateway where I look sidewise at the Gurkha. He grins wryly at me, knowing that he holds my fate in his hands. A word from him to my parents would have me back in *Dar es Salaam* for the rest of the break. I keep my gaze straight ahead as we climb the driveway to the gym where the play will take place.

Terr has a minor role in tonight's play, a full-length version of *Jack and the Beanstalk*. Dave works in the box office, in charge of the ticket sales. Everyone knows he's good with money, so he is usually the ticket boss. Because of their involvement, Mom, Dad, and I are especially proud and eager to be there. I enjoy the play, but it's a bit childish.

A funny thing happens to the string pulling the rope ladder up from the well where Jack has thrown the beans. The string is supposed to be invisible. It is attached to a stronger thread of string, which is attached to a rope, which is attached to a rope ladder. "Leaves" are tied to the string, rope, and rope ladder. By the time the rope ladder part arrives, the leaves cover it so completely that people can climb up it to the "giant's land" in the rafters above.

The problem tonight is that the string breaks and the whole thing falls back into the well! Stunned at first, the audience begins to laugh. Jack and the rest of the cast are horrified on stage. In a flash, Jack begins to make up lines about the magic beanstalk flying up and down. A stagehand creeps from the back of the stage and into the well, where he fixes the string, and the beanstalk grows again. By now, the whole crowd is roaring with laughter and clapping at the way Jack has covered for the mistake.

On the way home, Terr tells us about the craziness behind the scenes as everyone tried to figure out what to do. We laugh all the way back to *Dar es Salaam* and our late supper.

Saturday morning is another beautiful Kodai day. After my usual bathroom nightmare and a quick breakfast, we head back to the campus gym once again. The curtain is drawn so we can't see the scenery for tonight's performance of *Jack and the Beanstalk*. But the rest of the gym has been laid out with rows of tables filled with stuff. Today is the second day of everyone's favorite "White Elephant Sale." All kinds of things are for sale at modest, missionary-affordable prices. Such things as embroidered clothes, doilies, tea cozies, clothing, and small furniture come from cottage industries that the missionaries have helped to establish. None of that junk interests me, but Mom makes a beeline straight to those tables.

I have been saving my allowance for several weeks because I know what I want. I head directly to the tables filled with used comics. Unfortunately, the pickings are slim because some kids got here yesterday while I was still in class. But I do find a Superman issue that I haven't read, and there are a couple of Mickey Mouse and Donald Duck ones which are cheap.

From the comic section, I wander over to the Lucky Dip booth. Mom walks up to me and whispers, "Are you sure you want to do this?"

Startled, I respond, "Yeah." I don't know what's up.

"Well, be careful, because this is a lot like gambling." I know that gambling is a definite no-no for us mish kids. But I don't see how the Lucky Dip is like gambling.

Upset by her comment, I respond, "It's for a good cause, so it can't be that bad." Turning away from her, I hand over my few annas to play. The attendant gives me a fishing rod with a fake "fish" tied to the end. I extend the rod over a cloth screen and begin to "fish." On the other side, another attendant ties something to my hook, and I feel the pole being jiggled and some weight being added.

When the jiggling stops, I draw the rod back over the screen and grab my "fish." I'm disappointed. I know that some kids have "caught" Dinky Toys and new tops, but I only get a piece of candy. I could have bought ten of them for the annas or coins I spent on the Unlucky Dip. Maybe Mom was right.

"Hello, *Sahib*, efery-body OK? Beauty day, efery-ting beauty, *Sahib*!" It's the day after the White Elephant Sale, and we're just finishing a late lunch when we hear someone inside our gate calling out to us. The man climbing our steps wears a ratty white suit that hasn't been cleaned in years. Its sleeves and worn cuffs sprout tiny strings that hang like torn fringes. Just behind him is a *coolie* balancing a large, metal trunk on his head. The trunk weighs more than the old porter wobbling underneath it.

"*Sahib*, felly beauty day! How efery-body, efery-body good?" the suit man continues in a loud and jovial voice, as if we're long-lost friends.

He shakes hands with each of us, smiling from ear to ear to make us think we've been waiting all day for this happy occasion.

"*Sahib*," he addresses Dad, "I must show so many kind, wonder tings!" Before we can reply, he gestures to the *coolie* to put the trunk down. We're too caught up in the action to say anything yet, especially as we stare at the *coolie* who looks like he will fall over if he doesn't put the trunk down.

The man in white, sensing our feelings about the poor porter, indicates the *coolie* is in complete control of the situation.

The *coolie*, who had arrived with a blank look on his face, now has an expression of utter exhaustion that makes it clear it will be a long time before he has the energy to carry the trunk again. We might as well pay attention to the trunk's contents.

Before we know it, the man is in our living room commenting on the beautiful view from our bay window. "Beauty window! Wonder view!" Somehow, the trunk flies in while no one is looking, and it magically appears in the center of our living room floor.

"So, many wonder tings I show you!" the salesman promises as he opens the trunk with a big sweep of his hand. I remember hearing a story about Pandora's Box and all the bad things that came out of it.

As if to add to the magical mystery, Sousai comes silently into the room with a tray of goodies, and we're all served tea and sweets. Outside, it grows chilly as a mid-afternoon fog rolls in and a drizzle starts. Sousai lights an instant fire in the fireplace. As the room warms up, the salesman begins to spread out his wares.

Soon the entire floor space and all the empty bookcase shelves are covered with "wonder tings." Bolts of *sari* cloth, trinkets of ivory, silver and gemstones, statues in brass, wood, and ivory, handmade metal objects are spread all around. I can't imagine how all of this stuff fits in the trunk. Or how the *coolie* was able to carry it on his head!

Our living room now looks like a museum shop. Mom praises the eager merchant for the beauty of his treasures. He glows with hope about the killing he's about to make.

I like the carved wood animals. They're so real looking. I wonder how someone could carve a piece of wood or ivory into such little treasures. My favorites are seed elephants, tiny hollowed-out seeds the size of a lima bean with one open end that is filled with a dozen, fifty, even a hundred miniature ivory elephants. It takes a magnifying glass to appreciate the details.

Each elephant is hand carved and unique. It's unbelievable so many elephants fit in a seed and were carved by hand.

"Thank you for taking the time to show us these wonderful items," Dad says after we've looked at everything. Dad's voice tells all of us that we are done looking. We have heard that tone before. My brothers and I straighten up and return to our seats. Mom stops handling the *sari* material.

"My joy for you to see," the salesman says, giving no sign that he has taken the hint to leave.

"*Sahib* so much rain," he mutters as he looks out the bay window at the downpour. He wants us to know that it's raining too hard for him to go outside.

Dad falls silent, and the salesman finally takes the hint, slowly wrapping each item in paper or cloth. He takes his time and looks carefully at each item so we can get a final peak at it before it disappears into the trunk. I sense a growing awkwardness in the room. Without saying anything, his body language and facial expressions say, "I've gone to all this trouble showing you my precious items, so now you need to buy something."

We pick out a few inexpensive things and thank him profusely, expressing our appreciation for how nice his things are. We promise that we'll tell our friends about his treasures, but we make it clear we're about to eat supper, so he needs to leave.

"Your family is cheap!" his eyes say as he leaves.

I stare back with an expression that, just as silently, says, "Duh, we're missionaries! What did you expect?"

As if to punish us for our cheapness, the next day Mom is ripped off. Twice. She has such a good heart that she doesn't seem to realize what is happening—or, if she does, she doesn't mind being taken advantage of. About mid-morning, when Mom is the only one in *Dar es Salaam*, a man approaches the house and asks to speak to the Lady of the House. Mom likes his nice words and quickly thinks he is an honest person.

"Please Madame, I chop wood for Madame?"

"No, we don't need any wood cut."

He breaks into heavy sobs, explaining that he can no longer do his regular job since his ax is broken. Mom doesn't realize that this is such a well-worn story that it should have been retired years ago. The man goes on to say that because his ax is broken, he can no longer feed his family. He describes in grim detail how his kids suffer from hunger and his wife cries all day long. Mom takes it all in and ends up giving him twenty rupees to buy a new ax. Twenty rupees is about as much as a man could make in two weeks of full-time work. He is one happy guy as he struts away, probably hoping he won't run into any of us know-it-all kids.

Later in the day, the *dhobi* returns one of Mom's favorite, pleated skirts. Two days before, she asked him if he could take out some tar which had spotted part of her skirt. Mom had tried a number of ways to get the tar out, but it wouldn't go away despite all her efforts.

"Yes, Lady, no problem," he assured her, and took the beloved skirt along with our other laundry.

In the late afternoon, when Mom goes out to pick some flowers from the garden, she finds that the clean laundry is in its bag on the porch, and her pleated skirt is hanging from a hook. The *dhobi* is nowhere to be seen. Usually he makes a big show of returning the laundry, hinting that an extra tip would be welcome. But today he's gone.

To her surprise, the skirt seems to be tar-free, so Mom is very pleased. She brings it into the house with the rest of the laundry and shows it to Dad and me. We're playing chess and are the only ones home just now. The *dhobi* had succeeded when all the chemicals Mom could find had no helpful effect.

"I think I'll put it on for supper," Mom says. She walks into the bedroom to change. A moment later she yells out, "Oh no! I can't believe it!" Dad and I jump up, knocking over a couple of chess pieces. I'm glad the game is over, it hasn't been going well for me.

Mom comes back into the living room holding her skirt around her waist. It isn't fully zipped, and it is very tight on her. "He cut out the pleat!" she groans. "Look how he's sewn it back together." Sure enough, the *dhobi* had solved the tar problem creatively. Dad and I chuckle a bit, but Mom is really mad.

Two weeks later, as the end of Mom and Dad's vacation approaches, I can sense a growing pit of loneliness in my gut. Coming home from one more play on a Saturday night, I ask Mom, "Who do you love the best?"

"Well, Paul, that's an unusual question. I guess I have to say that I love God the most." I had expected that. "Then God would be followed by Dad and then you boys, equally." I am disappointed that I come after Dad. As we walk in silence the rest of the way, however, I realize that this is true. Mom and Dad will be returning to Bahrain together tomorrow, and I will be staying here with Dave and Terr. It hits me that living with Mom and Dad will no longer be normal. While they will always be together, it will be more like a privilege for me to be with them. From now on, I will be a temporary visitor in their home.

Miss Lange is my sixth grade teacher, and I can't be happier. She is about thirty, pretty, and caring—kind of motherly. She is different from all the other teachers, and we all like her; in fact, I have a hidden crush on her. She is so nice that we wonder why she isn't married. A bunch of us talk about how we'd be glad to marry her someday. It's a good thing she doesn't know our comments or dreams!

But things don't start out well with her. She is shocked to learn that I don't know the order of the months. "Every sixth grader should be able to list the months," she tells me in front of the class on the first day. Then she patiently recites, "Thirty days have September, April, June, . . ." I don't hear the rest I'm so embarrassed. Then I wonder what that poem has to do with the *order* of the months. I just hope that my relationship with her improves as the school year continues.

Sixth graders are supposed to live in Phelps Hall, but there are too many elementary kids this year, so my new roommate, Teno, and I are moved up to Block. Block Hall is the home of seventh and eighth graders, so they don't want us there. Teno and I are stuck in the last room at the far end of the hall where it is far too quiet, dark, and scary. After lights out, I am too afraid to venture down the veranda to the bathroom. The whole place gives me the creeps. When I wake in the middle of the night and have to go to the bathroom, I think, "What would Bosch do?" No problem. I head out my door, lean over the veranda wall in front of my room, and water the lawn, always keeping a sharp lookout for my new house parents.

Teno is a handsome, athletic kid and is very popular with the girls. He is good at any sport he tries, and I hope that some of his skills might rub off on me. Despite all his gifts, Teno suffers from bad headaches, and his grades aren't very good. I would trade my better than average grades for his athletic ability in a second.

Mail call this afternoon brings sad news.

"Dear Paul," Mom's letter begins, "I'm sorry to have to tell you, but Grandpa Gran passed away. He had a stroke last month while bowling with your cousins. Unfortunately, we've just learned about it." I can feel myself tearing up. Bowling with my cousins. That's how Grandpa would want to go, having fun with his family. I'm jealous that he was with my cousins, not with me. Minnesota seems a long way from Kodai.

As I sit on my bed in my empty dorm room, memories of Mom's father come rushing back. The strongest are the smells of the sharp Norwegian cheese he ate all the time. In fact, the whole house reeked like dirty socks because of that awful cheese. And pickled pigs' feet. He loved to eat white, withered pigs' feet which came from an unlabeled jar with cloudy juice in it. It turned my stomach to see that bottle; it looked to me like it came from some biology lab with body parts in it.

I remember his stories of Norway and homesteading a farm in Minnesota and years as a conductor on the Empire Builder Railroad Line which ran between Chicago and Seattle. Grandpa's stories gave me my love of train riding. He is the first person I know personally who has died. I'm sad, but I can't really share that sadness with anyone; I have to take it like a man. Terr and Dave are probably sad themselves, so I can't bother them.

In July, more parents go home and more kids come back to campus. A bunch of new sixth graders move up to Block from Phelps. At last we have some company. One day, Teno and I are moved into the social room in Block. It is the large room where we usually have our dorm meetings, but now it will be used as a dorm room. Six more kids move in with us, and it soon becomes crazy. Teno and I have had too little time together for his athletic abilities to rub off on me, but now we have six other kids to get along with.

Along with my old roommate, Teddy, the new group includes Paul B. and another Paul. That makes three Pauls in one room, which is really confusing. The newcomers are Hannes, Lansey, Kaz, and Riggs. We are packed in like sardines; all of us have to share two dressers and squeeze into four bunk beds. Known bed-wetters take lower bunks so they can get to the bathroom quickly—or change their sheets easily; fortunately I am in an upper bunk. In spite of being crowded, it is a comfortable room with plenty of space, high ceilings, huge windows, and the only wooden floors and fireplace in Block.

Above the light switch hangs a picture of an Indian lady. We don't know who she is, but she stares at us no matter where we are in the room. Her steady gaze gives me the creeps. None of us wants to turn the light off at night and be the last person she looks at. So, we each hustle to bed to avoid being the one to turn the light off. We are convinced Chrome Dome, our completely bald, new housefather, put the picture there as a message: "I'm watching you!"

It's amazing we get any sleep with eight sixth graders packed into one room. The first night sets an unfortunate pattern. It is filled with a pillow fight, an extended story telling time (we each have something that has to be shared), several trips to the bathroom, hurried searches for lost pens and books, and last-minute homework. Just as I'm about to fall asleep, someone passes gas—the intentional, high-pressure, multi-toned type—and the entire room erupts in noisy laughter and shouts of rage. It takes forever to get to sleep.

In the middle of the night Teno wakes up Paul B., in the bunk below him. "Paulie, d'ja see that?"

"See what," Paul B. mumbles, half asleep.

"D'ja see the tall, white-robed man in our room?" Instantly Paul B. is wide awake and sitting up. In fact, we're all awake and moving around.

Suddenly, the Eye Lady crashes to the floor, and eight throats scream out together. "The White Man must have done that when he left the room," Teno shouts. Lights flip on all along the corridor, and heads stick out of the rooms.

Shouts of "What's going on?" are met with, "Teno and Paul B. saw a Tall White Man in the room!"

"White Ghost? In the sixth graders' room?!!"

By now Chrome Dome is pulling on his bathrobe and

hurrying down to the social room, turning on the veranda lights as he goes. "Go back to bed. There's no one here," he yells, and slowly heads disappear back into rooms and lights go out.

When he gets to our room, Teno and Paul B. are scared. They explain what Teno saw. Chrome Dome assures them there is nothing to worry about, that the school's gate is securely locked—the Gurkha sees to that—and no one has come in. It takes us a long time to fall asleep.

The next morning the "White Ghost" is the talk of the campus. The little kids in Phelps Hall are eager to hear all the details, and Teno and Paul B. are the center of all discussions. That night, no one can sleep in Phelps Hall. The fourth and fifth graders are up all night crying, waiting for the White Ghost to make an appearance. Mr. and Mrs. Battleaxe can hardly get them to calm down and go to sleep. To make things worse, every tree branch the wind causes to scrape against a wall or every eucy nut falling on the roof brings ear-shattering screams.

In the early morning, Chrome Dome and Mrs. Battleaxe march into our room and wake Teno and Paul.

"Boys, you have caused a lot of trouble with your imaginary 'White Ghost.'"

"We never said 'White Ghost,'" pleads Teno. "I saw a 'tall White Man.'"

"Was your door closed?"

"Yes."

"Did you see the man go out of the door?"

"No. But the Eye Lady crashed to the floor, so he must have gone out."

"Now there was a lady in your room, too?"

"No. The Eye Lady is what we call the picture next to the door. It must have been knocked to the floor when the White Man left."

"But you didn't see anyone leave?"

"No."

"Paul, did you see anyone?"

"Well, not really. But I heard the Eye Lady fall. Something must have caused that."

"Boys, this has got to stop." Mrs. Battleaxe says sternly. "Teno, you must have had a nightmare, and your story scared Paul B. and everyone else. Now you have to help us stop all the rumors. Tonight, I want you to come down to the dorm meeting we're going to hold in Phelps, and I want you to tell the elementary kids that this is all a mistake. You did NOT see a White Ghost, a White Man, or an Eye Lady. Do you hear me?"

That night, when Teno and Paul B. return to the room from their meeting in Phelps Hall, we are all over them. "What happened?" Kaz demands.

"Well, we told them that Teno had a nightmare and I was so sleepy that I believed him. We told them that we didn't see anything and it was all a big mistake."

"Did they believe you?"

"No. They knew that Battleaxe and Chrome Dome made us come and talk to them, so they know we didn't mean it."

That night, things get worse. The jackals are out in great numbers, and their mating calls shatter the stillness. Some of them must be so close that it almost feels as if they are right outside our dorm room. Their yelping sends chills down our spines, keeping us all awake. They sound like tall, white men shrieking at eye ladies. When the hyenas join in with their crazy laughing, we all burrow under our sheets. Not only bottom bunk kids wet their beds that night, as we are all too afraid to run to the bathroom.

A few nights later, we are finally calmed down from the White Ghost excitement, and Kaz asks Lansey to tell us some

more stories. Lansey loves to make up stories, usually very sca
ones, which he shares with us at bedtime. It's amazing we ever get
to sleep. Some of his stories take many nights to be told. They
usually begin with something that actually happened, and then
spin into make-up land. Tonight, he doesn't want to continue his
story telling, but after a lot of wheedling from the rest of us, he
decides to do so.

"Once," he begins, "a black panther came onto the campus
in the middle of the night. It was found by a teacher who was
having a late-night smoke. The panther was like a dark shadow,
slinking between the campus buildings. It made its way to the
dining hall, prowling around for food that had been discarded
in the garbage cans. The teacher freaked out and screamed like
a crazy woman. The Gurkha chased the panther away with his
machete. In one bound, it jumped over the wall and ran into
town. The teacher reported that she could hear loud screaming
and cursing from the other side of the wall as Indians scattered
away from the charging panther.

"The next day, we heard that a young Indian boy had been
mauled by the panther." We're all wide awake now. Mrs. B. never
had a nighttime story like this. It's almost as good as the story of
the *Dara* sinking.

"As you know, Mrs. B. has a black puppy," Lansey resumes.
"A short time after the panther was chased away from campus,
Mr. and Mrs. B. took the whole Phelps dorm on a weekend
camping trip. Forty fifth and sixth graders in ten tents. On Friday
night, everyone shared their stories about the campus panther.
There were all kinds of tales about the teacher, the Gurkha, and
the kid in town that was mauled. When it was very dark, and the
last flames of the fire were dying out, Mr. and Mrs. B. made all the
boys go to their tents and get in their sleeping bags. Two seventh
graders, who had been brought along to help keep the little kids
in line, were allowed to sleep outside, next to the dying fire.

"Soon, everyone was fast asleep, dreaming of black panthers and kids being mauled. Suddenly, an ear-splitting scream cut through the night. Everyone was instantly awake.

"'Panther! Panther! Panther!'" yelled one of the seventh graders out by the fire. Heads cautiously peered out of the tents, as their kids wanted to know what was happening. Everyone was afraid of what they would learn.

"Then Mr. B.'s adult voice could be heard above the screaming, 'Calm down, it's only our puppy. There is no panther. Boys, go back to bed.'

"But no one wanted to sleep. Instead, they all gathered around the seventh graders to hear what had happened. It turned out that the puppy had come up to one of them and licked his cheek. When he woke up, he saw the muzzle of the dog up close, and it looked like the face of a huge, hungry, black panther. That's when he started screaming. The puppy turned and raced back to Mr. B.'s tent and hurried inside. Then everyone came running."

By the time Lansey finishes his stories of the panthers, we are so scared that we sit up the rest of the night retelling other stories about panthers, cobras, and hyenas. We are so groggy in the morning that we walk around in a daze. No one wants to go to class, but we make the best of things.

It is not easy being a sixth grader living in Block Hall. The seventh and eighth graders think the place is theirs, and they resent having to share anything. Especially the showers. The older boys don't like us punky kids using the main bathroom that is located right next to our room. They accuse us of using up all their hot water, which is not fair. There is never enough hot water for everyone.

So, we are forced to use the lonely, dark bathroom at the far end of Block near the science building. This is a spooky building where stuffed and bottled animals are stored. These are creepy enough, but I am also convinced some mangy dog or other animal might sneak into the dorm or bathroom to get out of the rain. The lighting is so poor, and the shadows are so deep, that dogs or even a couple of animal corpses—could hide in the shadows and no one would ever see them until they rotted and began to smell.

One night, while we sixth graders are taking our showers, some older boys sneak in and steal all our towels. We haven't brought any clothes to the bathroom because we usually wrap the towels around ourselves to get back to our rooms. Tonight is different. We come out of the showers and discover that we are towel-less. Our only chance is to race back to our rooms buck naked, hoping no one sees us.

We should have known better. Everyone else has been warned, and the hall is lined with a bunch of seventh and eighth graders whistling and clapping hands as we chug by. I even catch the sight of some girls looking out of the library windows up the hill. They're cheering, too, laughing at our nakedness. Where's Chrome Dome when we need him?

When we get back to our room we slam the door behind us, vowing never to go out again. It is totally embarrassing. In fact, we stay in the room all night. When nature calls early in the morning, we open the window and do our business right there. Fortunately it is raining, so the evidence is washed away. Unfortunately, one of us fails to open the window wide enough when it is his turn in the wee hours of the morning. Besides spraying himself all over, he "washes" Paul B.'s glasses which are sitting on the window ledge, making them totally unwearable. That's when we all break out laughing and appreciate the craziness of it all. All of us except Paul B., of course.

The next morning, a Saturday, I head down to Wissahickon, where Dave and Terr live. I have to get away from the tricksters in Block, and Dave welcomes me despite some of the other kids yelling out, "Scram, punk!"

"How about helping me out with some mimeographing?" he asks, knowing that I love to work with him on any project. Dave is an editor for the school newspaper, the *Thar*, named after an unusual and rarely seen mountain goat found in the Palni Hills around Kodai.

"You have to be careful with this mimeograph work or ink will get all over you," Dave warns me as he unrolls some of the stencils he has already typed. He then carefully separates the top page, which has typing, and the second page, which has red ink and is a copy of the typed page.

"I can do it," I tell him, not really knowing what I will have to do.

"Here, take this little brush and cover up that letter," pointing to a "q" which should be an "a." I dab at the ink page, splattering reeking liquid on my fingers and onto the red ink. Then Dave scrolls the pages back into his typewriter and makes the correction.

Soon, I am easily correcting another mistake, and then another and another. Each time I correct the stencil and splatter the awful smelling liquid around, Dave warns half-heartedly, "Don't make another smelly!!" I laugh in response. Before long, the whole place stinks of correction ink, and my fingers and sleeves are full of red ink. Dave shakes his head, but I'm having a great time with my big brother.

"I don't think I want to go to Hope College," Dave says while we're working on the stencils. "I think I would like to go to the University of Minnesota and study engineering. I don't want to be a minister or doctor." It makes me feel so grown up to have Dave talk to me about such important matters. "Maybe I'll join the Navy and see the world!"

When the stencils are completed, we put them in the mimeograph machine and add ink. This is another tricky part, because if I put in too much ink, it will smear everywhere. I have to adjust the ink several times, and each time I make the adjustment, I add more ink to my clothes and hands. At least it doesn't stink like the stencil correction fluid. Dave is patient, teaching me how to alter the ink to get the best balance. When the copies have been run off, Dave shows me how to sort and staple them. It feels very good to help Dave produce the school newspaper. Dave tries to clean me up, but it's not an easy job.

I love being with Dave, so when we finish with the paper and he asks if I'd like to go for a walk with him and Peggy, I eagerly agree. I think Peggy is one of the most beautiful girls on campus, and she is Dave's girlfriend. I know that most of my friends have crushes on her, too, so when they see me with her, they're all jealous. They're also jealous that Dave is the captain of the athletic club, and they envy me for being his brother. I'm learning that having people jealous of me is a good thing. Having Dave as a brother makes me cool.

This time, Peggy and Dave take me for a long hike along Coakers Walk. A lot of upper-class students are out on the Walk today, so we're constantly stopping to talk. Dave keeps introducing me as his "kid brother." I love it.

Coakers is the most beautiful hike around Kodai, because we can see seven thousand feet down to the flatlands below and across the valley to the non-volcano, Mount Perumal. In the distance, the horizon ends in the shimmering plains of South India. Walking with Dave and Peggy is wonderful; walking along Coakers is heavenly.

Paul B.'s parents come up to visit Kodai in early August and move into *Dar es Salaam*. They invite the Arab students to their home for supper, and I am really excited. Once again, I have the pleasure of home-cooked (meaning Sousai-cooked) food. It is a beautiful, cloudless day and Paul B.'s father, Uncle Don, suggests that we should go to the golf course and play a round.

I have never been to the clubhouse before, and I am fascinated by it. It was built by the British and made of hand-cut boards that smell of history. Its walls are lined with trophies and plaques with the names of past champions. There is a wood-paneled bar through a doorway, but we don't go in there. When we get our golf clubs, I am surprised to see that they are made entirely of wood, and they are ancient.

We head to the first hole and encounter an unexpected sight. There is a large water buffalo standing a few yards from the first tee, chewing his cud. Uncle Don is the first to tee off, so he sets his ball on the tee and warms up a couple of times. With all his might he swings away, expecting to clear the buffalo by ten yards. Unfortunately, his ball is a low line-drive, and it hits the buffalo right between the eyes. The bull turns and looks at us with a dumb stare, and we expect him to charge. Instead, he returns to his chewing as if nothing has happened.

"I think I'll try again," says Uncle Don, placing another tee in the ground. He doesn't want to retrieve his first ball until after the buffalo leaves. His second shot sails over the bull into the fairway. The rest of us tee off further down the hillside, using the ladies' tee.

It takes me several swings to complete the first hole, but we're all laughing and having such a good time that we don't worry about the score. As we make our way to the second hole, we notice that the fairway is lined by a whole herd of water buffalo, probably the brothers and sisters of the bull on hole one. We all shorten our swings so that we don't get too close to them. We know that buffaloes are not something to tempt. Another challenge is to avoid their droppings, which are everywhere. Fortunately, my ball doesn't land in any of the pancakes, but Paul B.'s second shot lands with a plop right in the middle of a big gooey one. He chooses not to clean it off, hoping that hitting it hard enough will do the trick. It doesn't, and he has to switch balls.

On the third hole, the fairway is lined by forests on each side. We lose a couple of balls in these forests, but no one is interested in going after them. Snakes, panthers, hyenas, massive wild bison called *gaur*, and other foul beasts live in the forests, and we don't want to meet any of them. Besides, we can hear the yipping of the monkeys and know that they've probably run off with the balls already.

As we begin the fourth hole, it begins to drizzle a bit, and we seek shelter under some of the trees on the fairway. The weather has turned bad very quickly, and an afternoon shower can't be far behind. Before we all complete the fourth hole, a thunderstorm rolls in, complete with flashing lightning, and we all run for the clubhouse. We flop down on the veranda, glad for the overhanging roof, and watch the amazing sky-fireworks. I notice that the bull that was at the first tee is still there, calmly chewing his cud and thoroughly enjoying the pleasures of a late summer rain. Uncle Don will never get his ball back.

Our conversation, however, is not so pleasurable. As we sit in the rockers on the sheltered, clubhouse veranda, Uncle Don reports that Iraq had attacked Kuwait in July, and the two countries are officially at war. Several missionary families have had to leave Kuwait for their safety, and Mom and Dad in Bahrain have moved from the mission compound to the greater protection of the oil company compound in Awali. It sounds like an exciting adventure, a huge slumber-party. I wish I could be with them.

There are a lot of stories about Chrome Dome. "Chrome Dome," the housefather of Block, is completely bald, his scalp as smooth and shiny as polished brass. While we never call him Chrome Dome to his face, I suspect he knows that's his nickname. Some of the boys in Block started a small newspaper called the "Ink Blob," a fun paper filled with make-believe and funny articles. The best series is called "The Adventures of Chrome Dome," and I guess he knows the stories are about him.

Today's issue has a nutty story about a fictional sailor in the Pacific during World War II. The story is about a U.S. destroyer that is trying to keep from being found by the Japanese on a night with a full-moon. Unfortunately, Chrome Dome has an upset stomach and heads to the deck. While he is leaning over the rail and puking, his hat falls off. The moonlight bounces off his bald head and signals the Japanese, giving away the location of the American ships and leading to a terrible defeat for our forces.

I read the story of Chrome Dome while I sit on a folding chair on the lawn outside Block Hall. I'm waiting for my turn in the barber's seat. The barber is known as Muthu, and he is the only one who gives haircuts to boys at the school. We don't know why he is the only barber. It certainly isn't because of his skills. There are rumors that he got his job because he promised that he would keep his clippers clean so that we wouldn't get lice. Other rumors are that he told the administration that he would keep our hair short. But no one knows for sure.

"Does anyone need a haircut?" he finally yells out. I'm sitting right there in the only other chair in the courtyard, and he calls out as if there were a stadium full of waiting clients.

"I'm next," I mumble, taking my seat in the other folding chair. "Please cut around the edges and leave longer hair on top."

"Yes. Yes." And then the clipping and ripping begins. Muthu is merciless on my hair, pulling out as much as he cuts. Before long, I realize that he has no interest in leaving anything on top. He just buzzes along without thinking.

"How's-Mummy-Daddy-everyone's-good?" he asks in a quick, slurred voice. His vocal chords are wrecked, and he sounds like he's been hoarse for decades. Turning to the side, he coughs and spits a big red blob of congealed spittle into the grass. The sounds are right by my ear and I feel like puking. I note where the blob lands so that I can avoid that part of the lawn. Then he dips his fingers into a snuff box and snorts another round. His hands are shaking, so I sit as quietly as possible, praying I won't be nicked.

"Ouch! Be careful." I check my ear and find that I'm not bleeding. Yet.

"You good boy? You get demerits?"

"Yes," I answer without explaining. I know he's looking for information that he can use against me some day. He's a warehouse of stories built up over years of clipping mish kids' hair.

"How's-Mummy-Daddy-they-coming-soon?" He is hoping to cut Dad's hair and to share information with him about me, perhaps getting a big tip for the gossip.

"They left last month," I respond. He's devastated.

Muthu mutters something to himself, but I can't follow what he's saying. In a slightly different tone, he then responds to himself. It's like a conversation between his good and bad voices. I'm not sure which will win.

"You sell me shotgun shells?" he asks, coming out of his personal dialogue.

"What? I don't have shotgun shells! Why do you think I would have such things?"

"Eh," he shrugs.

"What do you do with them?" I haven't heard of any Indians owning guns.

"Shoot pigeons. Make fine curry." My stomach turns over as I imagine pigeon curry with pellets in it. He smiles at me, but that doesn't reassure me.

Taking a leather strap from his bag, he attaches it to the back of my chair. Then he draws a huge, straight-edge razor from the bag and begins to sharpen it on the leather strap. His sweeping motions come too close for comfort, and I edge across the chair away from the strap. He continues to grin at me, whipping his razor up and down.

I close my eyes. Muthu snuffles again, sucks up another big wad of saliva, and spits it on the lawn. I close my eyes even tighter, remembering his shaking hands, and hope this round of snuff will help steady him. Soon I feel the cold blade on the back of my neck scrape away the hairs that are standing straight up from fear. Muthu works around to the hair around my ears, humming to himself. I hold my breath, praying madly that nothing gets cut off that shouldn't be cut off.

"Ha, ha. That good," he says. I open my eyes and let out my breath. I survive another haircut with all my body parts still attached. Prayer answered again.

"Does anyone need a haircut?" As I hustle off, I glance over at Lansey, who's white as a sheet from watching me live through the razor affair. He's the only one waiting in line, and he rolls his eyes as he ambles to the executioner's chair.

In late August my class hikes up to Wyadra Reserve, the site of the observatory which brought on the End of Time Panic. Wyadra is five hundred feet above Kodai, and the view of Kodai Lake and the school is wonderful. We settle down in the large, one-room cabin where we are going to stay overnight. The staff quickly sets up a curtain to divide the cabin in two. This provides the girls with protection from our prying eyes. Despite this flimsy barrier, the adrenalin is flowing, and we're all excited.

As soon as we've dropped our sleeping bags and backpacks in our section of the cabin, we head out for a hike in the woods. This lasts until almost supper time, and we return to a roaring campfire. Thanks to the *tiffins* which the staff brought with them, along with large vats of rice, we have a wonderful feast sitting under the twilight sky. It's a glorious evening.

When the supper supplies are cleared away (by the girls) and the fire has been stoked (by the boys), we gather around for singing. We all know a bunch of hymns and old campfire songs like "She'll Be Comin' Round the Mountain" and "There's a Hole in the Bottom of the Sea." When we've run out of songs, someone asks Lansey to tell a story, and he tells another tale about snakes, this time drawing out the legend part so well that some of the girls are crying by the time he's done. It's a great story with a whole village being killed and a snake that doesn't die. By the time we are told to head in to the cabin, we're ready for the sleeping bags. Before we get in, we each turn them inside out to make sure no snakes have snuck in.

Early the next morning, we boys quickly remember that there are a bunch of girls just on the other side of the curtain. This is too good to ignore. Jake crawls over to the curtain and tries to look under it. He raises it about a foot, and a girl screams bloody murder.

In an instant, the whole cabin is awake and noise consumes us all, the boys whistling and hooting, and the girls threatening to send us all to detention or even to hell. Several teachers rush in. Jake is hauled off by Mr. B., and I see a paddle in his hand. We all quiet down, waiting for the inevitable "whack" and crying, but Mr. B. must have taken Jake so far away from the cabin that we don't hear anything.

Slowly we get up and begin to prepare for the new day. We had been planning to take another hike along a mountain stream that runs beside the cabin, but after a cold breakfast the staff tells us that plans have been changed. Chrome Dome tells us that, after Jake's unfortunate behavior, we all need to learn some important things about birds and bees. Reluctantly, we boys follow him to a clearing where there are a bunch of tree-stump seats. We light a campfire and huddle around. The girls disappear back into the cabin, glaring at us in the distance. We all wonder what we need to know about birds and bees that we don't already know.

"Well, men," Chrome Dome begins, "you need to know that important things are happening to you and your bodies at this stage in your life. First, your bodies are beginning to change." We all look intently at our toes, wondering how they are changing. "Girls' bodies are changing, too." We all look up, wanting to hear more about this. But old Chromie isn't going there.

"You need to be very careful that you behave in ways which reflect well on your families and on yourselves. You must be gentlemen at all times, even when your bodies are telling you to misbehave. None of the awful behavior which we saw this morning in the cabin. Girls must be treated with respect. When you respect them, you are respecting yourselves. Remember, you are responsible for yourself and your own behavior. Am I clear?"

None of us have any idea what he is talking about. No birds. No bees. No sex. Just instructions on good behavior. We've heard that lecture before.

"Any questions?" Of course there are questions. We have a ton of them. How are girls' bodies changing? How come they are taller than we are? Why are they so snotty towards us sometimes? Why do they seem to prefer older boys? Why do they get in our faces and taunt us? Why can't we hit them when they deserve it? What is going to happen when we begin dating? Why do boys have to ask the girls for a date? The questions just simmer there under the surface, but no one speaks.

"Okay. I'm glad we had this little chat. Now men, please don't forget anything I've said. It will make life easier for everyone concerned." Does he really think we've had a chat? Men? Chrome Dome looks each of us in the eye, apparently getting the message that we men are all on board with his plan. "Good. You're dismissed."

We're stunned. That's it? Just be good. Where are the birds and bees? Is this all there is to learn about sex? We are almost eleven years old and have no better idea what we are going through than we knew before. Chrome Dome leaves the clearing, and we all look around not knowing what to do.

Finally, in groups of twos and threes, we get up and walk away, heading back to the cabin. When we arrive, we aren't allowed to go back in. The girls are still locked inside, so we mill around for a while outside, talking in small groups about how the girls' bodies are changing.

After what seems like hours, the cabin door opens and girls spill out. Some of them are red-faced like they have been crying. In little groups we corner the girls and ask what happened in the cabin. They tell us nothing. Even when we tell them about our weird talk with Chromie, they won't say anything. They just scowl at us with their arms folded. "If you don't know, then we're not going to tell you," says Bonnie unhelpfully.

I guess that girls are just too pure to talk about the biological details of sex. Besides, they were probably hearing about how to dress properly or how to iron clothes or how to cook. In any case, it is all a mystery to me.

The class trip to Wyadra had been so much fun that we decide to do it again the next weekend. Mr. Route leads a bunch of us boys there again. He's a young guy who has taken the place of Mr. and Mrs. Battleaxe in Phelps, who left in August for furlough in the States. Mr. Route enjoys battle games and tells stories that hold our interest. He has a wonderful sense of humor, and is fairly tolerant and easygoing. I only regret that he arrived in Phelps after I had moved to Block.

All week we are excited about returning to Wyadra, reminding each other of the fun experiences we had the previous weekend. When we arrive late on Friday afternoon, we have to set up camp by ourselves. But this time it isn't as exciting because there is no need for a curtain. There are no girls to tease or to taunt us. Or for us to tease and taunt. The whole thing is much more low-key, even boring. Supper is served, just like last week, but this time it just doesn't taste as good. And we have to clean up as well as collect wood for the fireplace. All around, it isn't as much fun.

In the evening, as we sit around the campfire, it is harder to get the guys to sing camping songs. No one wants to sing hymns. Although the roasted marshmallows are good, as are the stories which Lansey tells, we are all ready to hit the sack early.

"Let's go swimming," Teddy yells out after breakfast on Saturday. There is a swimming pool next to the cabin, so we're ready to join in. Teddy sports a particularly well-padded body, so when he plunges into the water, the rest of us follow. And almost die. The water is so cold, I am paralyzed from my chest down, gasping for breath. Despite my best intentions, I can't stand it and quickly scramble out of the pool. Everyone except Teddy follows me out.

"You kids are a bunch of wimps. I dare you to come back in. I'll save you if you can't handle it," Teddy taunts us. We stare in disbelief as Teddy paddles happily around the icy water, looking mighty proud of himself.

On the hike home, we all agree that we had a good time and want to camp out again. But we also agree that it wasn't as much fun without the girls, even though they could be pains in the neck. That is another mystery for me to think about.

September 9, my birthday, mail call brings me a surprise package. It is covered with Manila paper, lots of stamps, strings, and wax seals. I know that it contains wonderful secrets. My heart almost stops when I open it to find everything I could ever ask for: a model ship, a bunch of comics, and lots of food. Now I have another model to add to the collection already decorating my dresser-top and the windowsill. It will join models of ships, planes, and cars just waiting to take part in imaginary games and battles. Comics are a major source of entertainment and are bartering chips. I let other kids read my comics if they are nice to me. Also, I can trade comics with my friends, filling in the gaps in my reading pleasure. Food is always valuable, but it never lasts long. That's why food shopping is very important.

"Boys, let's hit the Budge," Mr. Sipanzi proposes the next Saturday morning, and my mouth begins to water. A small army of us agrees, running back to our rooms to pick up our meager allowances. We have to stick together as we head out to the local bazaar. It is a mile away, on a steep road, tucked in against the mountain cliff. Its small shops are filled with fruit and other groceries, hardware stores, clothes which we never look at, bakeries, and other goodies.

"We want to go to the bookstore," I beg Mr. Sipanzi. He's not fooled into thinking that we want to buy real books, but he nods and we all head for the comic book section. Pooling our money, my roommates and I buy four action comics, each choosing his favorite. We'll share them when we get back.

Next, it's Hamidia's general store with its display of sweets that draws our attention. Crowding into this eight-by-fifteen-foot box, the biggest "grocery store" in the Budge, we take our time picking out the most attractive Indian candies. Inevitably, we have trouble computing the prices, which are listed in traditional *annas*. I know that there are sixteen *annas* to the *rupee*. An *anna* is equal to six *naya-pice*, the new currency. Six *naya-pice* to the *anna* and sixteen *annas* to the *rupee*, should mean that there are ninety-six *naya-pice* in the *rupee*. But there aren't. There are one hundred *naya-pice* in the *rupee*. So we stand around for a while, trying to figure out if it would be better to pay in *rupees*, *annas*, or *naya-pice*. Only in India could the currency be so creative!

While a couple of other kids want to check out shirts and pants at the clothes store, I wander among the various bolts of fabric. Fortunately, Mr. Sipanzi is watching the serious clothes shoppers when I pick out the buy of the day. A pith helmet. It is a relic of the British Empire and fits like a crown. I don't care that it's mildewed and stinks like a rotten pear, I'm the only one with such a treasure. I go outside as quickly as I can so that Mr. Sipanzi can't make me take it back. Kaz says I look like I came out of *Beau Geste,* and Lansey calls me Gunga Din. I will be an instant movie star, walking along Kodai Lake in the most unique and recognizable hat around.

As we leave the clothing store, the next-door merchant calls out, "Magic treasure stones for sale here. Come, boys, come see!" He's holding a six-inch long, gem-like stone that has water in it. The water can be seen sloshing around inside the purplish, quartz-like stone, and we're all fascinated.

"How did the water get in the stone?" I ask.

"It very rare. Only few in the whole world. Water went in many thousands of years ago. Maybe time of dinosaurs," he explains. "Be very expensive in America. You get rich if you buy." Suspecting that the stones were somehow injected with the fluid, we all pass on the offer.

On our way back to the campus, we run into the Halva Man. He sets up his stand across from the front gate of the school, where seven roads cross. As usual, there is a traffic jam, with cars and cows and people all honking and mooing and yelling. It's a perfect place to buy some more sweets. The Halva Man's "shop". consists of a glass-enclosed counter which stands shakily on three-foot high, spindly legs. He carries his stand and glass counter with him, so when he goes home at night, there is nothing to show where his shop was except a bare spot in the grass where he always stands.

Halva isn't really candy, but it's close, and it's one of the few sweets we can afford. It's a greasy, sticky goo that's surprisingly good. The Halva Man doesn't know the word hygiene and doesn't waste any time on it. As we approach, he wipes his runny nose with his bare hand and resumes cutting wedges. When we ask for a piece, he slices a small slab off the large block and carefully weighs it on a hanging scale. Although I don't trust that his weights are accurate, I take what he gives me for my few *naya-pice.* "Just a little more?" I beg, looking up at him pleadingly. Grinning briefly, he slices off a sliver and adds it to my pile.

This time, my *halva* is wrapped in a page from an old class notebook that the Halva Man bought from some Kodai kid. I carefully unwrap my sweets and notice that the wrapper comes from a history notebook once owned by Dave's former girlfriend, Peggy. She has very whirly handwriting, and the page brings back fond memories of walking with her and Dave on Coakers Walk. Too bad they broke up.

For a change, the movie of the week is shown on Tuesday night. It's *Forbidden Planet,* and the whole school turns out to see Robby the Robot play the part of a hero. I love it. I decide that science fiction is the way to go. I especially like the realistic, otherworldly stage sets. The tension from aliens chasing innocent humans has us all on edge.

We have focused so completely on the movie and its scary plot that we haven't noticed that a monsoon is raging outside. When we head to the doors, the fierce wind and wild lightning adds to our level of fear. Could this be the beginning of an alien invasion from outer space?

My buddies and I run through the covered verandas, laughing and jostling to get into the lead. We're thoroughly soaked by the pelting rain that comes at us horizontally, making the roofs nearly ineffective. When we finally make it back to Block, we're all drenched to our bones. Changing quickly into our PJs, we head for bed, hoping to sleep the night away.

But the storm continues, getting louder and fiercer by the minute. After two hours the roof over Block Hall can no longer withstand the lashing gusts, and I can hear metal tearing as a large part of the roof is ripped off our dorm. I crunch down further in my bed, knowing that the aliens are coming soon.

In a couple of minutes, Mr. Sipanzi appears in our doorway and announces that Sammy and Riggs will be bunking with us for the night. They drag into our room, hauling their water-logged suitcases and clothes. For now, I have two new roommates. It isn't until after midnight that the wind begins to die down, and we all finally fall asleep, grateful that our section of the roof hasn't flown away.

Kodai abounds with mysteries. I find myself thinking about such things as: What lies beyond the next hill? What creatures make the eerie sounds coming from the forest at night? Who lives in the gated mansions up the hill? Who are the rich people who stay at the ritzy Carlton Hotel next to the school? Where do they come from, since no missionaries could afford the place? What is at the bottom of the lake? And many more puzzling questions. These mysteries bring a sense of adventure to everyday life.

Shortly after the night of the rainstorm, Bosch comes to our room and announces, "I have an idea." Remembering our allowances that disappeared in the watermelon business, we are all very careful when Bosch says that he has an idea. But his ideas are too much fun to pass up.

"There are tunnels all over this place," he continues as if we had encouraged him. "We're going to find some. I was talking with Mrs. Aung Twin and she said that the tunnels were carved out during World War II so that people could get between buildings without being seen. She's a survivor of the British campaign in Burma, so she should know." With that, Bosch turns on his heels, daring us to join him. So Kaz, Paul B. and I follow in his wake.

We begin by scouring the mountain walls that run behind Phelps and Wissy, but there is nothing there to crawl into. Up the hill are some large drain pipes which run under Block and the class building, so we head that way. Choosing the biggest pipe, we rip up a bunch of bushes to clear the opening. It's barely big enough to allow us to crawl on our bellies into the darkness. The trickle of water at the bottom of the drain, left over from last night's storm, looks very uninviting.

"You coming?" Bosch demands. Silently we each follow him into the opening, inching along by wriggling on our bellies from side to side. In a few feet we're drenched in the stinking rain run-off.

"What do you see?" I call out when the light from the opening fades behind us. I bet that snakes love this hideout. Or maybe a colony of rats. I'm no longer excited about this latest adventure.

"Not much here," Bosch responds. "In fact, I think I see where it ends. There's water dripping down from the top of the tunnel."

That does it for me, and I reverse-wriggle so that I can escape from this deathtrap, vowing to walk away the next time Bosch says, "I have an idea."

In late September I come down with tonsillitis. The glands in my throat swell so large that I look and sound like a frog. When Dave hears about my condition, he escorts me down to the Dishpan. Although I am not happy about going there, my throat is killing me, so I put up with it.

The Dishpan is run by a small, elderly nurse, Miss Annie Putz, an Austrian with a heavy accent. In her crisp white nurse's uniform, she brings a no-nonsense approach to nursing. Her strict methods may lack compassion, but Dave assures me that they are effective. For her, proper medical practice centers on cleanliness, silence, and staying in bed. As far as Miss Putz is concerned, all other remedies are much less important. Medications are expensive and hard to obtain, whereas bed rest costs nothing, so it will have to do.

Miss Putz leads me to my bed, one of four in the boys' ward, and tells me that I am not to leave that bed except to go to the bathroom. Unhappily, I climb into bed and look around. The Dishpan is sterile in all kinds of ways. The rooms are totally white and characterless. Even the bathrooms are totally white and smell of Dettol. Dettol is an antiseptic, disinfectant rinse that Miss Putz uses to clean everything. She tells me that anything touched by the magical power of Dettol, or even its fumes, is rendered germ free.

If Dettol is the magical cure for cleanliness, Icthyol is Miss Putz's usual cure for all body ailments. Miss Putz liberally slathers it to my neck, telling me that it will help ease the pain in my throat. As I lie there in agony, I notice that she puts Icthyol on the three other miserable kids in the ward, whether they have cuts, open sores, sprains, sore muscles, boils, or whatever else. One poor guy apparently isn't improving with this treatment, so she draws a curtain around his bed and gives him an enema. He doesn't look at the rest of us for an hour after this treatment.

As I lie in the Dishpan, I take stock of my misery. It is lonely and a little scary here. I don't know the other guys very well, and they don't want to talk for fear that Miss Putz will tell us all to shut up and get "bed rest."

By late afternoon, I am so bored I can hardly stand it. I've been lying here for hours, and my head is beginning to ache. I wish one of my roommates would get sick so that I'd have someone to talk to. For a while I fantasize about how contagious tonsillitis might be, hoping this would be my secret weapon to fill the room with friends. But no one new comes in, and the ones already here aren't talking. As I think about it, I begin to realize that the Dishpan is so awful, that we want to get better and get out. The whole miserable experience is designed to make us get better. I think about this for a while, and then abandon it. I'm too sick to care.

I nap for a while and then wake up while it is still light outside. On a shelf in the room is a stack of old comics, so I hobble over there and pick up a raggedy bunch of them. One by one I reject them because each one has pages missing right at the point where things are getting interesting. It is like some previous patient decided he was so miserable that everyone after him had to be just as unhappy. I read for a while, but even comics don't hold my attention. I stare at the ceiling, counting holes in the ceiling and following the cracks in the rafters.

Simone, Miss Putz's assistant, brings me my supper in the evening. I look at the glop and my stomach turns. It looks like yesterday's rejects from the main dining hall. Simone sees my disgust and stares at me. "Want an enema?" she threatens. I get the message. Simone is known all around campus as the enema queen. Holding my breath, I wolf down some of the mashed potatoes and peas and whatever the gristly charcoaled meat is. Simone grins threateningly at me, and I realize that the faster I get out of this place the better it will be for me.

Supper is finally cleared away, and I wonder what to do. I'm not tired enough to go to sleep, and the other guys are still not talking, so I walk over to the shelves. I decide that the comics are useless, so I reach for one of the well-worn novels. They have library numbers on their covers, but on the inside it says, "Rejected from Kodai Library." These are the castoffs of the school library, probably because they are so boring. I pick up a frayed copy of

Wuthering Heights because it has an engraving which shows a scary looking guy grabbing a frightened woman. But it is not scary, it is just boring, and after just three pages I'm fast asleep.

On Saturday morning, while I am still in the Dishpan, there is a big commotion outside. When I go to the window, I see a black limo drive past the campus and I recognize Jawaharlal Nehru, India's prime minister. The only reason I know it is him is because I knew he was coming to campus. He is going to deliver an address at Bendy Field, which can hold hundreds of people. While I know I'll miss his historic speech, I have heard that Miss Putz is going to let me out this afternoon, so that makes up for it.

I'm finally released from the Dishpan in the middle of the afternoon. The world seems like such a beautiful, exciting place again. When I see my friends walking around campus, eating in the dining room, playing games on the green, even sitting in the library, I feel happy all over. In fact, all of life looks more exciting and fresher than I remembered it before I was trapped in the Dishpan.

Although I'm disappointed that I didn't get to hear Prime Minister Nehru, the more I learn about his speech, the less disappointed I am. Teddy tells me that the only line he can remember from Nehru's speech is: "The Himalayas are more beautiful than the Palni Hills." Since the Palni Hills are our mountains, the ones crowned by Kodai no less, it seems rude that the prime minister would mistreat us in that way. I wonder why such an important man would waste his time coming here only to insult us. Doesn't he have better things to do with his time?

The movie that night makes up for any bad feelings left over from Nehru's visit. *Moby Dick* is shown in the gym, and for a change everyone is allowed to attend, since there are no scenes deemed unwholesome by the staff's censorship committee. We know the plot from having read the book for class, so this is an event not to be missed. In fact, the gym is packed to the walls with every chair that can be squeezed in. Sitting so close, we can feel each other breathing, the excitement growing as we wait.

True to the book, the movie is full of action. I especially enjoy the part where the great white whale eats a whole man. There are other dramatic scenes, full of wonderful action, which leave me deeply impressed. On our way out of the gym, we promise each other that when we grow up we'll work on a sailing ship together and learn how to throw harpoons.

Fall comes in October, turning the weather cold and telling us that school will soon close for our long vacation. We'll be going home! With Terr's help, I get my footlocker from the store room and fill it with all my earthly belongings. These things will be left in Kodai for the winter months, to be opened again in January. In between all the layers of clothes and blankets, I stuff moth balls. They are important to keep the moths from eating everything while I'm gone.

On Tuesday my class goes to the Dishpan for shots. It turns out this is something I have to look forward to every year. We all line up outside the Dish for our turn to get poked and re-poked. The line takes forever, so we have plenty of times to tell stories about shots we have received for cholera, polio, malaria, and other diseases we can see on the streets of Kodai every day.

"Last year, Teno paid Jake to take his shots for him and to fake his name on the sign-up sheet!" Teddy announces. We all oooh and ahhh about that.

"How much did he get?"

"A couple rupees. You should have seen his face afterwards, though, he looked like he had a roaring fever." We stop to imagine what it must have felt like to get poked on two rounds. Clearly, the payoff would be well worth it, even if it meant a roaring fever.

"I don't want a sharp needle," the girl three in front of me wails. "Let me check to see which is the dullest one!"

I watch her fuss and fume, trying hard not to laugh, as she feels the tips of three needles until she is sure she has the dullest one. She thinks that if it feels dull, it won't hurt as much. Simone grabs her arm and shoves the dull needle into it. The girl lets out a satisfying scream, and pulls away. "Duller, duller," she pleads, knowing that she hasn't had all her shots yet.

When it's my turn, I say clearly and loudly, "Don't use her needle! I want a sharp one." I look around and can't help feeling superior when several of my classmates nod and wink at me. Without looking at me, Simone grabs my arm, slaps some alcohol on the upper area, and then shoves in the second dullest needle in Kodai. So much for my logical reasoning. By the time she's shoved the third dullest needle into my arm, I'm ready to run out of there. Simone's reputation as the enema queen needs to be amended to account for her nasty shot-giving.

To add to the excitement about going home, the staff has posted all the travel itineraries for the Arabs, Burmese, Ceylonese, and Indians. I study the Arab itinerary over and over, memorizing all the stops which will take me home. The excitement is so powerful, that I can hardly sleep at night. Nor can I do any homework; concentrating in class is impossible. Fortunately, there are the weekend movies that we talk about over and over, recollecting all the details of the exciting scenes.

On Friday night, Teddy and I join the rest of the crowd and file into the gym. Tonight's movie is *Green Mansions*, a big Hollywood adventure in the jungles of South America. Like other movies on campus, we know that it was chosen in part because it has no sex, dancing, swearing, or drinking in it. As the plot plays out, we become totally absorbed in the tale of half-naked natives sneaking around in the jungle blowing poisonous darts at some lost Americans. Remembering a class I had recently about tree people who are hiding in India's jungles somewhere, I resolve that I will never go hiking in the mountains again.

At last, on October 17, we Arabian Mission kids leave Kodai, beginning the journey home with a bus ride down the *Ghat,* a trip we had taken the other way nine months ago. Once again, my gut is twisted by the harrowing drive down to the plains. This time, we are looking down the steep drops into the valleys below, and it seems much more dangerous. Sharp cliffs above and below make things even more scary, and I imagine what would happen if the driver made a mistake on one of the switchbacks. A minor error would send the bus hurtling thousands of feet into oblivion. Every once in a while we see signs of cars or trucks which have suffered such a fate.

About half way down the *Ghat,* the road narrows to one thin lane with no shoulders, and as we round a corner, we almost plow into another bus coming up the hill. The drivers beat on their horns a while and then get out and yell at each other, pointing at their passengers and at each other. Finally, the other bus driver shrugs and returns to his bus; he reverses it down the hill for several hundred yards until he comes to a wider section of road. We follow him and wave as we pass. I don't have any idea how they decide who should back off. Maybe we have more passengers. We resume our ride down the mountain, taking in grand views, sparkling waterfalls, and dense jungles. I love the monkeys, butterflies, cows, and snakes that make appearances along the roadway.

At the bottom of the mountains, there is a dry river bed with a bridge going over it. In just a few hundred feet, we travel from steep, mountainous land to the very flat plains. Just like that, we're out of the mountains and driving through open spaces, out of cool mountain breezes into hot and humid air.

We all cheer when we cross the bridge on our journey down the mountain because it means we are leaving school and returning to family and the comforts of home. It's been nine months since I've been off the mountain, but it seems like an eternity. It feels like ages since I was on the hot, flat plains, and I love the sensations it brings. Only now, with the stifling air streaming through the window onto my face, do I fully realize that I've been chilled to the bone for months. The heat, penetrating to the core of my body, is wonderfully refreshing.

The plains are pure India. As the bus meanders through village after village, the driver calls off their names. His announcements seem like mysterious chants: Botlagundu, Periyakulum, Vaigai, Shembaganur, KooKal, Trinchinopoli, Chinnalapatti. I feel like I am traveling through a magic land, somewhere begging for discovery.

We spend a lot of time at bus stops. The driver picks up or drops off passengers, catches a cup of tea, chats with his fellow bus drivers, relieves himself on the side of the road, and ambles back to the bus. Meanwhile, we haggle with hawkers, buy snacks, stretch our legs, go to the toilets, and wander about. We're careful not to walk too far, fearful that the driver may take off and leave us behind, surely the plot for future nightmares.

Resuming our bus trip, I am gently rocked into a thoughtful mood. The air smells of flowers and herbs, animal dung and human sweat, wet rice paddies and parched earth, fruits and forests. It is warm and comfortable. I watch lazily outside the bus window as a mass of people walk by. There are *coolies* carrying huge loads, gaily dressed women in flowing *saris*, little kids pushing barrel rings with sticks, cows roaming aimlessly, stopping traffic on a whim. Car horns blare whenever we're passing through towns. I can hear birds calling in the midst of the human voices. Trees rustle in gusts of wind while animals grunt and bellow at each other. Before long I am lulled to sleep.

In the late afternoon, as the sun's light softens behind the mountains, we eat supper in the small canteen at Kodai Road train station while we wait for the train. We order toast and eggs, and they taste wonderful; it is a delight to eat something that was not cooked in the school's cafeteria.

When we see the trail of engine smoke spewing on the horizon, we arrange ourselves on the platform, ready to find our compartments and board as quickly as possible. Kodai Road Station is a whistle-stop, and the train only stays for a few minutes. It's a mad scramble when the train chugs into the platform, and we run around searching for our compartments. In barely two minutes, we load our suitcases on the train, and the group leader signals that everyone is on board.

Somehow, the craziness of throwing my bags on the train and clambering in with everyone else gives me the feeling that I am now a part of India. This life seems "normal." The sights and sounds and smells are all familiar. The people, in all their differences, are familiar. Although India is not really my home, it has become part of me. I'm sure I will never forget any of this.

Sitting on my usual bottom bunk in the compartment, I stare in fascination out the window at the passing Indian countryside and farmlands. The farmers are still active in evening's dim light. Small farms, with their dirt-brown mud huts, water-filled rice paddies, rows of high cactus fences for livestock, dusty trees, and garden plots, dot the passing scene. Excited, scantily clothed boys and girls run alongside the train yelling something I can't understand. Young guards sit on makeshift platforms built in the fields, making sure that no man or beast tries to steal their crops.

Long-necked, white egrets stay close to the plow-cows, waiting for them to overturn dirt and unearth worms. Small brown birds stand on the buffaloes' backs and pick inside their ears for insects. Water buffalo chew their cuds, occasionally raising their heads to watch the train pass by. Pairs of oxen plod back and forth next to water wells, bringing up large buckets of water to gush into channels that feed the rice paddies.

As night falls, my energy runs out and I fall asleep to the gentle rhythm of the train. What a wonderful tune! In the middle of the night, the train makes lengthy stops in Dindigul and Trichinopoly, and we are roused by sleepy vendors outside the opened windows asking if we want food or drinks. We shake our heads, too tired to respond.

Something good happens in the morning when I wake with the dawn. Sitting on my bunk, staring out the window, absorbed in the passing scene, I notice a large white bird soaring above the train, gliding behind us. It's riding air currents created by the train. I can see the bird's head moving back and forth along the length of the train, surveying our little world. I wonder at the view it must have floating above us, and I can imagine that it sees all we're doing and everything around us.

I try to imagine looking at my world from the bird's view, and surprisingly I can do it. In my mind's eye, I see the train chug its way through the lush Indian countryside, trailing a tail of smoke, crossing rivers, and easing around villages. I can see the Kodai kids among the Indian travelers looking out the windows at the passing scenes. I feel completely content.

After spending two days crossing India by bus, train, taxi, rickshaw and airplane, we fly out of Bombay, headed for Arabia. As we sit in the plane during the four-hour flight home to Bahrain, I am overcome by the most wonderful feeling of well-being. All is calm and quiet in the plane's cabin. Bright shafts of sunlight stream through the windows, playing on the shadows inside. When the airplane turns and changes course, the shafts of light wander slowly around the cabin. I sit and think about the year in Kodai and all the adventures I've had. Now I am on my way home, something I've dreamt about for nine months. Life is good!

Typical small Indian temple

CHAPTER 4

Home Stay

We land in Bahrain three days after leaving Kodai. I'm barely off the plane when Mom grabs me in a big bear hug, kissing me on both cheeks. "Welcome home, Son," she murmurs in my ear. I don't even blush, it feels so good. Dad shakes my hand, just the way he does with Dave and Terr. We're all "men" today, and that feels great.

On the way home from the airport Dad and Mom ask a ton of questions about our trip and about the year in Kodai. I'm happy to let Dave and Terr do the talking while I stare out the window remembering familiar places along the way. "Paul did a good job of settling in," Dave assures Mom. The way he says this makes me feel warm inside. It reminds me that he was always watching out for me, like the times when he let me use his credit for food or when he made me go to the Dishpan.

I quickly stow my stuff, throwing most of my clothes in the laundry basket. I've worn the same clothes every day for almost a year, and many things have worn holes in them. I look forward to getting a new set of clothes. As soon as I empty my suitcase, I head for the storage room. On the way from the airport, Dad told me that my train set was up and ready to use, and I want to see it again after all these months. I love trains because they help me imagine little villages and broad countryside outside their windows. This time, I imagine Indian villages and farmlands, complete with the sounds and smells I had experienced just a day ago. My storeroom train reminds me that I will only be in Bahrain for a few months and then will return to Kodai.

While I'm playing with my train set, I hear the dinner bell ring and head back to the house. It is wonderful sitting around the dinner table again. Dad thanks God for the safe trip we have had and our good health despite the diseases all around us. He prays for each of us and even mentions some of the other mish kids. As he prays, I realize that he is talking about my new world, my Kodai world.

"Tomorrow, Mom and I will be going to the Arabic language service in the morning, and you're welcome to join us. We'll go together to the evening English service," Dad announces as we are served dessert. Mom has made an apple pie to celebrate our return. I don't know where she gets apples at this time of the year, maybe from cans.

"Thanks anyway, Dad," Terr says. "I think I'll sleep in, so I'm afraid I'll have to skip the Arabic service." Dave and I mutter our agreement. Even though all three of us have spoken Arabic since we first learned to talk, it has been nine months since we used it, so we feel a bit awkward about going to an Arabic service just now. For me, it is always weird to hear a service in Arabic. I know that Arabic is close to the language of Jesus, and I know that Jesus would feel more comfortable in an Arabic service than an English one, but I don't feel as worshipful in Arabic as in English. In any case, I agree with Terr that I'd prefer to sleep in tomorrow.

Except for year-long furloughs in America, my whole life before Kodai had been spent in the mission field, so now that I am back in Bahrain, living on the mission compound, I am back in my element. I take great pride in the work of the Arabian Mission. Its stories fill me with a positive, service-oriented attitude toward the world. Over the years, hundreds of missionaries and their families have come to this part of the world, teaching and healing and preaching. Like me, their kids have grown up on compounds and traveled to boarding school in Kodai. Some even come back as missionaries when they grow up.

My parents have served in hospitals in Muscat, Kuwait, and Iraq as well as in Bahrain. We have Arab friends in all those countries, people who have been cared for by my parents and the other missionaries. Whenever I come back to the mission compound, I feel especially proud and happy about all the lives that my parents have touched. This is where much good has been done and continues to be done.

At the center of mission life is the church, so my brothers and I are used to going to at least two services each week. On Sunday evening, we walk to the chapel with Mom. Dad has gone ahead because he is going to give the sermon tonight. Before he became a doctor, Dad thought he might be a minister, so he likes to preach from time to time. Tonight he's going to be talking about homecoming, he told us. Dave, Terr, and I are wearing our only suits, complete with ties. Our stiff collars itch in the Bahraini heat. For mish kids, formal church clothes are very important. We have to set the proper example of reverence.

The church is on the top floor of an old two-story, whitewashed building. As we approach it, my eye is automatically drawn to the square steeple and its famous clock. This is a huge timepiece high up in the tower which can be seen from all over the city. Bahrainis set their clocks by it. In fact, I have heard that sea captains use it when they are anchored in the harbor. Bahrainis call the steeple and its clock *Abu Sa-ah,* meaning "Father of the Clock."

There's only one way up to the church, an outside stone staircase that leads to a large veranda surrounding the main hall. I have climbed those stairs a million times, so it feels familiar to do so this evening. The whitewashed hall doesn't look like a traditional sanctuary. It has rows of about eighty wooden chairs with wicker seats. The walls are lined with large windows to let air pass through. I love this little old church on the second floor. It plays an important role in my life. It's where I have learned my beliefs and my way of thinking about the world. I wouldn't be surprised if God considers it one of his most sacred places.

We take our seats and get ready for worship. I look up at the ceiling fans that are trying, unsuccessfully, to cool us in the sweltering heat. Before long, I'm sweating bullets even though it's late October. As usual, I take a seat next to one of the windows. I like to be able to look outside during the service. That way, when things get boring, I have something to look at and think about.

By the time the service begins—as usual, it doesn't start on time!—the hall is full. In fact, the ushers have had to open folding chairs, but there are still people who have to stand. I look around and see many people that I know. There are Arabs, Indians, Brits, even some U.S. Navy boys who are in town with the Sixth Fleet. People are chatting quietly, welcoming strangers and renewing friendships. I nod at Swamakan, an Indian nurse who works at the hospital. He smiles back, tipping his head slightly. I like him because he always seems so calm and serene. That fits nicely with the expectations Mom has for me. As a mish kid, I am expected to be quiet and polite, especially during worship services. Tonight, I feel a special bond with Swamakan because I've just come back from India.

I settle in for the service, standing when the traditional hymns are sung and sitting with my hands folded when the preacher talks or prays. At one point I notice a gecko on the ceiling. He is working his way slowly to where a fly has landed. I watch him patiently inch across the ceiling, tail slowly waving to keep his balance. I can tell from his dark belly that he has had a feast tonight. Just as the gecko's about to pounce on the unsuspecting fly, Terr jabs me in the ribs. Startled, I bring my gaze back to the pulpit. Dad walks up to the platform and opens his notes, setting them on the Bible. I listen carefully as he begins to preach.

"As many of you know, my sons and the other missionary children returned from South India yesterday. It was a wonderful homecoming. Mrs. H. was so happy to have our boys home that she baked an American apple pie!" People chuckle and moan at this point. Dad continues. "It is a time of great family celebration, as I know many of you can imagine from your own experiences. I have heard you describe your happy homecomings when you returned to India or England or Pakistan or America. No matter who we are or where we come from, homecoming is a time to rejoice." Many people are nodding their head in agreement, although no one says anything. A few are dabbing at their eyes.

"But, no matter how wonderful, how enjoyable, how fulfilling our earthly homecomings are, they are nothing like the homecoming we can expect when we go home to our Father in heaven." Dad has done a nice job of tying in our daily lives with our eternal ones. Now the men are nodding vigorously.

Suddenly, the night air is broken by an amplified voice outside. From a minaret down the block, the *muezzin* has begun the evening call to prayer. It is time for all faithful Muslims to turn to Mecca and pray. Dad stops to let the call continue. "*Allahu Akbar.*" God is Great, chants the caller. Dad waits patiently for the call to end. It is too difficult to try to talk over the muezzin, so when his call happens during one of our services, we all wait for him to finish.

Finally, Dad continues. "When God welcomes us home, we will never want for anything again. He will shower us with love and with his awesome bounty."

Dad has me thinking. Life is pretty good these days, so I try to imagine how much better it will be in heaven. I imagine a world where I have a few more toys like the ones I've found in the dog-eared Sears Catalogue that Mom keeps on top of the toilet tank. More food would also be nice, although I don't recall ever being truly starving. I'd love to have membership in the local swimming club, where mish kids only get to go when their much wealthier oil company friends invite them. Perhaps heaven is like being in church all the time, listening to sermons and praising God around the clock. While I generally enjoy worship services, I'm not sure this is how I'd like to spend eternity.

As I think these big thoughts, I look around at the other people in the room. Most are listening carefully, sometimes smiling or nodding at what Dad has to say. I know that they are good people; Mom and Dad have said so. But I'm not sure what "good people" really are. I know that the hospital, where many of them work, does many good things, so that may be why they are good. But I have also heard my parents talk about some nasty things that a few hospital people have done to others, so that is not so good.

I may look like I'm bored or not listening, but inside I know that something special is going on in church. God's Spirit is present here, and I feel uplifted whenever I go to church. Tonight is no exception. Dad's sermon and my thoughts about coming home to Bahrain have made me feel very hopeful. God is good, and if we humans can work together with God, we can do good things, too. That's what Mom and Dad and the other missionaries are doing.

While I'm deep in thought about good and bad, I hear a car horn outside the window and crane my neck to find out what's going on. I can't see anything, but the horn's broken my train of thought, and I return my attention to Dad, who seems to be wrapping up. "So, while we can celebrate the little homecomings of this life, we can only imagine how splendid the homecoming will be for the next life. Amen."

"Amen!" reply many voices.

The service continues with an offering and then another hymn before it ends. We stand up and begin to greet each other, filing out to the veranda where it is much cooler. A festive air prevails, since everyone is in a good mood, probably looking forward to a homecoming to heaven. A lot of people come up to welcome me home, and some ask how it was being away for so long. Between greetings, I think about that. India, only a few days away, seems far away from Bahrain. I have become a Bahraini again. Three days ago, I felt like I was an Indian. Now I'm an Arab. I even find that my Arabic is coming back, although I can't understand everything that people say to me. The Egyptians are especially hard for me to understand, because I am used to Gulf Arabic. I'm like a chameleon that has to change its color depending on its surroundings.

Monday morning, before dawn, I am awakened by the raspy voice of the *muezzin*. As he continues his chant, I lie in bed listening. I know much of his call by heart, having heard it all my life. I can tell if he's in a good mood or a bad one by the way he calls. This, too, is a comforting and familiar voice. Even though I know that Muslims and Christians have many different views, I like the fact that they both worship God. "*Allahu Akbar.*" God is Great.

At the beginning of November, Sheik Salman Al-Khalifa, the long-time ruler of Bahrain, passes away. Within a day, his body is taken into the desert, and he is quickly buried without a funeral service. This is how Muslims do it. His son, Isa Bin Salman Al-Khalifa, becomes the emir and announces a period of formal mourning for his father. For two weeks everything, including all stores, will be closed.

Sheik Salman had been a good supporter of the hospital, appreciative of the many ways that missionaries have helped the Bahraini people. So the missionaries are genuinely sorry that he died. Representing the hospital, Dad visits royal family members and expresses his sympathy to them. He also attends official gatherings honoring the emir's life.

In the days to come, Dad is invited to formal ceremonies that mark the turnover of power to the new emir. Dad explains that these ceremonies are important historic and cultural experiences. "Would you like to go with me to the palace tomorrow?" he asks one day.

I eagerly agree, so Mom dresses me in my Sunday best, complete with suit and tie. As we drive along, Dad warns me that I am to be on my best behavior, serious and sad. Any misbehavior will be a black mark on the reputation of the entire mission. I'm not going to get into trouble, I promise him. While he talks, he steers the car to the south of town and into the desert. In the distance I can see the slight rise where the palace stands.

Dad pulls into a temporary parking lot where cars are scattered in an unorderly fashion. We get out and join a somber line of men entering the palace's main meeting hall. The weak glow of open light bulbs, dangling on long cords from the high ceiling, barely lights the whitewashed walls. The dim light filters down to a sea of red Persian carpets that flow from wall to wall across the large open area. Around the hall, dozens of men sit on over-stuffed pillows.

It looks like every man who is anybody in Bahrain is at the gathering to express his sympathy. Westerners dressed in dark coats and ties sit next to Arabs wearing flowing brown robes. A heavy mood is in the air as we wait in line to shake the hands of some royal family members. When my turn comes, I bow slightly, look as sad as I can, and shake hands. When we get out of the line, servants direct us to pillows, so Dad and I join the other men sitting around the hall. No one talks very loudly.

Through the silence and hushed movements, there is a strong sense of pomp and show. Dad, representing the health and medical establishment, sits with other professionals. They are all community leaders with important jobs. Their solemn whispers reflect the gravity of the gathering.

As the only child, I feel responsible to act like a man. I am uncertain exactly what I'm supposed to do, so I assume the saddest manner I can muster. Coffee is served, and as always I don't know whether to take the cup or not. Not taking coffee might offend the hosts. But I'm not eager to drink any of it because it usually tastes like burnt mud to me. This time I decide that I should drink a little, out of respect for the dead ruler and his son.

I do my best to disappear into the crowd. But I am the only kid and the only person with blond hair and skin as pale as a fish's belly, so I have a hard time blending into a crowd of swarthy, dark-haired adults. Occasionally people pat my head. I'm used to this; I have been told that some Arabs believe that touching a kid's yellow hair would bring them good luck. It sure doesn't bring me any good luck. If I got a dollar for every pat on my head, I could buy every comic book in the world!

I feel sorry that the old emir died, but what really makes me sad is that I have to spend two of my ten vacation weeks in official mourning. All fun activities are forbidden, at least outside the mission compound.

One beautiful afternoon, to break up the monotony of the mourning period, Dad takes me on a ride to one of my favorite places. We cross the long bridge to Muharreq Island where the British Royal Air Force base is located. Dad takes me up to the observation deck, and we spend the next few hours watching RAF planes take off and land. I especially enjoy the Hawker Hunter jet fighters. When they get all revved up, it sounds like thunder rolling across the sky.

The Bolton Beverly transport planes are huge and slow. When they lumber down the runway, I hold my breath, afraid that they will never get off the ground. I identify other aircraft, like the two Canberra jet bombers and the six scout planes. Dad explains what military mission each type is responsible for, and he even talks a bit about his pilot training during the War. Hearing his stories, I announce that I want to be a pilot when I grow up. To top off the evening, Dad takes me to the base theater and we watch a Three Stooges movie together.

Much too quickly, it is Christmastime. I get totally involved in all the fun activities around Advent and Christmas. I wander through the *suk*—a covered bazaar—shopping for the perfect presents for my parents and brothers. We go to parties at other missionaries' homes. And of course there are church services. I especially love the Christmas carol singing. The week before Christmas, we buy a scrawny bush and decorate it like a Christmas tree, complete with our special family decorations. I don't miss the snow of Michigan at all! It is a calm, cool night when we gather in the living room on Christmas Eve to open presents. My favorite present is a kite from Dad. It's a wonderful, family time, and it reminds me that I'll soon be leaving all this behind in order to return to Kodai.

It isn't until the day before New Year's that Dad has some time off from the hospital. All five of us pile into the car and drive through the desert to Jabal Dukhan, Bahrain's only mountain, in the center of the island. Jabal Dukhan is the perfect place to fly kites because powerful winds sweep across the open desert and build into strong updrafts when they hit the mountain slopes. We have brought several kites, all of which were made by Dad. Kites have been his hobby since he was a kid, and he loves to try different styles to see which one responds the best. Today Dad wants to see how different length tails change the kites' flight patterns.

"See how this longer tail creates more drag, but provides greater control," Dad says. "Did you feel that up-draft? You can anticipate when up-drafts will hit by noticing where the mountainside takes a dip or rise. The sun will affect up-drafts, too. When the day cools, there is much more wind activity, so you have to be more attentive and make the necessary adjustments." Whenever we go kite-flying, Dad likes to lecture about aerodynamics and to explain the science of aviation.

"What a grand thing kites are," Dad says as he grips the taut string and watches the kite flying high and steady. He uses the word "grand" when he is in a good mood. "I made this kite while you were in Kodai last year. Mom and I tried it out together. She said it was easy to fly, so I knew it would be a grand kite. Not like some of the designs I put together." Dad laughs to himself. He likes to draw up designs for kites and then assemble them with bamboo, paper, and yards and yards of string. More often than not, they take fatal plunges to the earth. The kites he has brought today are tried and true.

"Just imagine all that weight being held aloft by the unseen wind!" Dad points out to me. We think about that for a while, considering the wonders of unseen forces in nature.

"Can you imagine what you could see if you had a camera attached to the kite? The world from a bird's eye view, now that's something to spark the imagination!" And my imagination is sparked. I love to imagine what the world would look like from the air, and the idea that a kite might be used to make that happen is something that has my mind spinning.

"How big would the wingspan have to be? Would I have an automatic camera which took a picture on a timer, or would a motion picture camera be better? How would I aim or focus it?" I'm full of questions. Dad's ideas always get me thinking, and we spend the rest of the afternoon considering these questions.

Mom has packed a picnic, but I don't want to stop flying kites, so Dad and I munch carrots and egg sandwiches while holding on to our kite strings. Slowly the sun goes down and the evening chill sets in, telling us it is time to go home. After the long day in the windy desert, flying and chasing runaway kites and being gently burned by the sun and strong winds, I am wonderfully happy and totally tired. We return home for a quiet family supper. I can barely keep awake for midnight, dozing on the couch until Mom wakes me, wishes me happy New Year, and helps me mosey over to my bed.

My last thoughts before I sink back into sleep are that it has been a great day and a life-changing year. While in Kodai, I had learned that I wasn't the center of everything. Without Mom and Dad around, I discovered that not everyone loved me. I learned that I had to earn love and acceptance. I learned how to get along with my rowdy peers, even though sometimes I had to do things I didn't want to do. I learned that I couldn't take my family for granted, and that every moment with Mom and Dad and my brothers was precious. Wow, what a year!

New Year's Day is a busy time on the mission compound. Our tradition is to have a "progressive dinner," which means that we go from home to home and eat a different course at each. The main course is at our house this year, so Mom has gone all out to make a wonderful lamb curry, complete with chutney and freshly baked *khoubz*, traditional Arab flat-bread. Since this is the last time the whole mission staff will be gathered, Dad stands to give a little speech.

"I want to welcome all of you to our home on this New Year's Day. Thanks to all who have so graciously opened your homes to us. This is a bittersweet time, as you all know. While we celebrate together, we are conscious that we won't be gathered around a single table again for quite some time. On behalf of all the parents here, I want to say a special word of *bon voyage* to our children who will be leaving in the next week for Kodai." I look around and notice that there are a lot of teary eyes at the long table. "We love you and want this to be your best year ever. Dave and Nancy, since this will be your last year at Kodai, we want to wish you an especially good year. You have big decisions ahead, choosing your colleges and making plans to return to the States. God bless you."

Around the room people say, "Here, here!" "Amen!" "God bless you!" Now there are no tearless eyes. I sniffle a couple of times, myself. I hadn't thought about the fact that Dave would be graduating in May and would be leaving Terr and me behind in Kodai. More to think about.

On January 6, Paul B. and the rest of the mish kids from Oman arrive. They are followed in the next day or two by Teddy and the Kuwait bunch, and others from Iraq. While I love seeing my old roommates again, their presence is a daily reminder that I'll be leaving home for Kodai soon.

On Sunday afternoon, Dad drives Teddy, Paul B. and me out into the desert for one last kite-flying experience. I'm really not into it today, and we're all relieved when it's time to head home for supper. After supper, parents and kids pile into mission cars and head to the airport for our midnight flight to Bombay. When we check in we discover that our group is seventy kilos overweight, which costs the mission a lot of money.

This unpleasant detail sets the tone for our sad departure. When midnight comes around, we learn that the flight is delayed, making things only worse. In fact, the plane is so delayed that we don't get out of Bahrain until three o'clock on Monday afternoon. By that time we're all eager to get going; even our parents want us to get out of there. So maybe the delay is a good thing. Our sorrow about leaving home has been replaced by our anger and frustration with the delay. When we board the plane, no one has any tears left.

The BOAC DeHaviland Comet, the most advanced jet aircraft in the world, is to take us to Delhi. I marvel at the new interior and the unique smell of "newness," and I buckle in to my window-side seat. I wave out the window, hoping someone can see, but I'm mostly interested in the wonders of this new craft. The four jet engines are buried in the sleek wings, and they scream like banshees as they rev for take-off. When we hurtle down the runway, I am forcefully shoved back in my seat. The jet rises at such a steep angle that I feel like I am in a rocket taking off into space. What a thrill! This is the life.

It's not so nice on the next flight. After a brief layover in Delhi, we board a DC-4 for our flight to Madras. Just like last year, this old crate is unpressurized and has no soundproofing. I stuff cotton balls into my ears to block the noise, but the shaking and shuddering continues to alarm me. I barely sleep through the flight, and when we arrive in Madras in the morning, I am miserable. Not such a good life, after all.

Dave is in charge of the sixteen of us, holding our tickets, passports, and money. And our lives. He makes all the decisions, and we grudgingly go along with them. The first decision is that we have to lug our stuff to the train station to check it in. "If you hurry, we'll have some time for fun," he tries to bribe us. After no sleep, I'm not sure I have the energy to have fun. But we manage to get to the Egmore train station. We stow our luggage with the stationmaster, and Dave arranges for our tickets to Kodai Road. Then we're off for lunch at Buharis and then to the *gymkhana* for swimming. After lunch, we go to see *The Magnificent Seven*, starring Yul Brynner and Steve McQueen. We've all seen it before, but the action is so much fun that nobody objects.

We are in a much better mood after the swimming and movie. Heading back to Egmore station, we chatter happily. Dave assigns the older boys with half-hour "watch" duty over our luggage, and each takes his turn sitting with our bags while the rest of us roam the busy station. It's great to be with Teddy and Paul B. again. I can see that the older kids wander around with their friends, too. I think of us as a big, boisterous family on the loose at an amusement park.

Supper in the open-air cafeteria, with ceiling fans churning the air to provide a little relief from the oppressive heat, is a noisy affair. The hawkers peddling reading material and cheap toys hound us continually.

"Master, very good comic book, like new!" one screams.

"Master, very funny, everyone like, you much liking!" another promises, waving colorful comic books of Donald Duck and Bugs Bunny in our faces.

"Very cheap for you, Master. Good price!"

The word "Master" makes me uncomfortable. It doesn't seem right for a grown man to call a boy like me "Master." I can't get used to it. But I know that because I am a white kid, I will be treated with special respect by Indians of all ages. This is because the British Empire controlled India for so long.

"Velly, velly besta!" vendors yell in a singsong melody, sprinkled with similar chants in other languages. They appeal to potential customers who speak dozens of Indian languages as well as to those of us who speak English.

"So, velly tasty. Only velly besta and velly fresha!" they plead.

We buy peanuts rolled in newspaper, haggling to save a few *annas* over the already extremely low price. When we drop the shells in heaps on the ground, stray goats come in and eat them. Teddy buys a bowl of curried rice, but it's so spicy hot that he can't take it. We each try a forkful and agree that it's too hot for human use. This, too, we share with the goats, who seem unimpressed even if their tongues and throats are on fire. Goats will eat anything.

As night's full darkness settles on us, we board the overnight train for Kodai Road station. With the wind blowing cinders into the cramped cabin, the open windows are less than helpful. "I'll take the bottom bunk," I volunteer. No one objects, knowing that the lower bunk will be pelted all night by air-born sparks. I don't mind. A little discomfort is worth being able to watch the countryside fly by.

We're barely settled in when Paul B. announces, "I got a model of a destroyer. You wanna help me put it together?"

"It's too rough a ride. We won't be able to do a good job," I reply. But Paul is too excited to give up the idea so we start assembling the pieces.

"Ouch, that hurt." Paul B. slaps at his cheek. "We need to close the windows or we'll be burned to death."

"Then it will be too hot!" I respond. We argue for a while about what to do and then return to building Paul B.'s World War II destroyer. It's a mess, with many pieces slanting awkwardly. Not only are the train's motions making it impossible to put the parts together correctly, Paul B.'s not letting the glue set long enough for it to dry before he adds pieces. With his less than steady hand, it's a wonder the model is put together in recognizable form. Because I love to put models together, I help out for a while, but the long day is getting to me, and I lie down on my bunk.

"Hey Paul, turn the light off," someone hollers.

"I can't. I won't be able to see what I'm doing."

"Hey who left the bathroom door open? It smells like a barn in here!" It does smell like a barn. The flush tank must be empty. I shut my eyes, trying to block out the smells and the yelling. Then I feel someone sitting on the edge of my bunk.

"You doing OK?" Teddy asks in a quiet voice. He knows that I will be homesick soon.

"I'm all right, this is fun. Being a mish-kid is neat."

Teddy and I talk late into the night as the train chugs steadily through the dark. When he leaves, I stare out the window enjoying the rhythm of the train and the blur of the dark countryside. Before long I am lulled into such a deep sleep that I don't wake up for eight hours. Someone shakes me, "We're approaching Kodai Road station." I'm instantly awake, fully rested and ready for the bus ride up the *Ghat*.

We make a hasty departure from the train, managing to get all of our stuff out of the cabins just as the whistle blows and the train starts up again. Across the street, the rickety Kodai Motor Union bus waits for us, looking like it should be pushed into a landfill. We hoist our luggage onto its roof and watch as the bags are tied under the tarpaulin. Teddy and I grab the front seats for the four-hour climb back up the mountain.

For two hours we bump along the narrow, one-lane roads across the plains of India. Since cars and buses are coming at us, it's a scary, delightful experience. I hold my breath again and again, expecting on-coming vehicles to crash through the front window. The traffic appears totally chaotic as cars, buses, and trucks speed headlong toward each other. At the last minute one driver weaves to the side to let the other pass. There appear to be no rules of the road, but miraculously there are few accidents. Even those drivers who give way seem to hold no anger about "losing."

At each stop we tumble off the bus and head to the smelly latrines. We Arabs are such novelties that local people just stare at us, gawking in amazement with slackened jaws. They gaze at us without blinking, even when we are doing nothing in particular that might hold their attention. They stand next to each other, tapping their neighbors on the shoulder and pointing at us as if we had fallen from another planet. Perhaps, in their world, that is what has happened. Initially, the unwanted attention is unnerving, but we learn to cope with it and become good at ignoring it.

The ever-present beggars are harder to ignore. They stand outside the bus window haranguing us for alms. Holding out their hands, they plead, "No mama, no papa, no house, no food." The more nervy ones come onto the bus and stand right in our faces, "No mama, no papa, no house, no food." Even though they tug at our heartstrings, we don't give them any money. If we did, all their friends would pile into the bus and never leave us alone. Many of these sad souls suffer from physical deformities so gross they turn my stomach. The beggars make a point to display their defects, hoping they will move us to pull out wallets and provide some relief for the suffering.

It isn't long before I notice that many of the beggars are missing a leg below their kneecaps. The rest of their body is healthy, and they seem to be very alert. Beyond the missing leg, they don't suffer from the physical problems that so many other beggars have.

"Hey Dave, why do so many of these kids have one missing leg?"

"You don't want to know," Dave replies.

"Yes, I do!" By now other mish kids are listening intently, too.

Reluctantly, Dave answers. "They're from a particular caste of Hindu beggars. When they're baby boys, their parents cut off one leg so they can forever be legitimate beggars. That's part of the accepted social order, and it is how they make their living."

I'm stunned. This is too much for me to take in. The do-good philosophy of my missionary parents is so much part of my thinking that I can't even imagine parents deliberately hurting their child in order to satisfy some caste system. I'm so upset I want to vomit, and it takes the fun out of the rest of the trip. I notice that the other mish kids have grown quiet and somber, too.

As the bus slowly climbs up the *Ghat*, we begin to see glimpses of the mountaintop in the far distance. It is shrouded in clouds, which break up from time to time. Half way up the *Ghat*, the suffocating heat is abruptly relieved by the cool, clean mountain air. Eventually we enter the darkness of the clouds, and a moist chill settles over the bus. I shiver, huddling next to Teddy to conserve my body heat. Once again I have forgotten to keep my jacket handy. It's packed in the suitcase on the roof. At least it's not raining.

The driver turns on his headlights to penetrate the thick fog and turns on the roof lights inside the bus. They give off a brownish glow, and I realize how tired I am. In the middle of the afternoon, the bus pulls into the Kodai bus stop. It feels both familiar and odd to be back.

After dragging our suitcases to the dormitory and receiving our room assignments, we haul our heavy trunks from the storerooms to our bedrooms. Every item in them reeks to high heavens of mothballs. Grimly, I unpack my luggage and fill the dresser drawers. I'm thrilled to see my old friends, but I miss my parents terribly. As soon as the sun goes down, I get incredibly homesick. I keep thinking: my parents are half a continent away in the warmth of a Bahraini winter, and I'm stuck here in this cold, damp dorm. It is not a good beginning for my second year at Kodai.

Mylapore temple in Madras

CHAPTER 5

Kodai Kid

I click with Mr. Shaw right away. When I walk into his seventh grade class in June, he extends his hand and thanks me for Dad's advice about his back problems. Chuckling, he also reminds me that my brother, Dave, used to date his daughter, Peggy. I'm relieved to hear his chuckle, because I remember how much he liked Dave and how disappointed he was when Peggy and Dave parted ways. I was afraid he would hold the breakup against me. I know this is going to be a good semester. Mr. Shaw is my first male teacher, and that is going to be fantastic. I've had enough women teachers to last a lifetime.

Mr. Shaw wants us to get started with our science projects right away, so he has us all partner up for the lab sessions. I get to partner with Vivian, his youngest daughter. That can only help my standing with Mr. Shaw.

As we work on our project, which requires examining some animals that are stuffed and others floating in jars of formaldehyde, there is a low hum of conversation in the classroom. I'm really enjoying working with Vivian, who is as pretty as her older sister, Peggy, and who has her Dad's sense of humor.

Suddenly, Paul B. accidently drops a small vial of tear gas—a prank-toy he's secretly been saving since Christmas vacation—on the floor; it shatters and we all run to the windows, gagging as we go. We wipe away our tears and breathe deeply of the fresh air. Slowly our coughing subsides and the breeze carries out the awful odor. However, Mr. Shaw is still on his hands and feet, sweeping up the last of the broken glass. As a result, he's still tearing freely, with streams flowing down his cheeks. He stands up, wiping his eyes and blowing his nose.

At that moment, Principal Root walks in, leading a well-dressed American, probably a big-time donor. It doesn't look good; we're all out of seats and the teacher is crying! We freeze in place, holding our breaths.

"What's going on here, Mr. Shaw?"

"Oh, hello, Principal Root. I didn't realize you were coming around." Mr. Shaw sniffs and wipes his nose with his handkerchief. "What's going on? I've just heard this morning that Aunt Bessie, my favorite aunt, has died. I'm afraid I still haven't gotten used to the news."

We can't believe our ears. All eyes are on Principal Root. Will he buy this explanation? After a brief hesitation, he does.

"Well, you have my sympathy. I'm sorry to hear of her death. Extend my sympathy to Mrs. Shaw, too, please." Next to me, Vivian grabs my arm and leans into my shoulder, struggling to stifle a laugh. To Principal Root, it must look as though she is grieving the loss of her favorite great-auntie. The rest of us just stand there in awe. Mr. Shaw has just broken the adult code. He covered for Paul B.'s clumsiness. He is my new hero. Principal

Root and his guest quietly bow out of the room, leaving Mr. Shaw and Vivian to their grief—and the rest of us to our noisy relief. We clean up after the lab exercise, chattering about the close call we've just had.

When we return to our homeroom for English, Mr. Shaw reminds us who is in charge. "Sit straight, Kaz," he barks out. Kaz has been rocking back and forth in his chair, trying to find a comfortable position. Kaz slams the chair down on the floor, "Sorry, Sir."

At the end of the first day of class, when we have completed as much work as Mr. Shaw wants to put up with, he sits back in his chair and begins to talk about his life. No one else has ever done this in my classes; this is really cool.

"I was a nurse during WW 2." He says, "WW 2," not "World War Two." "We had some unusual experiences back then, I can tell you. We had all kinds of casualties come through our hospital tent." This is going to be good. I can picture the hospital tent, complete with operating theater, bloody body parts everywhere, and doctors and nurses huddling around the near-dead.

"Well, one day we had a couple of guys who were brought in on stretchers, and they were in bad shape. We hoisted them onto gurneys and began to strip them. Amazingly, during our examination they had turned into women, complete with breasts." He has our attention now. "We did what we could to patch them up, but that was some unexpected turn of events, I can tell you! Never knew what happened to those guys who turned into girls."

What a way to end the day. Stories about guys who turn into girls! I am spooked. Did God have that in store for me? Would I become a girl? How did that happen? What would my parents say? Would my dorm parents come and tell me to pack my bags and head to Boyer Hall? How humiliating that would be. I didn't even like girls' clothes.

That night I find out that several other guys have the same misgivings. "I've never heard of a guy becoming a girl before," Teddy reassures us, "but it may be possible. You never know." Teddy's father, like mine, is a doctor, so perhaps he knows something we don't. It doesn't help when we ask Bosch about this, and he swears to us that this kind of transformation has happened many times, right here at Kodai. I have a restless night, waking several times to see if my breasts are growing.

At breakfast, I finally talk to Terr about this episode, and he roars with laughter. "The doctors must have thought the casualties were men, but when they were stripped, it became clear that they were women. You dolt! They didn't turn into women like magic!" Terr's laughter attracts a teacher's notice, and she comes over for an explanation. Still chuckling to himself, Terr tells what has happened. I'm mortified and humiliated and red as a beet. The news of my stupidity is quickly shared around the dining hall.

Sheepishly, I enter class after breakfast, expecting everyone to hound me. Fortunately, before anyone can begin, Mr. Shaw stands up and hauls out a funny looking chair. It has only two front legs. Mr. Shaw must have chopped off the back legs. "Now, Men," he begins, "I want you to know, that if I catch any of you rocking onto the back legs of your chairs again, I will give you this one for the rest of the class session. Then you will see how well a chair works with broken back legs. Is that understood?" He looks pointedly at Kaz. We all nod, thinking evil thoughts about Kaz and what he has gotten us into. The girls giggle. But Mr. Shaw isn't done with his formal announcements.

"And Men, this weekend we are going to have a special field trip. Please be in front of the gym, ready to leave at 9 on Saturday morning. Wear athletic equipment because it may become muddy where we're going. We'll be back by lunchtime."

We know that Mr. Shaw likes to run three miles down the *Ghat* and back up every day. Perhaps he is planning to take us on an exercise run, a truly appalling prospect. No one has the slightest idea what he has in mind, but no one is going to pass on this mysterious adventure.

"Now, I'd like to turn your attention to the fish tank on the side of the classroom. It's a unique, tropical tank. The water is from the Indian Ocean. I've had to haul it two hundred miles. The last time I did it, it took four days to come up from Madras. I had to take it slowly so that the tetras, pearl danios, and angel fish wouldn't die." As we gather around the tank, we're mesmerized, watching the fish dart in and out of the fake seaweed. I imagine the little aqua-world of the fish and make up stories about their relationships. The day is off to a better start than I had anticipated.

Poffy is my new roommate. He has just arrived in India from the States and has never been out of the country before. "My parents are anthropologists from the University of Southern California," he tells me when we first meet. "They're studying life in a small Indian village while they are on sabbatical." This is news to me. Almost all of us are mish kids, with a few Indian and government children thrown in. All of us are Christians.

"What denomination are you part of?"

"None."

"Nun? Are you a Catholic?"

"No, Silly, 'none' as in 'nothing.'" He chuckles when he sees the astonished look on my face.

"You don't believe in anything?"

"That's right."

I'd never met anyone who wasn't a believer—Christian, Muslim, Hindu or something else. "I'm sorry," I mumble.

"I'm not," he responds, chuckling. "Are you a Christian?"

"Of course."

"Why?"

"I don't know. I guess because my parents are missionaries. I've always been a Christian."

"Oh, I'm sorry." His eyes glisten merrily.

"I'm not," I respond, smiling too. I know I'm going to like Poffy, whatever religion—or non-religion—he has. I like the twinkle in his eyes.

Vaguely, I wonder at my answer. Am I only a Christian because my parents are Christians? Is Poffy a nonbeliever just because his parents are nonbelievers? I've got to chew on this idea for a while. In the meantime, I decide I want to enjoy my time with Poffy. Live and let live, I figure.

Saturday morning finds ten guys waiting in front of the gym just before nine. Mr. Shaw hasn't said a thing all week about our field trip, but we've speculated about the hiking trails which might await us, or about the observatory we've visited in the past. Promptly at nine o'clock, Mr. Shaw chugs up the road to the gym. He has on his running gear, which seems to suggest that we're going jogging.

"Men, today we need to clarify some things which seem to have confused many of you. I understand that some of you misunderstood my comments on Monday about the two women casualties that I encountered in the field hospital tent. They were women when they came in, and they were still women when they left. A man doesn't turn into a woman by some mysterious transformation, so you guys can stop worrying about that. Is that clear?"

Ten pairs of eyes are inspecting the laces of our sneakers. "Uh, huh," we chorus. Teddy, standing next to me, gives me a poke in the ribs and mutters, "Told you." But he hadn't told me anything of the kind. He had said, "You never know."

"Today we're going to take a field trip to the government's veterinary and animal husbandry facility. When we get there, we'll observe and then talk about some of the basic facts of life. You are now young men, and it is time you learned about these things in a mature, adult fashion. No one will snicker or otherwise display childish antics. If you have questions, please feel free to ask them. No question is out of bounds. Is that clear?" Toes, again, are examined. What's clear is that no one will ask anything.

"In addition to observing how artificial insemination works in cattle," he continues, to our horror and mounting enthusiasm, "we will learn how cattle stocks can be improved by selective breeding so that the cows of the future will provide more milk and be extremely healthy." I quickly forget the second half of that reason for our field trip. This is not going to be a morning's jog, by any stretch!

Upon our arrival at the facility, we are ushered into a small, corral-like enclosure where an incredibly robust and contented bull stands in the corner quietly chewing his cud. He looks bored. It's a good thing we have on grubby clothes, because the floor is muddy and the stench of manure hangs heavily in the air.

Shortly thereafter, as we stand half-embarrassed and waiting for something to happen, two veterinary attendants open the gate and bring in a female cow. She seems even more bored than the bull. Despite his apparently detached state, he immediately knows the cow is in heat and turns his gigantic head, nostrils flaring.

In an instant, he awakens from his boredom and is transformed into an amorous predator. For the first time in my life, I actually see a facial expression on a bull. With a series of deep bellows and throat-clearing grunts, he approaches the female. His gait is awkward, almost sidling up to her like a crab. Moreover, he seems to use gestures with his tail, ears, and hind quarters designed to impress her. For her part, she is anything but impressed, and before long the expression on her otherwise blank face gives way to confusion and fear.

What follows is not a pretty sight, and it quickly dispels any notion that sex is a beautiful thing. We all stare in wonder and growing horror at the spectacle. There is nothing to indicate any sense of pleasure on the female's part; her terrified demeanor and pitiful bleating indicate that she can't wait to get rid of the bull and end whatever gruesome process is taking place as soon as possible.

As for the bull, he is completely out of control, and I wonder if even he knows what is going on. In his frenzied state, he seems uncoordinated and downright gross. There is nothing admirable in his behavior, in my mind, to make him the least bit attractive to the female.

We are deadly silent as we walk back up the hill to the campus. Even Mr. Shaw seems a bit shaken. I'm not sure he expected the grim proceedings, and he is not eager to entertain questions from anyone. That's okay, because each of us is lost in thought, trying to absorb the strange event. From having witnessed procreation in its rawest form, I am convinced that the true miracle is that it is ever successful—even with human intervention.

When we hit campus, we scatter, vowing silently to never speak of this expedition to anyone, ever. Even to each other. And especially not to Mr. Shaw or the girls.

Back in my room, I think about happy cows, hoping to put some distance between myself and the vulgar lesson in sex I've just experienced. I know that cows are "sacred" in Hindu tradition. They hold an elevated place in the steps of the Hindu reincarnation scheme, and they roam freely all over the country. Almost every time I head out of the campus, I run into at least one traffic jam caused by a cow who is sauntering unconcernedly down the middle of the road. I chuckle at the memory. This is working.

Since cows are everywhere, cowpies are everywhere, too. I've seen little kids scoop up big blobs in their bare hands, taking them home to dry for use as fuel or mortar. They must add a unique flavor to the food that is cooked on them. I concentrate on these fragments of memory and fact, trying desperately to get the image of the bull and cow out of my mind.

I scan my memory for more cow facts.

Cows appear completely content, and for that there's an endearing side to them. They have a calming influence over me, their antics a source of humor. Until today. Don't go there, I tell myself.

Cows deserve my respect because they are such lumbering creatures; no one can take them too seriously. They get stuck on narrow hillside ledges where they can't turn around, manage to get into gardens where they shouldn't be, walk through gates and can't get back out, wander into the lake and then fail to climb out, and stand in the middle of the road, blocking traffic and staring blankly at the cars and trucks blowing their horns. This is working. I haven't thought of the frenzied bull and hapless cow for two full minutes.

It's impossible not to step in cowpies, especially at night. A dripping shoe–or even a lost shoe–invariably incurs the laughter of schoolmates. Stepping in one is a messy and smelly affair, their wet consistency oozing into every nook and cranny of our shoes. Almost as repulsive as the amorous encounter of a bull and cow.

With these thoughts in mind, I know it's going to be a long day.

"Your room is too dark to study in!" Poffy's Dad announces a week later as he appears in our dorm room door. I'm reclining on Poffy's bed, doing some algebra homework while Poffy is working at his desk. Dr. Poffy has just come for a quick visit from his remote village. He speaks with such firmness that I look around the dimly lit room. He's absolutely right. A bare, 40-watt lightbulb hangs from the ceiling as the only light source in the entire room. All the dorm rooms are like this. There's not even a hood on the light to focus the rays on the desk or the bed area. The light casts a dismal, brownish, shadow-filled glow, making it difficult to read.

As a mish kid, I've grown accustomed to electricity being a rare and unpredictable thing. Also, it's expensive, so keeping the lights low is one way we all save on our electric bills. I had always accepted this state of affairs and didn't even consider complaining.

"We've got to do something about that!" Dr. Poffy declares. This approach to things is new to me. "Where do I buy light bulbs in Kodai?"

"I think the Budge," I reply. I have never gone bulb shopping, but that seems like a good guess.

"Let's go," Dr. Poffy commands, and Poffy and I jump up.

Twenty minutes later we're back in the room with a 150-watt bulb. It was the only 150-watt bulb I have ever seen in the entire Budge or anywhere. Once it's screwed into the socket, a whole new room greets me. It's grimmer and dirtier than I've ever imagined.

Word spreads quickly around the dorm that Poffy has a new light bulb. The room is soon crowded with silent gawkers. We've never seen such luminosity at Kodai.

"Where'd you get that?" someone asks. "The Budge?"

"Yup."

"I want one. How much'd it cost?"

While we're describing the terms of the transaction, our housefather arrives on the scene, plowing through the horde of gawkers.

"What's going on here?"

"Hi, I'm Dr. Poffy," Poffy's dad says, extending his hand to our housefather. "I was concerned that my boy's eyes would be strained by the dim light bulb hanging from the ceiling, so I ran out to the Budge–is that what you call it?–and picked up this one."

"Well, that's not the regulation wattage," our housefather responds. We sense an adult confrontation coming on, so we all watch and listen without moving. "If one boy gets a bigger bulb, then everyone will want one. That really costs too much and may prompt even more brown-outs than we already have. Anyway, we've learned that a 40-watt bulb is sufficient for everyone to read by. That's what we've used for years. I'd appreciate it if you would replace this one with the bulb that belongs there." This is getting good.

Dr. Poffy stands quietly for a moment, his jaw hanging a bit slackly.

"Well, I'm sorry. My boy needs the brighter light. You don't want to be responsible for him developing poor eyesight, do you? I'd hate to be in your shoes if I got the other parents to protest the dim standards that the school has. You wouldn't like that, would you?"

Our heads swivel from one to the other like we're watching a tennis match. The ball is in our house father's side of the court. But the fight has run out of him, and he turns and walks away, sputtering to himself about brown outs and uppity parents. The bright light would stay; Dr. Poffy has won the round. He is my new hero. I suspect, however, that the match isn't over. Enjoy your victory Poffy, I think. There are more rounds to come.

"D'ja hear what Sammy is doing now?" Paul B. asks Sunday afternoon. Homework is getting to me, so I gladly put it aside and get up. Sammy's last episode was preparing the campus for the clash of planets and the end of time, so anything could be happening this time.

"Nope. What's up?"

"He's preachin' on the hill overlooking Bendy."

"What's he doin' preachin'? He's only thirteen!" By now I've gathered my jacket and raced out the door. Poffy and I jog after Paul B., bound for Bendy Field.

When we get there, sure enough, there's Sammy in the middle of a bunch of young kids, mostly girls. "Prepare the way! This generation of sinners will see the face of God!" he proclaims. "The final days are just around the corner, fall on your knees and pray for forgiveness so that you will be able to walk through those Pearly Gates!" I try, unsuccessfully, to imagine people walking through the Pearly Gates on their knees and praying. "Those who don't repent will be cast into the depths of the everlasting fires of Hell!" Several of the girls fall to their knees, wringing their hands in prayer. Audible sobs can be heard.

This is weird stuff to me. I've been a Christian all my life, but I've never heard such hell, fire, and brimstone preaching before. At least not from an eighth grader! Sammy is the son of fundamentalist parents who are missionaries in Ceylon, so he's doing what might be expected of their offspring. I'm reminded that Poffy, the non-believer, is the son of non-believers and I am the son of Protestant Christians.

But, what if he's right? My Bible talks about the end of time and the return of Jesus to earth. Is that so different from what Sammy is preaching about? I begin to worry a bit. What if the end of time comes tomorrow, with my parents three thousand miles away? What if I never see them again? I know that my parents are good people, but what if I don't pass the grade and make it to heaven? "Like Sodom and Gomorrah, the unfaithful will be consumed in a ball of fire or turned into salt statues, forever regretting their denial of the One True God."

"Hmmph!" It's Poffy standing next to me. Clear-eyed, he is obviously not buying any of this message. "Let's get out of here. I've heard enough of this garbage."

Poffy's "Hmmph" has brought me back to a more observant state. I notice that there are more students on their knees, not just girls. And a lot of them are crying out loud, shouting "I repent! I repent!" I know several of them, and they're very religious goody-two-shoes. I can't imagine what they have to repent for.

I'm not sure that I can dismiss Sammy's message so completely, but the fact is that he's scaring me more than persuading me. What if he does something really crazy so that God feels the need to punish us all? I'm about to leave when I notice a couple of teachers standing on the edge of the growing crowd of students.

Suddenly, one of the girls falls over and begins to shake uncontrollably. "Satan, come out of her!" Sammy screams. The crowd parts so that she has more room to wriggle around. I'm really scared now. What has Sammy done?

"Enough. That's enough, Sammy. Okay, now we have to calm down!" That's Principal R. He wades into the throng, giving some kids hugs and gently helping others stand up. "Thanks for your message, Sammy, but it's almost time for chapel and everyone needs to get ready for that service." Chapel isn't for four more hours, but people begin to walk back to their dorms. Sammy is not sure what to do now, but he protests feebly, "I haven't finished sharing what God has put on my heart."

"Why don't you share it with me," Principal Root responds. I'll be glad to chat with you about it. With that, the crowd disperses.

"What a buffoon," Poffy murmurs.

"Yeah. But what if he's right?"

"Does he sound right to you? Do you believe the world is coming to an end soon?"

"No," I admit. That's not something I've thought about until Sammy raised the issue.

"Well, don't get carried away with his noisy pronouncements."

Whatever else it was, the afternoon's performance on Bendy Hill was exciting entertainment.

On Monday I wake up with a toothache. I'm not sure this has anything to do with Sammy's warning, but it sure hurts like hell. Poffy brings me to the Dishpan and Miss Putz agrees to set up an appointment with the dentist. The dentist is an expat from Britain–one of those Brits who stayed on in India after independence–whose training and credentials are questionable. We all suspect that he never completed dental training, but because Indian regulations are so loosely defined, he can get away with practicing dentistry here. In any case, he is cheap–a critical asset for all things missionary-related–and the only dentist in town.

Entering his outer office, I can hear groans coming from the drilling room. The dentist is trying, unsuccessfully, to get his patient to sit still. In the meantime, the sounds of the drill are irregular and ominous. All the way in this outer room, I can hear the pedal the dentist has to push in order to power the drill. Its squeak is a reminder of the primitive conditions of dental care in Kodai.

When it is my turn in the dentist's chair, I hold on tight to the armrests and try not to move. I'm reminded of the nicks in my ears that come with any movement under Muthu the barber's scissors, and I hold myself stiffly. The dentist prods around my mouth with what must be the dullest probe in the entire British Empire. I swear that he is intentionally trying to poke holes in my gums.

"There's a cavity in a lower bicuspid," he announces gravely. Nothing new there. That's what brought me to this torture chamber. "I'll need to drill it out." The words of an executioner.

After minimal preparation on his part and no anesthetic to dull the impending pain, I can hear the evil sounding "squeeeeeak" of the foot pedal and a corresponding "whirrrr" of the drill. It descends on my mouth. As I fight to restrain myself, the squeaking and whirring rise and fall. The dentist struggles against all odds to maintain a steady hand motion. I can sense, through his fist, the tension in him as he does his best with this antique torture instrument.

As soon as the drill touches my tooth it slows down; the momentum of the pump is not enough to counteract the added friction the drill has encountered. The whine of the drill falls lower and lower until, in frustration, the dentist takes it off the tooth and pumps like mad to get the speed back up. He then repeats the process.

I see sweat beading up on his forehead and tell by the look in his eye that he really wants an electric drill like a real dentist. I can't help but agree with him. At last he pulls back, and I begin to relax, although the image of myself in the overhead mirror certainly doesn't look like I'm relaxing much.

My buddies and I are sitting on the lawn in front of Block dorm, chewing on fresh shoots of grass and soaking up the sun on a lazy weekend afternoon. Suddenly, Mr. Mapp's dormitory door opens with a bang as he struggles out onto the verandah with his bicycle. It has all kinds of junk strapped to it. He pauses on the porch, examining the bike with frowning concentration to make sure all of the items are tied on properly and won't fall off. The bike is so loaded down that we wonder how he can possibly ride it.

The five of us walk across the lawn, out of the sun, into the cool shade of the veranda. We gather around and watch him in silence until our curiosity is too much to bear.

"*Que faites-vous?*" Kaz asks in his halting French. Mr. Mapp is our French teacher, and he's full of stories. Some of his tales about being a soldier of fortune who fought in the Mau Mau Rebellion in Kenya seem a bit tall. But, the look of fear that sweeps over his face when he tells it makes us believe it's real. Another of his stories— maybe just a legend—is that he was bicycling around the world when he ran out of money in India. Because he knows French and the school needed a French teacher, he was hired on. He was housed in a dorm room because that saved everyone money.

"I'm leaving." We stare unbelieving. It's the middle of the school year. What will we do? "Everything I own is on this bike, lads, and I'm heading out. I won't be seeing you all again, but I want you to know I've thoroughly enjoyed getting to know you."

"Can you really ride the bike with so much on it?" I ask. "It looks so overloaded."

"I think so," he responds, leaving enough doubt in our minds that we ponder the reply for a while.

Before heading off, he rides around the courtyard in a test circle, shaking and swerving. He looks like a clown in a one-man circus act. A butterfly net sticks out of his backpack, waving and shaking back and forth wildly. This only amplifies his unsteadiness.

"I'm off lads," he announces with finality. As he pedals down the driveway, he waves and shouts over his shoulder, "*Bon chance! Be proper lads, now!*" And then he disappears around the corner of the chapel.

A flood of regret sweeps across me as we stand there in silence, staring at the place that we last saw Mr. Mapp. I wish that I had listened more closely to his stories and had gotten to know him better. Anyone who can get on a bike with all of his worldly possessions and pedal off into the Indian mountains is free beyond imagination. I feel lucky to have known him, even if for only a short time. He has fueled my imagination and my love of faraway places and unmet people. I'll miss him.

That night as I lie in bed, I wonder where Mr. Mapp is and how he is doing. I picture him stopping by a small patch of forest and chasing butterflies, which he loves to do. I imagine him cycling through the small villages that pepper the vast plains of India. When dusk falls, I imagine him asking a farmer's permission to spend the night on his land. He'd set up a simple camp and stare up at the stars as he lies alone under the sky, eventually falling asleep knowing he is doing something unique and exciting.

I'm sure he gives little consideration to being robbed during the night. I think Mr. Mapp lives in a world even more trusting than the one I have experienced. Nonetheless, I expect that he'll sleep next to his bike with all his worldly possessions.

I visualize him waking in the morning, surrounded by small kids boisterously asking questions and dogs sniffing at his packages, hoping for a treat. He'll entertain them with tall tales and then be on his way again, continuing his solitary trek to points unknown. Thank God the world has people like Mr. Mapp.

It's Washington's Birthday, and all day long I enjoy the memorial activities in class and out. Here we are, Americans isolated in the southern tip of the Indian subcontinent, and we want to remind ourselves that we're still proud to be Americans. Washington's Birthday provides that opportunity, and every year we do it up right.

Supper is the highlight of the day, and my friends and I are eager to dig in. We're wearing our Sunday suits, a sign of the respect we have for the father of our nation. We arrive at the door of the dining room and crane our necks to see what's going on inside. There is bunting all over the place, crepe paper streamers and ribbons hanging from the rafters. The tables are festooned with candles whose flickering light makes the place appear more intimate—and casts the drab walls into picturesque shadows.

When the bell rings, we walk in—an unheard of polite entrance—and have to hunt around for our assigned seats. For a change, boys and girls are placed at the same table, so we know this is a formal event. Happily, Bonnie Bosch is sitting next to me, so I know at least one of my tablemates is in my grade.

After the prayer—a really long and patriotic one—we sit down in loud unison. Lively chatter quickly fills the room as we all greet our tablemates and speculate about the chicken dish we know is coming. The Indian waiters, dressed patriotically in white suits, scurry around serving us from large trays balanced on their shoulders. I can hardly wait to be served as I watch our favorite waiter, Vailu, attend the girls at our table first—another sign of formality that we rarely see. He is grinning from ear to ear as he serves Bonnie, next to me.

As he leans over to serve her, he tilts the platter too much and pours hot, greasy, brown gravy all over my suit. It runs down my shoulder and collects in a puddle on my lap. Through my clothes, I can feel my skin being singed. I jump up with a short gasp, drawing the attention of everyone in the dining room. The chatter comes to a halt, and I realize I am being watched and judged for my next actions.

Ignoring my scalded leg, I carefully mop the excess with my napkin and turn to the groveling Vailu. "It's okay. No harm done. Just get me another napkin, please." The chatter resumes as everyone returns to the business of eating, and I know somehow that I've passed the test. Rather than scream at the pain, or berate poor Vailu for his boneheaded move, I had forgiven him his debt to me. From a moment of embarrassment, I had transformed it into a moment of triumph. The gravy was still sticky on my lap, and the suit–which had soaked up the gooey mess like a sponge–was nearly ruined, but I had come through the crisis in good shape.

On Saturday I take my suit to the *dhobi* to have it dry-cleaned. I hang around the busy little shop to watch the action. I have never had anything dry-cleaned before. The *dhobi* wipes off the remaining gravy chunks and then takes out a bottle of mystery fluid. When he uncaps it, I can smell jet fuel and have a brief flashback to my flight from Bahrain to Delhi on the BOAC Comet.

Once the cleaning has been completed, I take a whiff of the coat. Sure enough, that has to be jet fuel. In fact, when I get back to my room, Teddy and Paul B. both swear it is jet fuel. I decide that I better avoid any fire source in the future. The whole suit could go up in flames in a second!

Beyond sniffing at my suit, however, no one wants to talk further about my encounter with the gravy. There is something else on everyone's mind. Two of our older fellow students had been kicked out of school for smoking. A third one, a classmate, has been put on probation, probably because he is younger and was led astray by the older kids. They had been here yesterday, but today their rooms are empty and all of their stuff has been packed to be shipped home.

"I can't believe their lives have been ruined because they wanted a smoke!" Teddy says. I have to agree. I resolve to be more careful in the future lest I get caught for doing something which would ruin my life and get me kicked out of school.

That night, things get stranger. Judy, the younger sister of one of my classmates, disappears from school. About seven o'clock, Terr stops by my dorm room. "They've asked all the junior and senior boys to help the police and faculty search for Judy. I'm headed into town to do what I can."

The idea that a kid could disappear is alarming for everyone. Rumors of kidnapping spread through the campus like lightning. The school is well known for taking care of its students, so to have one of them vanish for whatever reason is an awful prospect. I can't help think of the Gurkha thundering around, moaning about lapsed security. At the dorm meeting, our housemother prays that Judy will be found soon. A chorus of Amens echoes her prayer.

Finally, around midnight, Terr comes back. Everyone in Block is still wide awake, wondering what has happened. "The police found her hiding in the Budge," he tells us. "Apparently she ran away of her own accord. Nobody kidnapped her or anything. She had had a quarrel with her roommate, or something, and just wanted to go home. Stupid kid." Amid the general relief that ensues, I murmur a silent prayer of thanks.

"Oh, and you won't believe this," Terr continues. "They gave me two demerits because I missed the Wissy dorm meeting. Can you believe that?! They're the first two black marks I've received in more than a year. That really stinks." We all agree. It's a crazy place sometimes, when rules and regulations overwhelm common sense.

It's Field Day again, and the campus is abuzz with discussions about legendary past triumphs and failures. "I expect Laila to break all kinds of records," Kaz tells me.

"I can't argue with that. She certainly has the genes for it. Her older brother was one of the greatest athletes to come to Kodai." I'm particularly excited because Laila is one of the Arabian mish kids, and therefore she's like a big sister to me. Unfortunately, this year I can't compete because I've just recovered from a bout of stomach flu. But I'm not sick enough to miss the huge Indian banquet of *pilau* (yellow, flavored rice) and all the trimmings that is served on Bendy Field while the ribbons are being awarded. I cheer lustily when Laila climbs the podium. She's one of us.

That night the eighth graders go to Mr. Shaw's house for a taffy pull. Taffy pulls—especially when they're off campus—are great treats. After buttering my hands, I grab a wad of the hot, sticky goo—almost too hot to handle—and work it into a ball. Using all my strength, I pull the ball apart. As I do so, the ball begins to cool and becomes harder and harder to pull. Along the way, I have to test the quality of the taffy, so I nibble pieces of it. Eventually, the taffy has turned into a fluffy mass, ready to eat, and eat it I do. A perfect way to end Field Day, if I say so myself.

Easter Sunday plays a central role in school life, and I wake in the early morning darkness with great expectations. Since we're all at home during Christmas recess, Easter becomes the major Christian holiday we celebrate in Kodai. As I put on my suit, I notice that there is mold on spots where the gravy spilled. I try to wash it off as best I can, knowing I'll have to take it back to the cleaner for another round. To make matters worse, a strong stench of jet fuel still escapes from the coat.

Using my flashlight, I join the flow of well-dressed students who make their way to Coakers Walk. Unusually, no one is talking. The sight of all of us walking along in the dark, following our flickering flashlights, stuns the cows, who seem to feel that this should be their private time of the day.

The sunrise service on the top of Coakers is always visually awesome. Today it is spectacular to watch the red ball begin to make its appearance on the eastern horizon. It is a straight drop of almost six thousand feet from the side of Coakers to the plains below, which provides an unobstructed view of the sun growing bigger and bigger in the distance. The only sounds in the still morning air are the chirpings of birds protesting the human invasion of their sanctuary.

As I watch the glorious scene light up, complete with cloud banks rising from the valleys that cut through the mountain ranges, I think that this golden tableau is nature's way of honoring and celebrating our Creator. What more fitting way could I celebrate the rising of the Son on Easter morning? Before the service even begins, I am humbled by the renewing message of Easter. The words and music are a blur, only partly heard in the midst of my reverie.

In a happy glow, I walk back to the campus with the others. Again, other than a few students humming snippets of the hymns we just sang, no one is talking. Everyone seems to be wrapped in the same happy glow. Mornings on Coakers Walk can do that to us.

Following breakfast, we head to the gym. There, the school's band, orchestra, and choirs all join in a musical extravaganza. The church is just not big enough for the crowd that shows up. Huge bouquets of flowers and bright white lilies line the aisles of folding chairs. I love the pageantry. All the noise that was pent up during the sunrise service is released during this service. At the top of our lungs we belt out, "Jesus Christ is Risen Today!" The choirs and instrumentalists join in the fun. The gym rocks. I feel my eyes well up. Easter is wonderful! I wish it would last forever.

When I get back to the dining room, I run into Poffy. He is wearing his regular clothes. "Did you change already?"

"No, I didn't go to the Easter services."

"You didn't?! Does Mrs. Battleaxe know?"

"Yup, she gave me permission."

I'm flabbergasted. I know Poffy's family is not Christian, but he still has to attend every chapel service, just like the rest of us.

Mrs. Battleaxe had made that requirement plain to his parents. While Poffy doesn't complain, it is clear that he feels this is an unfair imposition on his civil rights. But that is the rule, and there isn't much that can be done about it. This is a Christian school, after all. And all of us—well, most of us—are mish kids. But not Poffy.

"How did you get her permission?"

"My dad keeps asking her to let me do some other sort of spiritual exercise, and she always says no. But this time, when Dad asked, she said that I could skip the Easter services if I wanted to. So I did. Maybe she thought I'd want to go because all of you were going, but I decided to get my beauty sleep."

I can't imagine why anyone would want to miss the unforgettable sunrise service and the heartfelt singing of the all-campus service. Poffy must really not believe if he missed those things. I wonder if Mrs. Battleaxe feels as though Poffy called her bluff. She must be sure that he's going to burn in hell. I'm not so sure. Poffy's a good guy, and I really like his mom and dad. I can't imagine all of them going to hell just because they don't say grace at meals or believe in Jesus. In any case, Poffy certainly has no regrets as he digs into the platter of roasted chicken that always accompanies Easter Sunday lunch.

Coming back from a wonderful "Doughboy Party," where we baked bread dough on sticks held over the fire, I am feeling particularly warm and happy. I have eaten three doughboys filled with hamburger meat and two more with veggies. Teddy comes jogging up to meet me as I descend the staircase to Block. He's out of breath.

"Paul, d'ja hear about Uncle Gerry?"

"No, I've been at Mr. Shaw's house. What happened?"

"He had a heart attack and died."

I feel my knees go weak. Uncle Gerry is—was—my dad's best friend and most loved colleague. They had worked in hospitals together in Bahrain and Iraq. He and Aunt Rose and their children were our closest neighbors. His daughter, Laila, had just triumphed during Field Day. It is hard for me to make sense of this awful news.

After surviving tuberculosis and the sinking of the *Dara*, after two decades of fighting all kinds of diseases from malaria to cholera and dysentery, Uncle Gerry is dead. He was always so active, a great tennis player, and so full of energy. How could God let this happen to such a saint? It is incredibly hard to absorb. What will his son and daughters do? What will Aunt Rose do? I can't imagine. I know in the old days of the Arabian Mission, back in the last century when the pioneers went out, many of the people—men, women, and children—died in the field. But modern medicine and modern transportation mean that those days should be gone.

"I wonder how Laila is," I say to Teddy. "Let's go and talk with her."

Neither of us speaks as we trudge over to Kennedy Hall. My legs are like lead, and my mind runs pictures of Uncle Gerry. He's always doing things and smiling. Doing and smiling. That's how I remember him.

There are a bunch of girls, along with the housemother, standing around Laila. Terr has his arms around Laila. She looks like she hasn't slept in a week. Her shoulders shake as she tries to control her weeping. Her pain cuts me to the core. "Hi, Laila," I start lamely. "Teddy and I wanted to let you know we're sorry for you."

She looks up at me, and I can't hold back the tears. "Uncle Gerry was a great man, a saint of God," I sob. She breaks down and cries harder. I don't know what more to say. Teddy and I just stand there in the crowded room, sniffling our sympathy. Finally, Terr motions toward the door with his head, and Teddy and I back out. As we wordlessly head back to Phelps, I pray to God that nothing like this happens in my family, because I know beyond a shadow of doubt that I couldn't handle such a personal tragedy.

"I can't believe you'll be leaving soon," I say to Terr later that afternoon. "I'll be on my own." I'm still wallowing in the sour mood created by the news of Uncle Gerry's death. "I don't know how I'll cope."

"You'll do fine," he replies. "You have Teddy, Paul B. and the others. Soon you'll be the oldest Arab kid and leading the young ones to Kodai." I think about that scary thought for a few minutes, and it is even more unsettling. I can't help thinking about the time when Dave and Terr were about my age and a student leader had left all the passports in a taxi in Bombay and lost them forever. That was before my time, but it's a story told over and over as a wake-up call for all later leaders. Before they could continue traveling, they had to get a letter from the U.S. ambassador to assure the Indian and Arab immigration authorities that the students were all Americans who were returning to be with their parents in the Persian Gulf region.

Terr is reclining on his bed in Airlee Hall, thumbing through the Eucy, our yearbook. He stops at a page of pictures showing students in various extra-curricular activities. "I took those three shots. And I edited the whole extra-curricular activities section." He keeps thumbing through the pages. I think about how he and our brother, Dave, have been involved in the newspaper and yearbook, and a shiver of pride ripples through me. My big brothers.

"Here, have a snack," he says, pushing a half-eaten candy bar at me. I grab it.

"Look at her," he points to one of his classmates, a real beauty. "Took her out to the *Gunga Din* movie a couple of weeks ago. Real nice." I nod in agreement. "Saw her with Steve this week, though." He looks a bit dejected at the prospect of losing her to someone else.

"How's your fingernail?" he asks.

"Are you still checking up on my nail chewing? I suppose Mom put you up to that."

"No. The one you lost?"

I have almost forgotten. Before we left Bahrain, a gust of wind slammed a door on the index finger of my left hand. It turned all black and blue before I left home. Dad assured me it would be okay. But shortly after I got back here to Kodai, the nail fell off, leaving an ugly nailbed exposed. I went to the Dishpan and Simone swabbed it with iodine and put a bandage on it. The wrap went halfway around my hand, making it difficult to close my fist. At least she didn't give me an enema, although she did threaten to give me a tetanus shot. Fearing that I would be maimed for life, I wrote home. Again Dad reassured me and promised that the fingernail would grow back. It did, but it took its time.

I hold up my hand to Terr. "See, it's almost like new." He grunts and returns to the Eucy and the pictures he had taken and formatted. "I guess I'll see you later." Another grunt.

I am almost back to Phelps when I realize I haven't thought about Laila or Uncle Gerry or death for at least half an hour. Terr has worked his magic. I smile to myself as I realize how he's played me. I'm still the kid brother.

"Well, men," Mr. Shaw announces in class. "The weather seems to be freshening nicely, so I think it's time to take another camping trip. This time I'd like to hike up to Lake Berijam.

We'll leave right after school on Friday and be home in time for vespers on Sunday. Be sure to bring changes of clothes. Hiking shoes would be good, too. And canteens." I'm elated; the rainy season has driven me nuts, and I'm ready for communing with nature again. I have forgotten my fear of snakes, jackals, panthers, bison and other wild beasts. And of tree people swinging between branches in the forests of South India.

Friday afternoon Mr. Shaw is waiting outside the gym with a bunch of tents, shovels, and packaged food. We all trundle up with our packs stuffed with clothes and a sleeping bag strapped on our backs. As usual, mine came right out of the storage room and stinks of generations of sweaty, dirty, Kodai hikers. We cram the food into the last spaces and strap the pieces of the tent and our rolled sleeping bags to the undersides of the packs. I guess that my full pack must weigh about forty pounds. Maybe four hundred. I sway as I stand up, and Kaz—who is behind me—reaches out to steady me.

After several hours of hiking through beautiful but rugged mountain paths, we break out of the forest into a clearing. The sun is almost setting, so we have to work quickly, setting up the tents and—most importantly—digging a latrine. While most of us are building the camp, Teddy and Paul B. are busy getting supper ready. They gather wood, enough to last the whole night, and light a fire. Carefully setting the cooking pans on the coals, they stir in the prepared ingredients.

"D'ja hear about the cobra on campus yesterday?" Kaz asks as we sit around the campfire. The supper and campfire have created a mellow moment. We're all relaxed after the invigorating climb and the hard work of setting up camp. Just the right atmosphere to recount the excitement of the week.

Of course every one of us had heard about the cobra on campus, but Kaz feels the need to fill in the details in case anyone was unconscious in the Dishpan for the last forty-eight hours.

Since he is a principal actor in the episode, we all agree that it is appropriate for him to give the official account.

"I was walking with Steve out of the gym when I saw something slithering along the driveway," he begins. The driveway curls uphill from the main gate where The Gurkha has his guardhouse, runs past the chapel and the gym, and ends at the flagpole circle in front of the main class building.

"I realized it was a six-foot-long cobra, so we backed off and watched from the gym door, ready to bolt if it came our way. It glided up towards the flagpole green and then suddenly turned into that drainage pipe that runs under the driveway. You know it?" A dozen heads nod. The drainpipe is a little bump in the road, and it's so narrow that it doesn't do any good when there is real rain falling.

"Anyway, Steve and I each grabbed a large rock and rammed them on either side of the drainpipe, blocking the snake inside." This was assuredly a heroic action that demands our quiet attention and approval. We all stare into the fire, imagining boulder-sized rocks blocking the ends of the drainpipe. The darkness of the night seems to close in on us. The periodic sparking of the fire sends off fireflies of light which float into the trees above. We huddle closer to the flames, knowing that the fire wards off all kinds of beasts, including king cobras and banana vipers.

"By now, there were a dozen kids hanging around, so we explained what we had done. 'I better get Principal Root,' Steve said and ran off to the admin building and someone else ran down to the guardhouse. Soon Principal Root showed up, and the Gurkha came chugging up the road.

"'Step back!' Mr. Root yelled at us. We inched away. The Gurkha scowled at us, so we all moved back twenty feet.

"'I've called the mongoose man, Sahib,' The Gurkha said to the principal.

"'That's good,' was the reply."

Kaz takes a deep breath and looks around. Although we all know what was about to happen—several of us had even been there—we hang on every word Kaz has to say.

"When the mongoose man arrived, he plopped a canvas bag on the grass and took out a wriggling mongoose. I think the mongoose had already caught the scent of the cobra and couldn't wait to get at it. While holding the wriggling rodent, the mongoose man chatted briefly with the Gurkha, probably getting caught up on the details of the situation.

"He nodded a couple of times and then knelt down at one end of the pipe. We all moved back another ten feet, almost up against the wall of the gym, ready to run through the doors if the cobra charged us. In a swift set of movements, the mongoose man grabbed one of the rocks, moved it aside, shoved the mongoose into the pipe, and then slammed the rock back in place."

At this moment, a branch in the fire lets off a cloud of sparks, lighting up the horror-stricken faces crowded around the campfire. This is what camping is all about: a warm fire, filled bellies, and stories that could make your hair curl. I resist a smile of happiness. Kaz resumes.

"You wouldn't believe the snarling, hissing, scratching sounds that I heard!" We believe. We believe. Keep going. "And then everything went quiet. It was eerie, all that racket and then total silence. We edged back toward the mongoose man and the drainpipe. Slowly, cautiously, the mongoose man knelt and listened to the drainpipe. We all strained to hear, too. But there was nothing to hear. Just as slowly and cautiously he reached down and lifted the rock. Like the little superhero that he was, the mongoose trotted out of the drainpipe, dragging the six feet of cobra behind him. The snake's neck had been broken, and it was a bloody mess. Once again, the mongoose proved that it is faster than a striking cobra!"

I want to applaud, although I'm not sure if it's for the mongoose, the cobra, or Kaz the storyteller. Kaz has kept us on the edge of our seats and has us all worked up to a fine anxiety. A story perfectly told!

After a pause to let us absorb the magnitude of the struggles that nature has built into it, our conversations begin again. In small groups we chatter about the cobra, about other deadly snakes we've seen, and about the wonders of Indian flora and fauna. Before long exhaustion sets in, and we filter back into our tents and snuggle down in our sleeping bags. It has been a great start to the camping trip.

Saturday morning, after a hasty breakfast, Lansey yells out, "Skinny dip time!" strips off his clothes and barrels into the nearby lake. He doesn't even look for snakes, he just dives into the chilly, crystalline water. The rest of us follow, yelling and pushing as we go. In no time there are piles of discarded clothes along the lakefront, testimony to our readiness to follow any crazy leader into any crazy situation.

Skinny dipping is a mixed experience. While it is wonderfully freeing to remove the burden of a soggy swimsuit, it also exposes us to critical observations from the peanut gallery.

"Hey Paulie, where'd you get those . . . zits?" The pauses are almost as devastating as the words being used. While I'm conscious of the crop of zits I grow every day, like my peers, I'm also constantly looking around and comparing. On some comparisons I win, on many others, I don't. So, when I hit the lake water, I remain mostly submerged, splashing and pushing anyone who gets too close.

"Hey, this is the men's camping trip, the ladies are back on campus."

"Wimp, shrimp. You call yourself a man? Anybody here got a magnifying glass?"

"Whoa, look at that joke!"

"And how old are you? How many years before you expect to hit puberty?"

The jibes fly around the lake, striking home on more occasions than not. I'm more than mortified, but I join in the jesting, too, shooting an arrow or two at likely targets. There is always someone who can be targeted, and we're pros at it. Mr. Shaw just sits on the bank of the lake, listening and chuckling to himself. I sense that there will be a new topic of conversation around the campfire tonight.

Indeed, there is. "Men," he begins. "You should know now that we all mature at different rates. Some of you have advanced further in the process than others, but the late bloomers should take heart. You'll catch up."

The fire draws all of our attention. In some way or another, we are all late bloomers. "You need to know that Mother Nature works uniquely in each of your bodies so that some of you will be bigger and stronger, others smarter and quicker, and still others more creative. These are all part of God's great creation, and you are one of the unique images of God in that creation."

All of a sudden the monologue drifts from sex to theology. Mr. Shaw is good at this. He's trying to get us to think about the higher things in life, not the lower ones. But I can't help thinking of the lower ones, and I'm not sure that I will ever truly catch up with my classmates. Maybe I started school too young, and if I had waited another year, I'd be right in the middle of the maturation pack. It's with this ambivalent idea in mind that I slink off to my tent and sleeping bag. A lot to think about as I drift off to sleep.

The unfortunate episode with the spilled gravy continues to haunt me. No matter how much jet fuel is poured over my coat and pants, they still develop mildew and stink like gasoline, so in

April Mom sends me some extra money to have a new suit made. With cash in hand, I head off to meet the legendary Mr. Peter.

Mr. Peter is the town's tailor. I can't say if he is a particularly skilled one, since he is the only tailor in town. I suspect that he isn't on the high end of the skill scale because he's stuck here in Kodai. On the other hand, he possesses a good imagination and is resourceful at making us believe he can create anything we challenge him to sew. All we need to do is show him a picture in an old Sears catalog and he takes it from there.

Mr. Peter hangs out in front of his shop waiting for Kodai kids to pass by on their way through the bazaar. When I arrive, he's standing in the doorway, his enormous smile revealing huge white teeth.

He yells out compliments at another student who is wearing one of his creations. "That shirt is good. I make it. Pants need replacing. Come in, I make you new pants to match shirt!" The student waves hurriedly and keeps on going. Not a good sign.

"You bring Sears picture, Master," he tells me when I ask about a new suit. "I make and bring to you in few days." He is so confident in his promise that I quickly agree to his terms. Having heard from Terr about Mr. Peter's methods, I hand him a picture I have with me of a boy's suit, which I had found in one of Mrs. Sipanzi's magazines. He promptly measures me up and down, writing the measurements in a lined notebook. We agree on a bolt of cloth for the suit, and he assures me that all is "good, good, good."

In three days' time, as promised, Mr. Peter arrives at Block with a boy's suit. It looks nothing like the picture I had left with him, and I'm not even sure it is made out of the cloth we had agreed to. On the other hand, it fits me snuggly, making me look trim and well dressed. No more gravy stain or mildew blotches. I gladly pay him his wages, and he leaves with hearty invitations for me and my friends to buy more clothes from him.

We have time for one more excursion before my parents return for Terr's graduation. After much debate, we settle on a night time bike ride down the *Ghat* and then a hitchhike back up the mountain. Since I don't own a bike, I have to rent one from Shadrach, so on Friday afternoon I head over to his little shop just outside the campus gate.

Shadrach isn't his real name, of course. Since Indians find that we Westerners can't handle their lengthy names, they regularly adopt names that they think will be easier for us to handle. Knowing that we are a Christian group—except for Poffy, of course—they often adopt biblical names. So the bike man uses the name "Shadrach," and for generations of Kodai kids, that's how he has been known. That's no different from some of the other names local merchants have chosen; there's a Methuselah, an Ebenezer, a Sampson, and a Moses nearby. Biblical names run amok.

I notice that his shop has a "selection" of reconditioned clunkers that Shadrach has picked up from roadside ditches and garbage dumps. They are minimally reconditioned into moveable crates, pieced together from other wrecks. Parts and wheels are strewn around the shop, waiting to be grafted onto new relics as Shadrach finds them. But the price is right, and being in no state to haggle over the rental fee, I'll be glad to find one that is serviceable.

Like all of his bikes, the one I pick is dull black in color, has large wheels, and creaks as I pedal along. I take it for a quick trial run and realize I won't be doing wheelies or spins; it waddles even when I peddle in a straight line. I'll be lucky if I don't drive off a cliff as I wend my way down the mountains. But it is sturdy enough to make the trip, and I ignore the bald tires, knowing that it is better to be on a bike than on no bike at all.

When I have my bike picked out and paid for, I ride it back up the driveway to the middle of campus. I park it next to the gym and head over to the dining hall for supper. We are going to leave about 9 o'clock, so that we can be flying down the *Ghat* when midnight hits. Supper is bearable, and we eat a lot, knowing that we won't have another hot meal until tomorrow night.

At last it's the appointed hour, and we gather in silence in front of the gym in the nearly pitch black night. As we had planned, a full moon is breaking over the eastern horizon. I'm the only one who has had to rent a bike. Kaz, Paul B., and Lansey have all retrieved their new bicycles from storage. They make a big show of wiping them down and shining up the fenders and handle bars. I look at my jalopy and rub a hand over the seat. At least that can be dust free, if not shiny. I check my canteen and backpack, making sure they are securely fastened to my belt and shoulders.

When everyone's ready, we set off. There is a gentle breeze tonight, now with an almost full moon shining down. We can see the stars through the trees, glowing brightly in the sky. The Gurkha checks us out as we pass the gate, grunting his best wishes, I imagine. He knows we love to bike down the *Ghat* at night, but he doesn't like it when we're not nearby so that he can keep his eye on us.

We're already heading downhill at a controlled pace when we clear the village limits. Beyond there is only darkness under the thick tree cover, the road dimly lit by the blazing moon. It is a wonder how well lit the terrain is, given the prevailing darkness. We have to watch carefully as we fly along, because potholes are everywhere, and there are always fallen branches and twigs on the road. Fortunately, as always at this at time of night, there is little traffic, although I do have to dodge a lorry about fifteen minutes into the run. The noise it makes as it lumbers up the *Ghat* provides ample warning, so we slow down and head to the side of the road.

An hour later the road levels out, and for a few kilometers it is even going uphill. Shadrach's old crate makes the going really tough at this point, and I have to grind to get up the shallow grade. I am elated when I begin to feel the pull of gravity drawing me forward. When I glance at the valley side of the road, it's straight down for a thousand feet, with nothing but trees to break the fall, so I hug the mountainside even more tightly. My front tire hits a stone and veers off the narrow lane of tarmac, but I am able to right myself before the bike tips over.

We come to a gentle downslope, and I become totally absorbed in the glory of the night, glancing up at the moon and stars as they shimmer through the forest overhang. It doesn't get any better than this. Returning my eyes to the road, I see a fallen branch ahead and begin to steer clear of it. Then it begins to move, and I realize it's a snake, slithering across the warm asphalt pavement. It must sense me coming, because it suddenly bolts for the drainage ditch, and I narrowly avoid running over it. "Snake," I half whisper, and the guys behind me yell out, "See it?"

As quiet as we tried to be, our conversation could wake the dead. Instantly there is loud chattering in the trees on both sides of the road as a colony of monkeys warn each other of impending doom. I feel the hairs on the back of my head stand on end.

"Monkeys," Paul B. half whispers from behind me, as a deep rumble echoes the monkey's high-pitched chatter. My heart is racing along with the bike. Unconsciously, we pedal a little faster, pushing our bikes to get past this section of the jungle. Shadrach's make-believe bike seems to slow down no matter how frantically I push the pedals. In a couple of miles, we begin to relax our pace since we haven't heard any animal sounds for some time. With all the trees hanging over the roadway, it feels like we're driving through a tunnel, aiming at the light at its end.

"I love this trip!" I scream out. My scream is echoed by a chorus of "Hi-ho-Silver!" and "Wheeee!" I am so euphoric that I lift my legs and sail along without brakes. Fortunately, the road begins to level out again, so I slow down. Unfortunately, I hit a patch of loose dirt, skid to the side, slam my feet down on the pedals, grab for the brakes, and tumble head over heels onto the ground, skimming along the roadbed for a dozen feet. Laughing all the way.

The others pull up and drop their bikes on the side of the road, running up to check on me. I'm still laughing, which only convinces them that I must have bashed my head and knocked myself silly. I stifle the laughs, gasping for air, and try to stand up. I'm wobbly, but with a little help, I right myself and check for broken bones. Although there are scratches everywhere, everything seems to be working. My pants are ripped in several places, and I have blood dribbling down my right arm. Grease from the bicycle chain has left a streak across my right pant leg. I'll need to see Peter the Tailor soon, I think.

"I'm okay."

"You sure? Do you need help?"

"No, just scrapes and bruises. Nothing serious." Almost disappointed in that admission.

I retrieve the Shadrach crate, make sure that the wheels aren't bent too badly, straddle the front wheel and straighten it, and declare, "Let's go!" As we resume our trek, I review the steps in this crash and plan how I will retell the story.

It is still dark when we sail across the bridge that divides the mountain range from the broad, flat plains below. Each of us lets out an exhilarating yell, "Whahoo!" Under my breath I murmur, "Yay, we've survived!"

But there is another test to come. Since it is harvest season, the villagers have scattered piles of rice in a thin layer, about an inch thick, on top of the road surfaces. They do this so that passing trucks and cars will thresh the grains and the wind will carry the chaff away. Kaz and I both take spills as we wind through this grain mine field. Fortunately, I don't add to my collection of injuries; the rice acts as a natural cushion, protecting us from the uneven roadbed.

Soon, we're gliding into a small hamlet on the edge of the plains, looking for a truck to take us back up the *Ghat*. Although the dawn is just beginning to break, there are already people on the streets, walking to roadside food and tea stalls or to their rice paddies. Women are carrying bundles of straw and sticks on their heads for the family fire, and young kids are everywhere. In fact, it is just a matter of minutes before we're surrounded by a swarm of jabbering children, "Engleesh?" "How you, Joe?"

We head over to an outdoor tea shop and find an empty lorry. "Can you take us up to Kodai?" we ask the lone customer, presuming him to be the truck driver.

"No, Master, I have cousin," he says, confusing us. "I take," and he beckons us to follow. We're reluctant to go with him, but then he points to another truck on the other side of the road. "Cousin lorry, Master," he announces with pride.

Before long, our bikes are stored in the truck bed, and we flop down on and around them. We're exhausted but thoroughly happy. As the sun begins to climb overhead into the sky, we make our bumpy ascent back up the *Ghat* to our beloved Kodai school.

A flower lady

CHAPTER 6

Transitions

On January eleventh, we Arabian Mission kids fly out of Bahrain, spend a night in Bombay, and then fly on to Madras where we catch the overnight train to Kodai Road. We arrive in Kodai after a too-quick, two-day trip. The sense of adventure that I used to experience has been lost on this too-rapid trip. I prefer the longer journeys of the old days. They made the transition between home and boarding school much easier, allowing more time for me to get used to leaving home and to savor the joy and wonder of seeing the wider world.

When I arrive in Kodai, I find letters from Mom and Dad awaiting me. Since it takes at least a week for mail to get to Kodai, these must have been written while I was still in Bahrain. Mom and Dad knew how lonely I would be with Terr and Dave gone to college, and also my friends Poffy, Paul B., and Bosch being on furlough back in the States.

Being in boarding school is a mixed blessing. Spending months away from home is harsh, but at the same time, I love being with friends and all the excitement generated by having dozens of adolescents living together. An unexpected blessing of boarding school is that I never once consider running away from home! As a consequence of being gone so much, when we are together as a family, we make an extra effort to enjoy each other's company. From all the special activities my parents plan when we are together, I sense how much they love us, even though we have to be apart so much. We don't hold our separations against our parents because we know that is how life has to be in the mission.

On my return to Kodai, I move back into Airlee with my new roommates, Kaz and Teddy. I miss my best friend Poffy, but I quickly become best friends with Kaz. Kaz has a wiry, compact build and is a self-confident, risk-taking type, with an adventurous spirit. I have to be careful about "daring" Kaz to do something, because he can't turn down a dare. His self-assuredness probably stems from his unusual background. His family are refugees from the Soviet Union. He hasn't told me all the details, but they must have had a harrowing escape to get to Ceylon where they now live.

Our housefather, Mr. Sipanzi, is an Armenian Orthodox minister. He tells hair-raising stories about the Armenian Holocaust. Some of his relatives were killed during the massacres that happened in Turkey in the early 1900s. His scary tales open up a whole new window into the world of evil I'd never imagined possible. It is such a stark contrast with the wholesome outlook on things that we have developed in our little corner of the world. Mr. Sipanzi also tells stories of the period in his life that he worked as a chaplain in an insane asylum. We wonder if that experience is what got him the job as our houseparent.

I'm on my way to class after lunch, bright sunlight is streaming through the hallways from the windows above. I'm in a good mood and surrounded by and happily bantering with friends. Just before entering the classroom I catch Vivian's eye. She's staring at me as if she wants to say something. "Prepare to be embarrassed," she whispers.

"Why?"

But she returns to her desk before I get an answer.

I'm clueless as to what she is talking about until I stroll apprehensively into my oddly silent class. There, pinned to the bulletin board for all to see, is a pair of dirty underpants. Everyone's staring at me and stifling giggles. Mercifully, Vivian isn't looking at me.

Like a moth to flames, I'm drawn to the bulletin board.

All our clothes in Kodai have our names sewn on them, and my name is clearly emblazoned on these undershorts. Our teacher, Miss Slifer, stands stoically at the head of the class, clearly aware the shorts are hanging there. She has done nothing to remove them. It feels as though she is silently condoning the humiliating display.

I stuff the underpants in my pocket and slink to my seat like a wounded puppy. I'm embarrassed beyond words; my life is in ruins. Why anyone did this to me is utterly beyond me. I try to think of who I might have offended. No one comes to mind, but whoever it is, he certainly got me in a painful manner. I wonder if anyone else has had such a despicable thing happen to him. More painfully, how can a teacher be complicit in such degrading behavior?

Too baffled to be angry, I decide to silently take my licks. I have learned to take care of myself without the aid of adults, so I will get through this setback. It crosses my mind that this never would have been allowed to happen to one of the girls in the class, but because I'm a boy, I'm expected to get over it.

Not long after the underpants incident, I take another emotional blow.

On Wednesday night we hold our usual weekly dorm meeting. Since Rev. and Mrs. Sipanzi are absent from campus, Mrs. Henderson is our substitute house mother. I like Mrs. Henderson because she is an "old school" Scottish woman who has lived in India since the dark ages—well, at least since India was part of the British Empire. Mr. and Mrs. Henderson are proper, loyal British subjects, proud of their queen and country. Having no children, they expend most of their attention on their two dogs. The dogs are better taken care of, better groomed, and better fed than us school kids. However, the dogs are also generally better behaved than we are, and this fact doesn't escape the notice of the Hendersons. They are constantly watching out for any signs of mischief.

Mrs. Henderson is a gifted storyteller, spinning spellbinding tales. We can actually immerse ourselves in her riveting accounts of adventure and heroism, and they make us feel like one day we might do something heroic like that. We are all convinced that the stories are real. She is also one of the few adults willing to gossip and fill us in on some of the juicier happenings in Kodai.

When we have all gathered in a circle around her chair for the night's dorm meeting, Mrs. Henderson sits down. She looks like royalty in the glow of the fireplace, with the room lights low. In a slow-paced, official-sounding voice, she passes on the news from the school. It's like being in court with the queen giving her subjects their marching orders. Because it is hiking season, she discusses the various hikes that are being planned, and wishes us well in our efforts to earn the school's annual hiking pin for most miles completed.

"Mrs. Henderson," Fletch interrupts, "I heard that some of the guys are going to hike down the *Ghat* and then hitch rides to come back up." He knows this will set Mrs. Henderson off, and he glares smugly at Kaz and me.

"Riding on trucks is a bad idea, since trucks only carry boxes," she announces with grave concern. I'm not sure what carrying boxes has to do with it. It has been my experience that we can easily fit in with the boxes.

"Mrs. Henderson," Kaz ventures, "I've hitch-hiked a number of times. A lot of us have." Several others murmur their assent, and a few heads nod.

"Trucks only carry boxes!" Mrs. Henderson states once more with a tone of finality. She is ready to move on to the next subject at hand and looks down at her notes.

"That's not true, they carry sacks too!" I blurt out, not considering my words with care. The manifest truth of my statement evokes animated whispers of agreement.

"Hey, Paul's right!" a few emboldened students agree.

Mrs. Henderson turns her chair to face me with a steady gaze that never lets up. I assume she is thinking about the reasonable argument that I have said and, realizing I have set the record straight, she would give me a little approving smile.

Boy, am I wrong!

Mrs. Henderson launches into an impassioned speech, during which she never stops staring at me. "You are the cheekiest, most impertinent, ill-mannered boy I know...," she begins. She then goes into great detail about how I am the most immature, impudent, insolent child she's ever met. Her speech is one of the most eloquent, smoothly delivered, knock-down speeches I've ever heard. It probably only lasts five minutes, but it seems to go on for fifteen tortuous minutes. It stretches out like one, long, fiery blast; she does not even pause for breath.

In spite of the frigid night, I run a cold sweat and want, as never before in my life, to melt into the floor. The room is utterly silent and, other than an occasional crackle from the fireplace, no sound competes with Mrs. Henderson's cold, fully controlled, accusatory voice. I'm not sure why she reacts in this strident manner; perhaps she has had a bad day. Or maybe she feels I have attacked the Queen of England herself.

After her speech Mrs. Henderson quickly dismisses us, and we all leave, exhausted from the emotional intensity. I feel pretty bad, but after the meeting several classmates congratulate me for putting up with such a verbal barrage and bashing. Everyone knows that I haven't done anything wrong, and the measure of my manliness is in my steady response. At least I learned what "impudent" and "insolent" mean.

When trouble comes, it all comes in a rush. Shortly after the episode with Mrs. Henderson, the principal calls all us Airlee Dormitory kids into his office and accuses us of wrecking a boat at the boathouse. We haven't done the deed and, with difficulty, we make him believe it. Nonetheless, Mr. Root leaves us with a warning that he'll be watching us for the slightest mistake, threatening to punish us harshly should he discover any misdeed. Go figure. We didn't do anything, but the next time we did, we'd be in real hot water.

In early April I am given a day's notice that I am to move out of Airlee and transfer down to Wissy, the high school boy's dorm. I've made it to the big time! My new roommate is Peter Kapenga, a fellow Arabian mish kid. Wissy has its own traditions, including an initiation rite for newcomers. For a few days, I have to wear short pants with diapers, carrying around a brick wherever I go. On Friday night, before supper, I have to clean the steps of the dining room with a toothbrush. For the final secret rite of initiation, I am lined up with the other newcomers, and we have our bare butts stamped with the Wissy Seal. We are now proud members of the secret society of Wissyites. We are told that we need to keep the Wissy secret, because no outsiders—especially the females and the staff—know of its existence. To make sure we don't wash off the stamp, we are checked in the showers for the next week.

Wissy has other traditions I have to learn. I discover the first night that the "Lights Out Monitor" is a revered position in Wissy. It is the monitor's job to ring the gong at night to tell everyone that it is bedtime. We are supposed to turn out our lights at that signal and to head straight to bed. Because this job involves some real power, it is supposed to be passed around to everyone. However, in Wissy some guys are terrible at it and can't be trusted. They ring the gong too early—which only aggravates students, or too late—which aggravates the house parents. For that reason, some boys don't like the job, rightly fearing that their peers will give them a hard time. However, some boys like the job, and they become very good at treading the tight line between pleasing the house parents by getting everyone to bed on time and not creating too many enemies with the kids who don't want to take the routine too seriously.

Our current monitor is Curry, who's so good at his job that he earned the nickname "Lights-Out." He takes great pride in the role he has to play and has developed some distinctive skills. At the designated hour, he prowls the hall yelling, at the top of his lungs, "Li-i-i-i-ghts ou-u-u-u-u-t!" We can hear him shouting from the first bellow, and it becomes funnier and funnier as he shouts again and again while he walks around the corridors. He's cagey; he can't be criticized by the house parents because he's only doing his job. And the humor of his routine makes the announcement palatable for us students. In this distinctive way, he lets everyone within half a mile know that the high school boys in Wissahickon Dorm are going to bed and everyone else—especially dorm parents—can now breathe a sigh of relief.

April is filled with plays and choral recitals in the gym, taking advantage of the parents arriving for the summer season. I join the stage crew to work the spotlights for the season's most extravagant production, *The Sound of Music.* The spotlights are on a precarious and seemingly dangerous platform mounted between two girders of the gym's roof. Getting to it is a feat in itself. I have to climb a long ladder up the gym's wall, then carefully walk along a girder to the center of the gym's roof, and then sit on the eight-by-eight-foot platform with two very hot, steaming spotlights.

I like the little perch high up above the audience because, in subtle ways, I get to "direct" the play. The actors take their cues from the lights, and by spotlighting different actors, it feels like I am calling them into action. I also like the fact that I can observe the audience and its reactions to the production. When the little kids stare up and point at me, thinking I am somebody special, it reminds me that I did the same thing when I was their age.

To earn spending money, I work in the library. I enjoy my work and marvel at the intricacies of the Dewey Decimal System. I love discovering interesting books and the smell of old volumes. This is the perfect job for me.

Watson is my supervisor. No one knows if Watson is his first or last name; it is the only name he has, and everyone knows him simply as "Watson." A round-faced and chubby Indian, he has managed the library forever, an icon of the school and inseparable from it. He knows everyone, from faculty and staff to students. Like the Gurkha and Muthu the barber, Watson also knows everyone's older and younger siblings and can tell good and bad stories about each of them. Since we all spend a lot of time in the library, Watson has the perfect position to know about all that goes on at Kodai. In fact, it is impossible to think of Kodai without Watson.

The pay in the library is miserable, twenty *naya-pice* an hour. Given the rate of exchange, I think I'm making about $.04 an hour. About four pennies an hour! I have to work three hours to buy one *dosa*, an Indian crepe. But the side benefits make up for the lack of compensation. I learn the Dewey Decimal System, get to walk around the library and hang out in the book stacks where I can sneak peeks at the pretty girls, and I can give people a hard time about their overdue books.

As May approaches and Watson knows that my parents will be returning to Kodai, he turns on the charm. "Paul, my friend," he oozes. "I would like to ask your parents to bring me some things from Bahrain. I have a small list here which would be very helpful. My family and I can use these items which are very difficult to find in Kodai." I chuckle to myself. My parents will hardly have room to bring gifts for me. I can imagine what they would say to Watson's request.

"Let me see what you want, Watson." I take the list and have to stifle a guffaw. He asks for pens, tennis rackets and balls, watches, radios, record players, and tape recorders. Plural. "These, my family could use." At the end of the list is "player piano"! I shake my head.

"I'm afraid my parents won't have any room for these things. Maybe I can get them to bring a few pens." Although he says these items are for his family, I know—and he knows that I know—they are really things he'd like to sell on the black market. Most are very difficult to find, and they're all in demand.

When Mom and Dad arrive for summer break, we move into a house across the lake. The days are filled with the usual vacation events: boating, school plays, occasional movies, hiking, golfing, the white-elephant sales, and many walks with Dad.

While Dad and I explore the hills overlooking Kodai, we talk about medicine, science, life, family. I especially like hearing about his journey from his childhood with simple, down-to-earth farm folk in rural Minnesota to his life as a globe-trotting doctor. He doesn't tell the story in a bragging manner, but rather to impart the lesson that life and success take hard work. He had struggled to get where he is, and he wants to impress on me that I will have to struggle too. But he feels strongly that I can rise to the occasion if I apply myself.

He also believes that God has a hand in it, and that God will see me through in my life. "God's plan for me was to serve people in the mission field, and to bring them to Christ. He has a plan for you, too."

"Dad, I don't recall many baptisms in the Bahrain or Iraq missions in the years I was at home," I venture.

"Yes, I know. I'm not sure what God's plan is for converts. All I know is that I am called to bring Jesus to the people of Arabia. God will have to bring their hearts to him; all I can do is be a witness to God's presence in their lives through my medical work and through my Christian life in their midst. I know that we are loved and appreciated," he continued, "but Muslims are reluctant to take the final step and become Christians."

We're in the midst of an early morning stroll along Coakers Walk, watching the sun break through the cloud banks that cover the plains below. Dad is in a reflective mood. "Almost every male missionary has a graduate degree, either in medicine, ministry, or educational administration. With few exceptions, the women—like your mother—also have college or professional degrees. We have all worked hard to get where we are, and we're committed to sharing the Good News of Jesus with the Muslims of Arabia."

"While we have all kinds of success in the classroom, *meglis*, and hospitals, we still have few souls which can be counted for Christ. I know the Arabs deeply appreciate our work and have strong affection for missionaries and what we do. I just don't get it. Perhaps this is God's way of testing our commitment. In any case, I know that I am fulfilling a 'call' that I received from God."

"It's time for our walk, Paul," Dad announces one night after the supper's dishes are washed and put away in the cupboards.

I love our walks and talks. We stroll through town as sunset's darkness settles over the houses; the lights come on, casting a pleasant glow of soft yellow from their windows, a glow which spills gently onto the walking paths.

"What are you learning in your science classes?" he asks. We love to talk about science.

"We're covering the size of space and the universe. It's unbelievably big, and it's hard to comprehend."

We walk in silence for a while. The stars begin to jump out of the darkness overhead. Dad pauses and points to a constellation above us.

"That's the Seven Sisters, the Pleiades," he says. "They're named after the seven daughters of Pleione in Greek mythology." Dad and I enjoy studying the constellations in the crystal clear skies of Kodai. Every northern constellation sparkles through. "I'm glad you're studying the universe and the enormity and majesty of God's creation. When you look up at the Pleiades, think of me in Arabia. When I see them there, I'll think of you here in Kodai." We walk on in silence, each of us absorbed in thoughts of the wonders of nature and the fact that it can bring the two of us together when we look at the same night sky, whether in Arabia or in India.

"Dad, is there still a place for missionaries in the new Arabia? Aren't the national hospitals and schools being well funded by oil income? The Arabs don't need us like they did when missionaries first came. Can we still be of use to them?"

"Those are hard questions, Paul. I've had to think about them very carefully. The world is changing so fast, I confess that I have questioned if there is still a role for missionaries in Arabia."

"Is there?" I ask anxiously, fearing that my whole world might come tumbling down. Are Mom and Dad contemplating leaving the mission field? Is that why we're having this late night walk and talk?

"Yes, it's not quite the same role we had in the past; but, yes, God still has a role for us in Arabia." I breathe a sigh of relief.

"Our mission, I believe, is different now," he continues, "I'm not sure my work should emphasize medicine as much as it has in the past."

"I have trouble thinking our lives might change so much. I've liked being a missionary kid and don't want to be anything else."

"Don't worry, Paul. As I often tell you, God has called me and our family to do mission work, and that is what we'll do."

"For how long?" I need reassurance.

"Well, in 1932, when my father agreed to send me to high school and later to college, I made a commitment to him that I'd go into the ministry. Those were tough years, during the Depression, and letting me leave the farm made extra work for the whole family."

"Are you in ministry now?"

"Yes, my ministry is being a medical missionary."

"How long does your commitment last?"

"For the foreseeable future. I'm happy with what I've accomplished, so that means we're doing the right thing."

"I don't want our mission-life to change." I say anxiously.

"Neither do I, but you're right, oil is transforming the Arabia you and I know. I'm not sure they need us in the same ways anymore."

"Are the changes good?"

"Some are, some aren't."

"How can they not be?"

"I'm concerned for the collective psyche of the Arab people. Unearned wealth, wealth that one doesn't work for, is dangerous. It tends to have undesirable consequences and create a skewed view of reality and of one's place in that reality."

"You're worried about them?"

"On a daily basis I watch money destroy the soul of the noble Arabs I have known for three decades, spoiling and corrupting them. It's happening so rapidly that I can scarcely fathom it. They are jumping into the future so fast, leaving behind cultural traits that made them great: patience, generosity, moderation, trust in God, and a reflective approach to life."

"So...do they still need us?"

"Well..." he pauses, struggling for an answer.

A dog yelps at us as we pass its yard. "Go to your pen, you should be on a farm where you can do an honest day's work!" he mutters toward the dog.

"I fear missionaries will become a thing of the past unless we change our role significantly," he continues. "You know that two of our Arabian mission hospitals have already closed, and now they're considering closing another mission hospital. Many Gulf countries can now afford to hire their own doctors and give free medicine to their people. We can't compete with that."

"If our hospitals continue to close, there may come a time when I'll have to return to the States and start a private practice. One thing's for sure, that would provide more financial security for Mom and me than this mission work. Sometimes one must choose between a life with money or a life with meaning," he laments. The tone of this conversation is out of character with his usual optimism.

I admire his honesty, for admitting to his doubts and for sharing his weaknesses. I can identify with those doubts and weaknesses. I admire even more that he intends to stay the course, in spite of uncertainty. His approach to these tough questions is a great lesson for me.

As always, Dad's words are instructive. He is an honorable man with a keen interest in making the world a better place. His confidence in his calling to be a missionary and his reassurance that I will have a meaningful life are extremely important to me.

"You see, part of the problem is that our motive has been to serve the poor, and now some argue that the Arabs are no longer poor. However, I would argue that they are poor in spirit, and that we can respond to their spiritual needs. In part, we can do that because our medical service has a 'caring' aspect that can't be bought for any price."

"So, what do you think will happen?"

"I wish I knew. I never imagined the riches that oil would bring to Arabia. We came to serve the poor and destitute, and Arabs know that and respect us greatly for it. So, maybe it's good to stay and show we still care."

"So what do we do?"

"We adjust. It's a new world and we have to adjust to it."

"I don't want to adjust. The world I grew up in was a good one. I want to stay in that world," I whisper.

This is really a long walk; the sky is pitch black now. Our path takes us from lamppost to lamppost, illuminated islands floating in a darkened sea. It's our last walk before Mom and Dad leave for Bahrain.

Late in July we have Christian Emphasis Week led by the Reverend Jake Holler from the Arabian Mission. This seems like the ideal time for me to renew my Christian commitment, so I sign up for all the sessions. I go to lectures, discussion groups, and prayer meetings.

The week is capped off by the Christian Emphasis Retreat hike to Poombari. We leave at two-thirty on Friday afternoon and hike through a series of downpours. It is, after all, in the middle of monsoon season. Three hours later, when we arrive at the campsite in Poombari, we are sopping wet and chilled to the bone, shaking with the cold.

In the continual rain showers, we boys have to set up our tents. It doesn't seem fair that the girls can all go to the dry hut with its blazing fire. We're stuck in these moldy, damp tents. Once the tents are up, we meet for supper and a final prayer meeting. It is hard not to pray for dry weather and a warm, fire-heated hut.

It's impossible to sleep. I crunch into a ball in the driest center of the sleeping bag, a World War II surplus relic. When rolled up, it is about two feet in diameter and weighs half as much as I do. It smells heavily of mildew, mothballs, and the dirty feet of the World War II soldiers who used it.

Due to the continued rain, my sleeping bag doesn't have a chance in a thousand of drying out. And it doesn't. Even my clothes are damp and chafed when I walk in them the next morning. Since we boys are only allowed in the fire-warmed hut when a religious meeting is going on, I attend every meeting and sidle up to the fire as close as I can get. With the others, I pray fervently for my family, for my friends, for my countries, and for warm, dry weather.

In spite of the sleeping bag experience, the CE Retreat has a profound impact on me. The outside speakers are excellent, and I am moved by their message. I greatly appreciate all the work that the school's staff has put into the varied Christian events, and I resolve to pray regularly and to renew my faith.

When I get back to my dorm, I write to Mom that I had a wonderful experience on the CE Retreat, and that I am going to pray more often. I don't mention the monsoon that blew through or the fact that girls were high and dry and boys had to survive World War II tents in our muddy trenches.

My religious fervor is still running high a week later when the choir takes an unforgettable trip to Madurai. It takes us seven hours to bounce down the *Ghat*, pass the turnoff to Kodai Road railroad terminal, and shudder into the holy city of Madurai. After a quick supper, we present a concert to the Indian students at the Lady Doak College. I really love gospel spirituals, and with my choirmates, I bellow out "Climbing up the Mountain," "Children, Don't Get Weary," and "Good News." For our Indian audience, this is totally new music. However, they respond enthusiastically, so we all turn in to our dorm beds feeling satisfied.

The next morning, we tour the famous temples of Madurai. They are adorned with countless stone statues, depicting scenes from Hindu mythology. This city is truly an architectural wonder and a piece of art like no other in the world. The statues have just been repainted with bright, gaudy colors, and although many of them have eight arms, two heads, or an elephant's trunk for a nose, they look real enough to come to life. Huge, windowless interior halls lit by nothing more than the light of flickering candles throw shadows that dance around the statues, playing ever-changing shapes on the carved stone walls. The surreal aura bears no similarity to any Christian house of worship I've ever seen, but the whole scene is surprisingly reminiscent of our Sunday school pictures of Jerusalem's temple in Christ's day.

Hindu pilgrims parade silently by, periodically prostrating themselves before stone deities and leaving dishes of food or other gifts. The heavy smell of ancient, damp stones is barely broken by the smell of so many humans and the sweet aroma of incense that is burning in urns or of jasmine flowers that are strung around the statues' necks. In the stone corners and recesses lurk *bandicoots*, monster rats the size of small mongooses and just as mean. Their beady eyes follow us as we tour the temples. While the pilgrims are there to worship and share their faith, I realize that I am just a tourist. For them, this is a sacred place; for me it is like a museum. No wonder the rats glare at us like interlopers.

Now that we are in high school, we are allowed to dance, and we do so often. Every Wednesday is Canteen Night: with candlelight setting the ambiance, we chow down on handfuls of popcorn and drinks. The record player broadcasts our favorite songs for dancing, slow or fast for different occasions.

I like dancing because there are so many attractive girls to dance with. The "innocent physical contact" is intoxicating. My first time out I ask Susie to dance a fast dance with me. Despite her shocked look, she extends her hand and we hit the dance floor to do the twist. I steer Susie to the darkest corner, hoping to hide from my friends' prying eyes. I know this is going to be a challenge.

Sure enough, in spite of being in the bleakest corner of the dance floor, I might as well have been on center stage all by myself. Casey, a senior jock everyone listens to, says in his loud voice, "Look at that uncoordinated idiot!"

Such a judgment from one of the senior jocks is instantly taken as gospel. I have been skewered for life. Trying my best to ignore the chuckles, I continue to gyrate in a more controlled fashion. I pray for the song to end, but the music goes on and on so that I feel like I'm stuck in a moment of time that won't end. I feel sorry for Susie, who condescended to dance with me. She bravely continues, ignoring my dancing as well as the taunting hoots. Mercifully, the song ends and we part. I know she'll never dance with me again, and I know I'll never do another twist in public!

The last weekend of August, our class hikes down to Tope again, this time for an overnight stay. The rugged trek covers eleven miles and descends precipitously six thousand feet to the grassy plains below. The hike is deemed too strenuous for two of the girls, so they ride down with the truck carrying our luggage. The rest of us brave the steep downhill trek, slicing our exposed upper limbs on razor-sharp elephant grass as we plow through. Teddy finds an Indian man to lean on for support part of the way down in exchange for a handout from Teddy's picnic lunch.

Hot and weary at the end of the trail, we scour the welcome pools for signs of snakes; not seeing any, we jump in with abandon. As we began to swim, it becomes very clear to me that something has changed dramatically since our last class trip to Tope; a new dynamic is in play that I have not discerned before. There isn't quite the pal-like interaction among the boys and girls. Our new relationship tone is more standoffish than it had been on past camp-outs.

For the first time I am aware that our female classmates are turning into young women. Until this time we have considered them to be more like sisters than anything femininely provocative. But it is very apparent that, in body as well as mind, they are now way ahead of us boys. Things are changing, and I'm not sure I like what is happening.

My lessons in the differences between boys and girls continue in all kinds of contexts. Like playing chess.

The student council has organized a chess tournament. Dad taught me how to play and showed me many tactics over the years. As a result, I decide to join the tournament and show what I can do. I easily win a number of rounds, progressing up the tournament ladder towards the semifinals. After sailing through the first few matches, I begin to dream of standing in front of the gym with the whole high school looking on and clapping as I am awarded my trophy. This would be the first public recognition of my intellectual skills.

I am waiting in the library for my semifinal challenger. It is four in the afternoon, school is done for the day, and I am relaxed as I wait. Abruptly, the library's double doors swing open and she enters, looking around as her eyes adjust to the dimmer indoor light. She strides up to the edge of my table and looks down at me.

"Are you Paul?" she asks sweetly, sitting down across from me. "We're scheduled to play each other today."

I nod confidently, and then my confidence disappears. I've never been so close to such a beautiful girl-woman, and my eyes are wide as saucers and my mouth is agape. She is dressed fit to kill, and I struggle to keep from staring. My voice falters into a stutter. I hadn't known her name, but I had pictured her with perfect clarity in so many of my dreams. Her curvaceous figure contrasts starkly with my physical immaturity. Under any other circumstances a senior like her would never condescend to talk to a lowly underclassman like me. I can smell a light scent of perfume. My head spins.

She positions herself across the table so that when I look at the board I can't help being distracted. When I glance up, I realize that she is staring me in the eye to make sure mine don't wander. She smiles knowingly. I am totally unnerved, can't think straight, or even talk sensibly.

The match begins with her opening. I don't know where to rest my eyes; my field of vision is filled with the chessboard, the face and hair of a goddess, and her chest. I am in sensory overload, eyes darting around self-consciously.

One of her hands rests besides the chessboard and sometimes comes close to mine as we move the pieces. Her fingernails are well manicured, in sharp contrast to mine, which display the tell-tale signs of an immature teenage fingernail biter. I wonder what it would feel like to touch her hand.

I'm a caged tiger being teased by someone holding a flank steak just outside the bars. I'm overwhelmed with a mixture of longing and anger, a toxic potion which scrambles my mind and destroys my strategy. My classmates are all girls becoming young women, but here is a woman in full bloom. Her "checkmate" comes quickly, as I pay the penalty for not concentrating on the board.

"Thank you," she says in her sweet, lilting voice. Then, as quickly as she had arrived, she is standing and gone.

I know that I am the better player, but I sit there in a daze, utterly devastated while I ponder the worst, most memorable, chess game I have ever played. As I make my way out the library door, I want to kick the nearest big boulder. Maybe the pain will shock me out of my stupor. I have been slyly played, and it hurts.

After the match I drift over to supper and join my friends.

"You look like you've been hit by a train," Teddy opines. "Aren't you hungry?"

"Nah. It's nothing." I sit morosely all through supper, picking at the chilled food on my plate.

"Hey, Paul, you have to snap out of it!" Teddy says, again.

I can hardly tell them that a beautiful goddess just ambushed me on the chess board. I'd be laughed off the campus.

When I leave the dining hall, I happen to see the goddess with a couple of her friends. She walks right past me and doesn't even acknowledge my presence, although I know that she can't miss me. I'm a bug which has been squashed and doesn't deserve another thought. With furrowed brow, I return to my dorm room and shut the door. How can I ever show my face again? Tomorrow the campus will know that I was bested by a lesser player, and my friends will begin to question me. Tonight I just want to curl up and pretend I don't exist.

In September, Teddy receives a telegram from Kuwait saying his father had to go back to the States because he "had a serious medical problem." Teddy is very anxious because he doesn't know any more details, and that night, after lights out, as Teddy and I lie quietly in our beds in the dark, I can sense his agitation and pain. From the sighing and rolling in bed, I know he is in anguish.

"I'm so afraid for my father," he finally says, his voice quivering.

"He'll be OK, he's in the States," I respond, not knowing what else to say and implying that being in the States means that any medical problem is fixable.

"No one's telling me what's going on. Maybe they're keeping the bad news from me. They think I can't take it."

It seems a logical conclusion to draw. When crises come to mish kid families, the distance between home and school seems to multiply. Kuwait feels like it's a distant planet from Kodai.

"Teddy, I'm sure God is watching over him." I invoke the consoling formula we mish kids all know.

"Yes, that's true, I know he is."

The fact of the matter is that, as I lie there in the total darkness, I too fear for Teddy's father. I struggle not to imagine the unthinkable. It had happened to Uncle Gerry last year in Kuwait, and that memory still burns painfully. Uncle Gerry was taken up into God's kingdom. But his death had to be an aberration, a once-in-fifty-years tragedy. It couldn't happen again so soon. Losing another missionary doctor in Kuwait is more than God would want the mission to endure.

I listen to Teddy sigh heavily, roll over, and sigh again. Gradually, the sighs become quieter and less frequent until the regularity of his breathing tells me he is finally asleep. I lie on my back staring at the ceiling, barely able to discern the high rafters in the black of the night. I can't imagine being in Teddy's shoes. I wait anxiously for the light of morning to come and wash away the darkness. I know that the glare of the sun and the constant activity of school will mask morbid thoughts or feelings.

After a few very stressful days, word arrives that Teddy's father had a brain embolism and that his surgery had been successful. Teddy is spared unimaginable heartbreak. We put the incident behind us, avoiding any discussion of it, unwilling to handle such heavy matters. In fact, I don't raise the issue with him again.

One evening in September, the acting principal hauls me out of study hall in the midst of my focused studying. He brings me to his office, shuts the door, and then begins to yell at me.

"You will never amount to anything! I can't believe that you have misbehaved so badly again. You've been sassing the staff." I stand there, confused. He must realize I don't know what's going on.

"The supply room clerk told me that you talked back to him when he was handing out your new notebook and pencil. We will not have our students treat the Indian staff that way! You should know better." I am really confused now. I try to recall how my last encounter with the supply clerk went. I know that I was in line with a bunch of others, and someone may have said, "It's about time," when the clerk finally brought our stuff to us. But I didn't say it, so I know this tirade has nothing to do with me.

"I didn't say anything," I protest feebly.

"But I know that's the kind of thing you fresh-mouthed teens will do!" At this point his voice is high and pinched. I'm afraid he's going to have a heart attack and I'll be blamed for bringing it on. In a flash, I see myself being expelled and never readmitted to any decent high school in the world. No high school diploma, no college. My life is ruined.

"I'm sorry, Sir," I offer. "It will never happen again."

Somewhat mollified, he sputters to a close, "Well, see that it doesn't. Now, get back to your studying."

During this entire exchange, one phrase keeps running through my mind, "You'll never amount to anything." I've got to think about that.

Our new housemother's daughter marries an Indian man in late September. Our housemother is one of the American teachers, and the marriage—an elopement, really—is the talk of the campus. The housemother has real trouble coping with the mix of the two cultures, and she lets everyone know it. I find her attitude hard to comprehend. Having been raised in three cultures—American, Arab, and Indian—I can't understand someone focusing on the minor differences between people. I know that there are good and bad people in each of the societies in which I've lived. Some people are richer, some are poorer. Some better educated. But basic virtues like honesty, love, and hard work are found in all the cultures I know personally.

It's strange, when I think about it, to realize that as a mish kid, I have come to a very broad-minded understanding of people who have different languages, religions, and cultures than my own. While my parents and the other missionaries are intent on bringing Christianity to Muslims and Hindus, I am inclined to appreciate the differences and not want to change them. Perhaps I'm too naïve to see the seamier sides of life—although the image of beggar boys with missing limbs is always in front of me— but I sense that people from Muslim and Hindu societies have somehow made sense of their world in much the same way that I have in my Western Christian one. By and large, they seem happy, too. I've seen too much of the world and life not to conclude that all humankind has much in common and we are all essentially equal. So I don't understand our housemother's obstinacy. She should embrace her daughter and son-in-law and wish them well. At least, that's how I see it.

October brings bitter cold weather to our mountain retreat, infecting us with vacation fever as we anticipate traveling home later in the month. The school always puts on Christmas plays and parties during our last weeks of the semester to send us off in good spirits. Maybe they think that will encourage us to give positive reports to our parents and assure a good impression of Kodai School.

Whatever the motivation, the Christmas events are some of the highlights of the year. I particularly look forward to the fun of the long anticipated Christmas play and the unforgettable Christmas banquet. That is one of the few times in the year that we get chicken. Chicken is the best, most expensive meal in Kodai, and we thoroughly relish the two pieces allotted to each of us.

On Saturday morning of the Christmas banquet, I spend an hour and a half in detention for a minor infraction. Perhaps the teachers think that the detention will take the edge off my having too much fun. I make up for the slight at dinner. During the evening's Christmas banquet, I eat half a chicken, sneaking more pieces than I should have. Life is good! The dinner is followed by an evening of entertainment that includes skits, songs, and games in the gym.

On Sunday evening there is the annual Christmas Vespers. It is held in our little stone church with its romanesque, granite design and arched windows. With its dimly lit sanctuary and scattered Christmas decorations, it looks like a Christmas card scene from Victorian England. Vespers brings my Kodai family–for that is what my two hundred fellow students feel like to me–together for an evening of worship and good will. The service is filled with Christmas carols that invariably bring tears to my eyes. The Christmas pageant recreates the wonder of the day that Jesus was born, complete with angels, shepherds, and wise men. I am totally wrapped up in the moving experience.

The scripture reading for the evening is the first chapter of the Gospel of John. At the moment that the play's narrator says, "...and the light came into the world," the electricity fails. The chapel is thrown into complete darkness.

The coincidence of the lights going out just when the Bible passage announces the arrival of the Light of the World is a shocking one. The congregation lets out a collective, muted gasp. There are mysterious forces at play tonight. We know power outages are common, but the timing of this one is a direct affront to our Maker. I almost expect some sign of God's wrath to fall on the congregation or on the incompetent perpetrators of such mockery. I shudder to think about such vengeance.

We sit and sit in the pitch black, trying to absorb the full meaning of the situation. The quiet is incredible; I never imagined two hundred people could be so still. Eventually, as it becomes clear that the power outage will be a long one, candles are called for and the pageant resumes. I can't focus on the action because my mind is reeling over the timing of the power outage that occurred at the very words, "...and the light came into the world."

Before long, the absurdity of the coincidence takes on the aspect of a joke, and I wonder if maybe God has a wry sense of humor. Perhaps he is trying to tell us to calm down and not take our relationship with him with such stern seriousness. I wonder if perhaps God has very logical reasons for letting the outage occur at this juncture. Maybe the power failure has even saved someone's life. Perhaps, with the bad wiring that exists throughout Kodai, someone was about to be electrocuted but was spared when the power went out. As I consider this possibility, it occurs to me that our loving God would, indeed, put the importance of one person's life way ahead of the convenience of the vespers service.

It gives me a lot to think about, and the more I think about it, the more loving God becomes in my mind. To my surprise, this conclusion is just the opposite of the vengeful God I first imagined when the lights failed. The Christmas message of hope and promise is renewed in my heart. Life—even in darkness—is blessed.

Kodai Lake with Perumal Mountain in background

CHAPTER 7

Coming Home

As I pack my bags and say goodbye to Mom and Dad, I have mixed feelings about going back to Kodai. It's been a year and a half since I was there. In the intervening period we spent a year in the States on furlough. Now we're back in Bahrain, and a return to boarding school stares me in the face. When I'm in Kodai without my family, I'm often homesick. When I am at home with my parents, I'm lonely and miss my Kodai friends. Of the two emotions, I find loneliness the harder to bear, so I'm excited to return to Kodai for the last half of my junior year and first half of my senior year.

The reality of India strikes me most poignantly when we wait for the train at Egmore station in Madras. As in years past, we arrive in mid-afternoon and kill time until early evening, when the overnight train to Kodai Road departs. It is a long wait, but it's never boring, for the station is abuzz with activity.

215

People live their full lives right in middle of the station. Women congregate around a public water pump where they wash clothes, rubbing and pounding them against large cut-granite stones to get the dirt out. They then hang the clothes over nearby rocks to dry. Families cook, eat, and go the bathroom in the open for all to witness—there is no wall or toilet to hide their intimate daily routines. They brush their teeth and even bathe, lathering each other up at public faucets and then dousing themselves with pails of water. Children are undressed and washed and allowed to air dry (who can afford a towel?) and run around in their birthday suits. Perhaps their running speeds up the drying process.

The next day, when we begin the ascent to Kodai and the bus slows its pace, straining up the inclined road and sharp curves, I focus on the moment. Focusing on the sights and sounds, I block out all other thoughts, putting my full attention on the here and now. All my senses are engaged in an intense survey of the environment. I notice butterfly varieties that are different here at lower altitudes from the ones up in Kodai. I hear different bird songs—loud squawks and clackings—which are unfamiliar in the higher altitudes. I hear deep rustlings—even above the engine noise—in the jungle that I've never heard before; it is as if some giant animal has been spooked by the bus's sounds and is in a life-threatening retreat, leaving tree branches and tall grasses swaying in its wake. Low, distant barks of monkeys emanate from deep within the jungle. I smell vegetation that is unknown in Kodai, and I can even smell the moist air of streams when we pass over them. At these lower altitudes even the sun has a different character. It's more diffuse, with fewer defined shadows, than our sun in Kodai.

I have a window seat, as I always do, sitting next to Teddy.

"How's it feel to be back?" he asks, shaking me out of my reverie.

"Good! I want to see all my friends again! Do you think they've changed?"

"Naw. But there's a new kid in our class, Bugs, you'll like him."

Teddy always looks after me, like a big brother wanting to know how I am doing.

The name "Bugs" makes me grin, and I look forward to meeting him.

"How are the teachers?"

"The same," he says without elaboration. The teachers are a constant in Kodai, and it's clear Teddy doesn't want to think about schoolwork yet.

"How's the food?"

"As bad as ever!" he laughs.

My stomach twitches.

I am enthralled by the familiar scenes as our bus struggles up through the mountain valleys and passes, wending its way through the Indian jungles.

"It's good to be back," I say again and fall back into my reverie.

While I'm settling into Wissy with Teddy and Bugs, Dad and Mom are busy moving from Bahrain to Muscat, Oman. We had lived there before I first came to Kodai, so both my parents know the country and its people well. Dad will be filling in as director of the hospital for a colleague who is going home on furlough. In a letter I receive from Mom and Dad in early February, they wax eloquent about how wonderfully things are going. Mom loves setting up her new home; she "feels like a new bride," she writes. Dad re-embraces Omani society and says that even I am not forgotten. In fact, "Many of them ask about you. I am sure that your close identification with the community in so many ways will be remembered for many years. Two days ago, one teenager in the Bazaar insisted on carrying some of my things home. He wanted to know all about you. He had spent many hours playing with you when you were small here."

The only sour note in their move is that they had to sell our wonderful Persian carpets. "They were too heavy to send on the *dhow* with the other fifty-three boxes of household goods," Mom writes. It saddens me to lose this intimate part of our family history. I have spent countless hours driving my Dinky toy trucks and cars along their intricate roadways. They were magic carpets for me and my imagination.

Bosch, back in Kodai for his senior year, has a new motorcycle—an old classic-looking British one—and he takes me for a ride. It is a wonderful, liberating venture as we wind our way through the Kodai hillsides, up to the observatory and then back to town. I fall in love with the freedom it creates, and I resolve to get one as soon as I can.

The next day, Bosch crashes his motorcycle. A day or two later I go to the Dishpan to visit him and find that his leg is trussed up in a cast. It had been fractured in multiple places, and Bosch will be confined for a couple of weeks. He's really depressed. I've never really seen depression before, and I have never imagined that someone as smart and fun-loving as Bosch would succumb to such a miserable condition.

In an effort to cheer him up, I steer our conversation to future motorcycle jaunts we can take when he's up and about. We speculate on the most challenging, steep roads around Kodai and promise that we'll ride and explore them together. By the time I leave the Dishpan, I think he's feeling a bit more upbeat.

Claire is my first steady girlfriend. She is a real beauty, and I can't believe that I'm so lucky. We're among the first in our class to date regularly, so I have to deal with jealous dorm mates who constantly razz me.

I thoroughly enjoy dating. Life is suddenly much more lighthearted. On the other hand, I find it hard to believe that anyone—especially someone as pretty as Claire—would want me as a steady boyfriend. Soon I learn that my misgivings are well placed.

"I have a weak heart," she tells me one day. "I was born this way."

"Are you going to be OK?" I respond with genuine surprise and just a hint of sympathy.

"Yes, but I think dating is more than I can handle right now."

So, with the knowledge of her grave physical disability hanging over our relationship, I reluctantly give up my love and my lightheartedness after barely two weeks of bliss. Feeling abandoned, I console myself in the belief that I've done the noble thing by breaking up and thus protecting her delicate health.

Then a miracle occurs! A few days after breaking up with me, Claire starts dating Jake. Her congenital heart problems are miraculously cured. Although I am only sixteen and am no medical genius, it crosses my mind that medical journals might be interested in documenting how such a congenital defect, having threatened one's life for sixteen years, could be cured so suddenly. I briefly contemplate writing an article for a medical journal recounting this wondrous recovery, but then I reconsider my decision. Claire's new boyfriend is three inches taller than I am and may take exception to my scientific revelations.

Instead, I work out my frustration by writing to Dad about the "medical miracle," expressing how upset I am about breaking up. Maybe he'll want to submit an article to a medical journal.

Two weeks later I receive a letter from Dad expressing his sympathy but making no judgment on the level of divine intervention which might have affected Claire's medical condition.

"We appreciated your comments about the girl you had been dating. Your breakup should not concern you. Yes, boys and men find the female sex a bit confusing. That's their nature. They live by emotions and feelings and not so much by reason as males do. It's well for you to find these truths by practical discovery and to learn the give-and-take that goes with them."

Another opportunity to do research on this perplexing topic arrives with the junior-senior prom. It is held annually in the Kodai Missionary Union Hall, since that is the largest room in Kodai. It provides the optimum setting for a lavish meal, entertainment, and dancing. So it is that, with high anticipation, we spend weeks preparing for the prom. Girls have new dresses made (I'm not sure whether they go to Peter the tailor, or not), boys buy hand-me-down white jackets from the previous years' stock. I'm glad about this, because when I haul out my Peter-made suit, I find that it has shrunk in the intervening years, so I need a recycled one.

We boys carefully track who is asking whom to the prom. Having lost Claire to alleged heart disease and the taller Jake, I'm scared to invite another girl who has caught my eye. She's a year ahead of me, and that is a major drawback. Finally, bucking up my courage, I take the plunge. Much to my surprise, she readily agrees. I wonder if she knows about my humiliations on the dance floor and in the chess match. If she does know, she seems to be overlooking them.

I'm sure the girls talk among themselves about the prom too, but they play coy and pretend not to be thinking about it when we're together. As in most things, we boys have no real idea what the girls are discussing among themselves. Once or twice I catch a glimpse into their secretive world when one of them comes up to a boy and suggests that so-and-so would welcome an invitation. Usually the guy is so dumbfounded that he just goes along with it, even if he really has someone else in mind.

Two days before the prom, Bugs, Teddy, and I head into the woods to scout out the best orchids we can find. This is crucial, because we have to make our own corsages on the day of the prom. We're excited to find a whole patch of orchids in full bloom. We carefully cover them with vines and leaves so that no one else will pick them before Saturday.

The morning of the prom we hike back into the woods, pick our orchids, and then gather in the social room where our housemother helps us construct the corsages. Along with the orchids, we bind ribbon, baby's breath, and other floral paraphernalia into the corsages. Our housemother pronounces them "beautiful."

However, it quickly becomes apparent who has the best corsage when we're all together in the Kodai Missionary Union Hall. The honor goes to Pope, Bosch's roommate, who earned his nickname thanks to his serious demeanor. His stately countenance and slow movements remind us of movie clips we have seen of the Vatican's incumbent, the officious and plodding Pope John XXIII.

Pope won't divulge where he found the singular flower in his corsage, but a few of us ferret out the story.

Bosch and Pope had gotten up at four in the morning for a motorcycle ride to Shembaganur Monastery. We call it Shumbug. Shumbug is a Catholic monastery which lies deep in the woods a couple of miles from Kodai School. The towering eucalyptus trees that surround the monastery block much of the sun's light, leaving an other-worldly, reddish glow covering the forest floor.

Bosch and Pope coast the last few hundred yards so as not to make any noise. On an earlier visit, they have seen a strikingly beautiful orchid in the monastery's garden. Their stealthy scheme came off as planned, and in minutes they'd clipped the flower and were on their way back to school with their prize orchid. As far as they could tell, no one was the wiser for their outing. It is this prize that Pope's date is sporting tonight.

My first prom is delightful. I only dance slow dances, so that keeps the laughing hyenas away. The brief speeches are bearable. My date, the senior catch, and I are a good match. We talk together easily, and we dance enjoyably. But my eyes are elsewhere. I'm constantly checking out Pope's incredible, one-of-a-kind orchid corsage and the beautiful girl who is wearing it. There is hardly a prettier place imaginable for an orchid to be pinned!

At one in the morning, with a full moon frosting the mountains in a silver sheen, I walk my date home. It has to be the most romantic setting I've ever been in. I drop her off, but nothing special happens. We exchange hugs and a peck on the cheek, and the romantic atmosphere dissolves when she turns to enter her home. During the two-mile trek back to my dorm, clouds roll in, obliterating the moon and sending the world into such darkness that I can barely make out the path. It scares the daylights out of me. I imagine snakes and panthers jumping out of the shadows and putting me out of my fearful misery. I consider returning to my date's house to wait out the night, but I don't want to look like a sissy. My stumbling walk back to the dorm in complete darkness puts a damper on the fun night.

The next morning, a rumor is quickly spreading through the dorm. Pope wakes me early and recounts the story.

"Bosch and I have to go to the principal's office. I don't know what it's about, but it can't be good," Pope says.

While Bosch has visited Mr. Root on a number of occasions, this is a first for Pope. When I see Bosch, however, he too is unusually nervous about the meeting.

That night, while taking a break from studying, Pope recounts what happened in the principal's office. "Mr. Root opened with, 'Did you know that one of my students' father is a missionary?'"

"This was such a strange statement...we just stood there looking like dummies. Most of his students' parents are missionaries, so we didn't know where he was going with this. Not waiting for a response, Mr. Root continued, 'He is not only a missionary, but has studied orchids extensively and is something of an expert on their varieties.' We were still in the dark, but now the dark was looking even darker.

"'He had been in communication with the Jesuits at Shembaganur Monastery about a rare orchid that only blooms every fourteen years. The monks told him the orchid was about to break out, so he set out to see it. Can you imagine his grave disappointment when he arrived and found the orchid was gone? Can you?! It had been heedlessly picked by some vandals, a tragic end for this rare plant.'"

Pope pauses for the gravity of the situation to sink in. Now, I'm duly impressed. I realize Pope and Bosch are in a heap of hurt.

"'It turns out, young man, that your date was wearing that exceedingly rare flower. Everyone saw her brilliant corsage on Saturday at the prom, and when my student's father told me about the tragedy, I put two and two together. You, young man, are to go to Shembaganur immediately and apologize to the monks for what you have done!'"

"So Bosch and I rode right back to the monastery. Bosch told me to let him do the talking. Much to my amazement, the head monk knew Bosch and quickly forgave us for taking the orchid. I couldn't believe it. They were so nice.

"On the way home, Bosch told me that his father had done them a favor this past summer by giving them one of the Arabian mission's used projectors.

"'I guess they figured they owed me a favor. One orchid for one projector. Not a bad trade.'"

Mom and Dad arrive in Kodai at the end of May. Together we move into *Tonawanda* cottage and begin to adjust to each other's routines. Once again, it is a disorienting experience to go from the independence and self-absorption of dorm life to the more emotional, care-filled environment of home and family life. But Mom and Dad are old hands at this process. They've been making this transition for almost twenty years, starting with Dave's arrival in Kodai in the early 1950s.

As usual, they smooth the transition with a couple of thoughtful gifts, providing good and healthy meals, and sharing news about the family. Dad gives me a tape recorder, complete with the Beatles' *Rubber Soul* album. I'm taken aback, because I know the Beatles are considered too risqué by most missionaries. I had expected a tape of gospel or classical music. It is a wonderful gift, and when he hands it to me I see the glint in his eyes. I know he's pleased with himself.

"Paul, let's have a talk." As always, I've been looking forward to our talks.

"Sure, Dad."

Mom picks up her cup of tea and moves into the living room, so I suspect a less than pleasant discussion. He always uses such statements to precede serious conversations. I am concerned we are going to talk about my less than stellar grades. So I make a quick mental review of my classes and prepare to point out how much I have studied and how many other things have intervened to take me away from doing my best in class. Images of Bosch, Pope, and nicely placed orchid corsages float through my mind.

But to my great surprise he begins on a very different note. "Paul, your mother and I are very proud of you. We know that you have a lot of potential, and we are pleased with how nicely you are maturing. Now that you're about to start your senior year, you will be making a lot of life-determining choices. We want to help make sure that the choices you make are the best they can be."

He pauses to let this serious message sink in. Frankly, I'm not prepared for such a heavy conversation on our first day together. I guess the fact that he's only going to be in Kodai for a couple of weeks means that he doesn't want to waste time.

"Your mother and I were wondering if there is anything in particular that you want."

"I want a motorcycle!" I blurt out, as if I had only heard the last sentence of his talk. "That will help me grow up," I continue as my mind races to defend my first life-determining choice. "It will make me feel more self-confident and independent." I hope these are the words he wants to hear. Then, in an effort to appeal to the scientist and explorer in him, I back this argument up with, "I want the adventure of driving around Kodai and discovering new places." I breathe more easily, thinking I've just issued the *coup-de-grace*. I know that those are things Dad would love to do.

During the long pause that follows, a hundred arguments run through my mind. I know that a motorcycle would be very expensive. Perhaps I should have asked for something cheaper. But that is what I want, so I stare pleadingly at him and watch his eyes and expressionless face. I can tell that he is stunned with the request and trying to consider all the implications of it. Finally he responds.

"That's a good idea, let's get a motorcycle," he says in an even, low voice.

I am speechless as the words and reality set in. I can't believe I've won! In my mind, I'm already spinning around the Kodai hillsides, chasing Bosch up and down mountain trails.

"Maury, can I talk to you a minute," comes Mom's firm voice from the living room. Could she have been listening in?

Mom leads Dad into the bedroom and closes the door. I can hear just enough high and low tones to know a spirited discussion is going on.

After ten minutes, Dad emerges from the room.

"Paul, we've decided to buy you a camera instead," he announces. "You'll be able to take it on your hikes into the mountains and record the beauties of nature with it."

I know that Mom hates motorcycles, and her quiet firmness has obviously won the day. I didn't even get a chance to make a counter offer or present a more detailed explanation of my choice. I'll make do with the camera.

It is not long before I have the opportunity to use the gift. As soon as classes are out, Mom tells me that we are going on a family tour of southern India. I'm elated. I haven't been out of Kodai for months, and the damp and cold have chilled me to the bone.

We set out by taxi, descending the *Ghat* to the plains. As we cross the bridge separating the mountain passes from the flatlands, I let out our usual cheer. Mom and Dad chuckle; they've heard about this tradition, but the taxi driver looks quizzically at me in the rearview mirror. It is a wonderful day, and Dad and I keep up a constant stream of chatter about the sights and sounds that have become so familiar to me. Steam engines, wash-and-wear clothes, bridge structures, the wonders of concrete, the power of gas engines, space exploration, and much more draw our attention. Dad asks me about my opinions of these technological innovations and comments on the changes they have brought that he has personally witnessed since his days as a kid on the family farm.

When modern technology isn't our topic, we turn to religion. The cows, which crowd the streets and seem to be everywhere, prompt comments about their revered status and about what might have caused that religious tenet millennia ago.

We see Indian holy men trudging along the side of the road, and Dad comments on the power of pilgrimage in the lives of Hindus and Christians. He talks about a book on Buddhism that he is reading. It suggests that there are more parallels for Christianity with Buddhism than with Hinduism. Mom has no taste for such discussions and sits in silence.

At Kodai Road we have a pleasant, lingering supper in a corner of a high-ceilinged lounge called the "Retiring Room." A single fan on the ceiling does its best to keep us cool. People are scattered around the large space, carrying on with life's many activities.

"Paul, do you see that man in the corner preparing to go to sleep?"

"Yes..."

"He's another holy man. We often see such men at train stations," Dad says. "They wander along roadsides, sit in contemplation under large banyan trees or atop large rocks. These itinerant pilgrims live simple lives with few possessions, not much more than a loin cloth. They are part of Indian culture and they are surrounded by many stories, some of mythical proportions, which attract followers. For instance, one may claim to see God in an anthill. Soon, he will begin to attract droves of pilgrims to hear about the divine anthill. Next, the religious fervor will give way to amazing tales of supernatural occurrences related to the sacred anthill: of holy men walking on water, of visions of fires floating in air, or of other captivating phenomena. Eventually, the tales may be molded into yarns to be passed from village to village. With each retelling they will become more and more colorful, adding spice and richness to the life of enchanted and magical India."

The holy man in front of us, fully absorbed in preparing for a night's sleep, unfolds his rattan sleeping mat with ritual attention, carefully flattening it out on the brick floor. He has a small bag of belongings, perhaps no more than six items, the contents of which he checks and rechecks. His scrawny, muscular legs are witnesses to months of walking.

"Do you notice how calm his demeanor is? That is because he is on a spiritual journey. His mind has risen above the daily concerns of life." Dad pauses as if to contemplate the calmness which would come with such a spiritual journey.

"Do you think man can find God in his wanderings?" he asks me, almost off-handedly. Dad fusses with his silverware, lining the utensils up in a neat formation.

"Yes," I respond bluntly. I'm uncomfortable with the direction this conversation may take. "One day I would like to live simply, like that holy man, and travel around by train. Which reminds me, I'm looking forward to our train trip tomorrow." I hope to bring the conversation down a notch or two, from the mysteries of religion to our excursion beginning the next day.

"Oh yes. Our train will take us up and over the mountains tomorrow. I never cease to be amazed at the power of steam engines. It's a wonder that they can pull hundreds of tons up such steep grades." The diversion has taken, and we return to the comfortable topic of scientific discoveries and technological marvels.

The next day, the train takes us north through the plains of Tamil Nadu and over mountain passes to Bangalore. Late in the morning, Dad has to leave us and return to Muscat, Oman. I watch his bus leave the Bangalore station, its fading image passing silently into the distance. The whole scene is indelibly imprinted on my mind.

Mom and I turn from the bus stop and make our way back to the train station, each absorbed in a quiet, personal cocoon. We're going to retrace our journey and head back up the *Ghat* to Kodai. In another couple of weeks, she'll be returning to Muscat, too.

There is a second international boarding school in Kodai. The Presentation Convent is an all-girls Catholic school that is housed in a grand, castle-like edifice on top of a nearby mountain. Surrounding this castle are majestic, well-manicured gardens. Since the convent isn't right next to us on Kodai Lake, and since its students are rarely allowed to go off compound, the whole operation is a mystery to us. The girls are a special curiosity in their modest uniforms. We rarely see them, except on the infrequent occasions when the nuns shepherd them through town for a short visit to the bazaar or Budge. Watching them with intense curiosity, we think they look like unruly sheep being herded.

In July, some of us high school boys are invited to a party at the convent. Initially, we are lukewarm about the invitation, but we finally decide that a promised bountiful feast would make up for the boredom of a Catholic girls' school.

When we arrive, we find the main dance hall dripping with decorations. Dance music is playing on the phonograph, and the girls are decked out in their best dresses. Some are lusciously pretty. All are eager to dance; there's a sense of nearly uncontrollable anticipation. I'm barely in the hall when a cute young woman grabs my hand and pulls me onto the dance floor. Much to the surprise of my friends, I do a pretty good imitation of a fast dancer. I don't even get a chance to learn what her name is.

The dance is barely done when another girl steps up, and we do a slow dance. The slow dance is intoxicating. My partner mumbles her name, something French like Monique, but I'm too wrapped up in her scented hair to hear very well. As I look around, I see that all my Kodai School buddies are in someone's embrace, and there are still a bevy of beauties on the sidelines, waiting for the chance to hit the dance floor.

When the slow dance comes to a close, Monique hangs on tight, fending off a couple of girls who swoop in from the sidelines. I have never before had girls fighting over me! I think I may be in love with Monique or Monika or whatever her name is. Maybe sometime she can sneak off her campus and we can meet.

But things get even nuttier at the end of the second slow dance. The nuns try to put fast dance music on, but the girls controlling the phonograph protest loudly and find some more slow music. The tugging and pulling make me laugh. I can't believe that nuns and high school girls could get into a pushing match over dance music.

As the evening progresses, I'm entranced with Caroline, Jasmine, and Philippina. At least, I think those are their names.

When we head for home, dazed—contemplating how unusual the evening was—and more in love with girls than we have ever been, we can hardly talk. The last thing I hear as we make our way through the convent garden is a nun's shrill voice: "We'll never allow those hooligans to come here again!" The whining and crying that follows that pronouncement just adds to the wonder of the magical evening in the convent castle.

"I thought we were well behaved." I say to the darkness.

"It's not us the nuns are concerned about," Pope assures me. "It is the girls. I overheard a couple of nuns remark, with considerable alarm, on the girls' aggressiveness. I kind of liked it, myself." We all agree.

"Hey, Pope. Can you imagine what it would have been like if we had brought orchids?" The hillside rings with happy, lusty laughter.

It's six o'clock on the evening of September 14. My friends and I are waiting in the supper line in front of the dining room, fidgeting while the waiters finish setting up the meal. An Indian postman, in a harried and agitated manner, approaches us holding up a telegram.

"Where house Mr. Root, please?"

We tell him where Mr. Root lives and return to our chatter as we move ahead in the supper line. The postman runs off to Mr. Root's house just as the last rays of sunlight are disappearing over the horizon.

After supper we all head to the evening "study hall" in the library. It's our nightly ritual–everyone is required to be there unless you are on the honor roll. From seven to eight-thirty each night, we sit at eight-person tables in our nightly solitude. It is a time to study, contemplate life, and slow down as we go over our individual homework lists and organize our thoughts and work. I'm immersed in precalculus problems, and it's going very well. Ten minutes into the hour, out of the corner of my eye, I see Mr. Root walk into the library. Everyone sees him enter and wonders what's up; it is most unusual to see him in study hall.

There is a growing sense of foreboding in the room as we each ponder what he came for and who the unlucky person is that he wants to see. I try to think of any reason he might want to see me, but can't come up with one. I am demerit-prone and have by far the most demerits of the three boys in my family, but I have been pretty good lately. I watch him stride through the rows, wondering where he'll stop. His path through the roomful of tables keeps bringing him toward me, and I suddenly have an incredible sinking feeling. He looks at me a moment and says, in a tone that leaves no room for question, "We need to go for a walk."

"Should I leave my books here?"

"No." The whole study hall has become deadly silent. All eyes are on me as I gather my books and follow Mr. Root out of the room.

We step out of the library into the bleak night and begin to amble down a path. He remains silent as we leave the library behind us, walking a hundred feet or so toward the gym.

"Your father has had an accident."

Mr. Root's voice is firm and measured.

The air is still; there is not a hint of the refreshing evening breeze that usually wafts through campus. The last streaks of daylight in the western sky, where Arabia lies, are being snuffed out by the descending darkness. As we proceed past the gym, the dim bulb on the front of the gym sheds some light on our broken path. There are a few ugly insects hovering in its weak glow; they look like little flying ants.

It's amazing how acute one's mind can be at times. This is one such moment for me. I feel suspended in space between two worlds—the world I know and one I have no desire to tread into. I hang for an eternity between the two worlds, wanting desperately to stay where time has stopped. All I know at the moment is that my father has been hurt, and it seems reasonable that since he was so near a hospital, his injury could be fixed. More importantly, it seems reasonable that God would take good care of his loving servant. That assurance of divine protection is written on my heart.

Mr. Root and I continue walking in silence as he lets his words sink in. His tone and demeanor are unlike any I've experienced with him in the past.

"Is he OK?" I finally ask, knowing the question has to be dealt with.

"No. He's dead."

Mr. Root's answer is so simple, it sounds like a gong to my ears.

I become aware of every step I take and how the dust billows each time I put my foot down. All the structures around me suddenly become very clear, as if outlined by a sharp pen. I wonder if we could just turn the clock back a few hours and stay there and avoid this new reality.

Dad is dead. I can hardly think about what might have happened to him. Instead, I quickly realize how much my life will change. My foundations have disappeared. I am no longer a doctor's son. I am no longer a mish kid. I realize I am going to be ripped—heart, soul, and body—from India and Arabia and the life and culture I know and love. It is not a parting I had ever imagined.

Mr. Root gently guides me toward the night-enveloped Coakers Walk. I am vaguely aware of some level of empathy emanating from him. Despite my grief, however, I have enough of my boarding-school wits about me to suspect that this is an exceptional and short-lived phenomenon. Such compassion will last for about an hour, never to return, and so there is no use indulging in it. I refuse to cry, assuming that is how he expects me to react.

Mr. Root and I walk in silence for about an hour. I am very conscious that the Pleiades are somewhere overhead gazing sadly down at me. But I don't look up from the path we're walking. After a time, Mr. Root brings me back to my room. I dread having to face my dorm mates, but when I get back I realize that they have already been informed. In spite of the semi-stupor I am in, it annoys me that my personal and ugly truth, this devastating experience, can't be kept a secret.

"We're so sorry, Paul," they say, trying to find words of condolence. It all sounds and feels so formal. These are my closest friends, and yet they are now far from me on the other side of an emotional barrier.

I sit unresponsively on my bed, feeling as if everyone is looking at me, as if I am some sort of invalid to be pitied. I wonder what I'd done wrong to deserve this. There must have been something more than a pile of measly demerits to bring such sorrow down on my head.

Finally, Mrs. Amstuz, our dorm mother, shoos everyone out of my room and puts me to bed. It is the first time she has been tender with me. This time, I appreciate her attention.

The next morning, the usual school-day routine consumes me, and I find the familiarity of it helps me survive my classes.

In the afternoon, I am instructed to see Mr. Cassidy, the school counselor. We call him "Mr. Peg Leg" for the artificial leg he sports, and we cruelly imitate his limp when he's not around. I find him to be extremely sympathetic, and as we talk I break down and cry. He sits in patient silence as the grief wracks my whole body. I shake and gasp for what seems like an eternity. The whole experience is both emotional and physical. I can feel myself shuddering; I can feel the sweat pour from my face and the tears from my eyes. Mr. Cassidy just sits and lets me be.

Before long, I begin to control myself and then bring the sobbing to a halt. I sniffle a few times, dry my eyes, and sit up straight. I pledge to comport myself like a man. Although he tries to engage me in further discussion, Mr. Cassidy runs up against a stone wall. I am ready to face the world again.

That night, while I am sitting alone in my room, I can feel Dad's spirit with me. I sense that he has come to say goodbye, and his presence dispels all my fears. The experience is totally unexpected, but its reality is palpable. In the midst of my profound grief, my dad's presence provides more comfort than all the other supporters combined.

As I lie in bed that night, my mind flies over the gigantic changes which have exploded in my life, my world, and my identity. They feel so comprehensive, so all-encompassing, that I hardly know where I am or how I am to fit into this new world order. One day I am the son of a hero-like medical missionary, and the next day I am struggling to retain my status as a member of a select family of mish kids, a family to which I am not sure I still belong. I feel like an intruder in a world that is no longer mine, and it breeds a painful sense of loneliness. Dad died exactly twenty-one years, to the day, from the first time he stepped on Arabian soil. I wonder if that had been on his mind while he lay dying. It was the kind of thing he would remember.

It's the afternoon of September 21, a week after I learned that Dad died. I haven't heard directly from Mom, and I don't know any of the details of Dad's death, except that he had been shot.

At the end of the school day, I slink back to Wissy, hoping for some quiet and solitude. Glancing at the green wooden mailbox where the dorm's letters are distributed, I notice that there's a letter in the "H" cubby of the mail box. It doesn't have an Indian stamp, so I know it's from Oman and it's for me.

Apprehensively, I walk up to the mailbox. I suspect the letter is from my father. Indeed, as I get closer, I can see that the handwriting is my father's. He who is no more.

It seems like someone should be holding my hand or wrapping their arms around my shoulders as I pick up the letter and prepare to read it. It strikes me that I shouldn't have to go through this alone. I return slowly to my room, opening the letter on the way. The dorm is deadly silent as I read the letter over and over, sitting alone in my room. I don't cry and vaguely realize I don't know how to any more. The very presence of the letter gives me the unsettling feeling that Dad is not really dead. The news is so routine, so up-beat, so like Dad, that he can't possibly be gone. He talks of all he is doing and all that has yet to be done. It all seems so impossible.

On Sunday afternoon, a memorial service is held in the chapel. The place is packed. The chaplain arranges for me to sit in his office in the front of the church so I can hear the service but so that no one can see me. As the service proceeds, my mind turns to statistics. Weird. During my time at Kodai, there have been more than eight hundred parents of Kodai kids. I remember only two parents dying during those six years. Why do I have to be one of those kids? What are the odds?

On Monday, a letter finally arrives from Mom, giving me the details of Dad's death. I take the envelope and head to my room and shut the door. Her letter tells me that on Wednesday, September 13, Dad woke early and in a good mood, knowing he was in a place of high responsibility where he could further God's mission. He was happy about how little sleep he needed, enabling him to spend more time at the hospital, pushing himself physically, mentally, and spiritually. In spite of the exceptional heat, Mom and Dad were busier than normal. Many of the hospital's Indian and American staff members were on vacation. Dad was acting senior medical officer.

Sometime around mid-morning, Dad gave blood, doing the procedure himself. He donated as often as he could, since there was always a strong need for blood and Arabs did not like to give blood. He knew the lost blood would make him light-headed as his body worked to rebuild the lost fluids, but replenishing the blood supply was a necessity. This was one more way for Dad to give of himself.

Dad held clinic that morning, a line waiting to be admitted to his office. A man arrived with his wife and walked to the head of the line, demanding to see the doctor immediately. He made such a fuss, the orderly couldn't handle the situation, and my father had to interrupt the patient he was seeing to come out and deal with the obnoxious man.

The man informed my father, projecting his voice so that everyone could hear, that he was a man of social stature, too dignified to stand in line with the less worthy ones. He and his wife needed to be seen immediately. Dad, already overworked, wasn't pleased by the interruption, the man's demands, or the implication that the others in line were lesser human beings.

"I am here to serve all people, rich or poor, the same! You need to wait your turn in line," Dad said in a voice loud enough to be overheard by those in line.

When Dad did see the man, it turned out that just his wife was ill. Dad admitted the woman to the examination room and told the man he could not come in with her. This was standard medical practice; men were not allowed in the room while their wives were examined. The man, already incensed, became irate but complied when he realized Dad wouldn't give on this point.

That evening, Mom and Dad went to supper at the home of fellow missionaries. There, they reviewed the preparations for the upcoming Mission Executive Committee meeting. Talk continued until ten o'clock, when Mom and Dad drove home.

Upon arriving home, Dad opened the gate and drove the car in. Mom went into the house while Dad closed the gate. The gate consisted of a large opening for the car with a smaller door in it for people to walk through—the biblical "eye of the needle." As he closed the large gate, a hand holding a 0.25-caliber revolver slipped through. When Dad turned around, walking toward the house, he was shot in the back at close range. He was hit three or four times in the left arm, left side and back.

Another missionary doctor, Fred Richards, who lived in an apartment above my parents, heard the four shots and Dad's distressed voice.

"Fred, Fred I've been shot!"

Dad limped into the house, told Mom what had happened, and lay down on their bed. Initially, Mom did not think he looked in great pain or in danger of his life.

"Can you think of anyone who has reason to shoot you?" Mom asked.

"No."

Fred ran to the house, following a trail of blood which started on the porch, ran through the living and dining rooms, and ended in the bedroom. Dad was in severe pain but lucid.

"Did you see your assailant?" Fred asked.

"No, he fired from behind. I know of no one who would have cause to shoot me."

Time passed quickly as Mom called the police, the mayor of Mutrah, and other missionary friends. "I really regret that I was running around doing all of these tasks when I could have spent that precious time talking to Dad," she wrote.

To relieve his pain, Fred had 20 mg of morphine sulphate and 0.4 mg of atropine sulfate rushed over from the nearby hospital and alerted the operating and x-ray crews that he would have to do emergency surgery.

After administering the morphine, Fred ran over to the hospital to scrub up. There, he dispatched nurses and others to retrieve Dad on a stretcher. By this time, Dad was acutely ill and, in spite of the morphine, was in considerable pain. He was carried to x-ray and, when his condition deteriorated, he was carried into the operating room. On the way to the operating room, just before being administered anesthesia, the anesthesiologist heard him say, "Father, forgive them for they know not what they do."

He was given a transfusion. The first pint was his own, which he had drawn in the morning. As his condition worsened, Fred gave him open heart massage, but Dad could not be revived. He was declared dead at 11:30.

As Mom recounted the grim events in her letter, she seemed to imply that the husband who had been so offended during the morning clinic was the one who had come in the dark of the night to settle a perceived score.

I finally know the details of my dad's last moments. Rather than comfort me, the information makes me more confused. What would prompt this devastating calamity? Could one's honor be so offended by a hospital visit that he might kill the person who had helped his wife heal? Could he be so bitter that the only way to respond to a minor affront would be blood vengeance? More importantly, how could God, who oversees everything, let such a trivial slight escalate to the death of one of his dearest servants?

What was Dad thinking after he was shot, during the thirty minutes he had before slipping into unconsciousness. Being a doctor himself, he probably had a good appreciation for the extent of his injuries and its likely consequences. Despite the incredible physical pain he was in, he must have thought about his family. His mind would have been racing, and he simply didn't have the time to talk about what he was going through. This is especially true because Mom was on the phone trying to get help, leaving Dad alone with his thoughts. Did he think about me? What did he recall about our times together? We'd been so close, we had so much in common.

In the midst of these questions, my mind keeps playing and replaying Dad's last words: "Father, forgive them...!"

That Wednesday, as I head to class in my usual daze, Teddy comes up and walks with me. "Hey, Paul."

"Hi, Teddy."

"How're ya doing?"

"Okay."

"Looks like you're doing pretty well. I know it must be a tough blow. I remember how you were so supportive when my dad had his stroke."

"Yeah."

"It must be tough. Well, see ya."

Without waiting for another "yeah," Teddy slips into his own classroom, and I head to mine. He's the first one who has spoken to me about Dad since the memorial service. I feel as though I'm being put in a separate box, no longer in the mainstream of the student body. Now I am just a child without a father. Even worse, I'm no longer the son of a widely respected physician. I'm floating on my own, unconnected. Am I still a "mish kid"? I don't know. This realization is devastating, for I have absolutely no desire to belong anywhere else. No longer an insider, I am on a slow and painful journey away from my home territory, gradually becoming an outsider.

In a last-ditch effort to comprehend what I'm going through, I turn to God in prayer: "Lord, what's going on, what are you doing? You who oversee your children on Earth, where is your loving care? I'm confused and distraught. This unimaginable loss is more than my young years can handle. Why would you allow the world to lose such a great man? My father's life was dedicated to the betterment of mankind in one of the most inhospitable parts of the world. He was doing your will and mission. Isn't that important enough to you, to let him continue?

"You've taken away my compass, my guide. This isn't your nature! Why did you not intervene? Why couldn't your doctors save him? Isn't that what they do? What good can come from this?"

Despite my pleading prayers, answers don't come.

The last day of October, school lets out for winter break. I've finished the first half of my senior year, and the future is not yet clear to me. I'm not sure whether I'll ever return to Kodai. I say my good-byes to Bugs and the others and suspect I'll never see them again.

I travel as far as Bombay with the rest of the Arabian Mission kids, unable to enjoy the journey as I have so many times in the past. When we arrive in Bombay, Mom is waiting for me at the airport. I half expect that Dad will be with her, too, and I look past her as if he may be at the ticket counter. His absence is another hard blow.

The rest of the kids drive off to their hotel, bidding us *adieu*, and Mom and I head our separate way. I feel the weight of their departure. While I have felt as if I was in my own bubble for the last few weeks, this physical parting signals my separation from the ranks of Arab mish kids for good. It's like another death in my life. Once again, I have no control over what is happening to me.

The one good thing that I cling to with all my might is that Mom has assured me that I will be returning to Kodai after Christmas for the last semester of my senior year. At least that part of me will hang on for a few more months. I resolve to make the most of those remaining days when the new year rolls around.

Temple and elephant

CHAPTER 8

Elephant Baseball

Mom and I make our way to the States for Christmas vacation, where we visit with family and friends. It is especially good to reconnect with Terr and Dave. Sharing a bedroom with them reminds me of all the ways they had nurtured and supported me when our times overlapped in Kodai. But now they are adults, Terr in the Navy and Dave finishing graduate school, so our interactions are more peer-like. We don't talk much about Dad and his death; it's still too painful for all of us. So much has changed in the blink of an eye.

For the first time since I began going to Kodai, I travel back there with my mother, not with the other Arab mish kids. We go directly from the States, not stopping in either Muscat or Bahrain. Apparently, I will never visit my Arabian homes again. When she departed in October, Mom left the major packing and shipping of our household goods in the hands of other missionaries. I wonder whether I'll see my things—like my train set—ever again. It is profoundly disorienting, to say the least.

While the sights and sounds and smells of India are the same, the experience is very different. It reminds me that I am in a new role this last semester. Mom will be living in a room at Kodai School, just a stone's throw from the dining hall. She's talked about assisting with the little kids on campus. I'll probably see her a lot.

Arriving in Kodai, I am determined to adjust to my new future. As much as possible I will return to the "normal" life I have come to love, one which brings with it familiarity, including old and new friendships. Once again I move into Wissahickon Hall, which I have been visiting since I was a fifth grader and Dave and Terr lived there. Once again, the passage of time and the events since those days seem overpowering.

I soon discover that my friend and classmate, Tom, has transferred, much to my regret. However, I can find out how he's doing though his younger sister, a frosh named Barbara. On the second day I'm back, I meet her in line for dinner.

"I'm 'BB,'" she says, extending a hand. "Tom told me all about you."

"I hope it was all good."

"Mostly," she smirks.

The conversation is corny, but easy. Her parents are working in Thailand, so I wrack my brain to find questions to ask her about Thailand. Although she's three years younger than I am, she is poised and bright. I love talking with her. It's easy and relaxed.

But she has a boyfriend.

So I bide my time, meeting when I can, often asking her more questions about Thailand just so I can hear her talk. It probably drives her nuts, but in the long run it pays off for me.

In February, she and her boyfriend break up, and I jump at the opportunity. I invite her to a Wednesday night canteen dance, and she quickly agrees. I soon discover that being with BB drags me out of my sadness; it's the first time I feel lighthearted since Dad's death.

I do everything I can to find time to be with BB, but I don't want my friends to know what's happening. She likes to skip lunch and head to the library to study, so I begin to eat early and rapidly so that I can join her.

"Hey, Paul, what's up?" Teddy demands. "Why are you always rushing off after lunch? Where are you headed?"

"I'm just studying," I reply lamely. He doesn't buy it.

While I fear that someone else may swoop in and begin dating BB, I can't bring myself to ask her to go steady. We still have a lot to learn about each other.

On February 21, we seniors head out for a few days of retreat. It's the annual "Senior Sneak," and all the plans have been made in secret. No one knows where we're going to spend the break.

One more time we head down the *Ghat*, pass the turnoff to Kodai Road station, and then to Madurai. From there, we travel four more hours to the east coast of India and the village of Mandapam. By the time we pull into a beach house we're renting from an elderly English couple, everyone's beat.

The girls head for the porch and spread their sleeping bags under the open air. We boys elect to sleep on the beach, where we set up a canvas lean-to and some hammocks. It is magnificent falling asleep under the stars, relishing the warm and gentle breeze that sweeps out to sea from the warmer plains. The palm trees lend an eerie "swish" to the ambience, like giant fans moving the air around.

Morning light rouses us early, and we hit the wide, sandy beaches. The high surf makes swimming difficult, but the effort is exhilarating. As we fight the waves and dive through the breakers, I feel transported.

Exhausted, I flop on the beach and take in the whole scene. Around the bay are a scattering of multicolored fishing skiffs, and we watch as they row out to their fishing positions. Framing the scene are the coconut palms, their branches clacking in the off-shore breezes. The sun soaks into my bones, and I feel as relaxed and comfortable as I have since September. I realize I haven't thought about my father all morning. I could stay on this idyllic bay forever.

That night, sitting around a huge bonfire, we sing folk songs along with a guitar. Exhausted, I head back to my beach-side hammock and snuggle in. The night sky is speckled with white stars that blink and hide behind the swaying palm fronds overhead. The nap I took in the afternoon has taken the edge off of my tiredness, so I lie awake and think. I ponder my years in Kodai and how they have formed me. How I am fully an American, but just as fully an Arab and an Indian. I think about how much fun I've had with BB, and how she has taken me out of my misery. Before I fade into sleep, I resolve to ask her to go steady as soon as I return to Kodai. I know I'm going to graduate in June, but even a few months together would be wonderful. In the dark, I fumble with my tape recorder and play "our" song, "Daydream Believer." I play it over and over until, sometime after midnight, the batteries wear out and I drift off to sleep with BB's image on my mind.

After three days of frolicking, we are all sticky and stinky. Salt has found its way into all our pores, and our hair is stiff with sand. Our skin is scorched, but we are happy. Before heading back to Kodai, we haul a hose out of the house and spray each other down.

"It's a communal bath!" Peck proclaims, a little melo-dramatically.

It's great to have some clean water to wash with; the last couple of nights we've had to fight with frogs, slime, and dead fish floating in the "fresh water" well at the beach "resort."

Driving back to school, we stop in Madurai where temple towers soar above the forests of palm trees. The temples would be famous tourist landmarks anywhere else, but here in the remote hinterlands of rural India these architectural wonders are virtually unknown to the rest of the world. We stop under the stern gaze of hundreds of gaudy statues that adorn the temples' huge sloping sides. In the temples' protective shade, we plow into a *biryani* feast and splurge on ice-pops. Even the teachers' warnings that they might make us sick are ignored; the ice-pops are too good to refuse. Although a dozen flavors are advertised by the vendor, it becomes clear that every ice-pop, no matter its color, has the same rose-water flavoring.

Returning to the reality of campus life, my worst fears are realized at Wednesday night's canteen dance. To my horror, I see BB dancing the first dance with a date. And she is thoroughly enjoying herself. I hang my head in disbelief and misery. I had such high hopes on the beach at Mandapam. Just when I think things can't get worse, she comes over and asks me to dance. Hallelujah! The night is saved! I dance as many dances as I can with her. My heart is soaring, but I'm still too scared to ask her to go steady.

On Friday evening, as we chat in the dining hall after supper, I find out that she is waiting for another date. My heart plummets.

Leaving her, I return to my room, depressed and convinced I've lost her. After wallowing in misery and self-pity for an hour, I decide I like her so much I have to risk one last gamble. The risk of being turned down is well worth even the smallest chance of success.

On Saturday morning, first thing, I search for BB. When I find her, I ask her out and she accepts on the spot. We have a wonderful conversation—about Kodai, not Thailand—and I'm convinced that our friendship is off to new heights.

"You're robbing the cradle!" Bugs ribs me when he finds out later that day. "The only reason she's dating you is because she's a lowly freshman and you're a vaunted senior!"

"She's too pretty and much too smart for you!" This from Teddy, the world's expert on dating.

There are elements of truth in these jibes; BB is very attractive and very intelligent. And maybe she likes me because I'm a senior. No matter, she's agreed to go out with me, and that's all that I care about.

BB lives off campus in Easthouse, a small boarding hall near Coakers Walk. The distance away from the campus turns out to be my good fortune. The next Wednesday night canteen dance I accompany her home after our date, and we are mostly alone on the way. As always, the nearby mountain peaks are beautiful as they glisten in starlight, so we stroll slowly, arm in arm, under the overhanging eucy trees. Our eyes are inevitably drawn to the lights that twinkle six thousand feet below us in the plains. The scene is right out of the movies.

We embrace for a few minutes in the shadows of Easthouse before Mrs. Shackleton, BB's housemother, comes out and looks around for BB. Mrs. Shackleton is another elderly British woman who has remained in India after the empire's collapse in 1948. Having a warm spot in her heart for wholesome young romance, she lets us have a few brief moments to say goodnight.

"I trust you to be a gentleman now," she tells me with a wag of her finger as she looks down from her pulpit on the porch. "Be a good boy and hurry home, Paul. Come in now, Barbara."

I blow BB a kiss and she smiles back. "See you tomorrow," she promises, and I am too overcome to say anything. The whole journey back to Wissy I float on air, not touching down until I hit the sack and drift off to sleep.

"So, it's agreed, we need to use our class's surplus funds to feed the hungry? Is that right?" Becky is trying to bring our class meeting to a close after a raucous hour of debate.

"Yes!" the girls respond eagerly.

"I know a charity which would be glad to have the funds; they're doing great things with the *dalit*," Karen shouts over the general clamor. "The untouchables are in desperate need of food and support." There are nodding heads all around the room—all of them are girls' heads.

"No, not them. *We're* the hungry ones. Feed us!" Fletch responds, just as loudly as Karen. "We want to go out to eat! After all these years of dining hall tripe, it's time we had a decent meal for a change. Who's with me on this?"

The boys let out a hearty cheer, and the girls groan in unison.

In general, the twenty girls out-vote the thirteen boys in our class, but this is serious business. It has to do with surplus funds that we have not spent on other class activities. Since there has to be consensus on the use of the funds, the money just sits there.

"I declare this meeting adjourned," Becky bellows, slamming down her fist like a fake gavel. The girls file out with dark mutterings of disdain for the "selfish, bottomless pits" in their midst.

But we boys don't leave the room.

"I declare this meeting reopened," Fletch asserts, slamming his fist in a noisy imitation of Becky. "Is there a motion for us to consider?"

"Yes, I move that the class hold a formal banquet tomorrow night at the Carlton Hotel. Furthermore, I move that the announcement of that banquet be held up until fifteen minutes before it is to begin, at which time all those who are not currently present should be informed of the event and invited to join us." Zorn always speaks with a flourish, and the motion carries his signature embellishments.

"I second that motion!"

"All in favor, say 'aye.'"

"Aye!" The motion is enthusiastically passed, followed by whoops and hollers.

The next evening, promptly at 5:15 as planned, Zorn runs into Becky who is standing in line for the dining room.

"Why are you all dressed up? And where are the other boys?" she asks, looking around warily.

"Well, Becky, I'm here to invite you and the girls in our class to join the boys for a banquet at the Carlton Hotel. Reservations have been made for 5:30, and we would very much enjoy having your presence with us!"

"You, but, you," Becky sputters as Zorn trots off.

As the thirteen boys walk into the elegant dining hall of the Carlton Hotel, just one block and several economic steps away from Kodai School, we are relieved to see that there are no girls waiting for us. That means more steaks, more boiled potatoes, more fresh-cut beans, more bread with real butter, more ice cream, and more tea and coffee for us boys. Waiters in fancy hats serve us as if we are special, and for one night we are. Without the stifling influence of a bunch of do-gooder girls, we have the time of our lives. The hungry are satisfied! At least for one night.

Chad's arrival in Kodai causes quite a stir. He has long hair–a first in Kodai School—dresses weirdly, and uses lots of slang words we don't know. As a new junior, he is assigned to Wissy, to a room down the corridor from me. His first night on campus Bugs and I stop in to welcome him.

"Where're you from?"

"I've just come from Milwaukee. Can't believe I've washed up on this backwater beach. Hey, you guys know where the action is around here?"

"Well, on Wednesday night we have a canteen dance, and that's pretty cool. With that and the movies or parties every Saturday night, you'll see that we're not such a backwater place."

Chad stares at us in disbelief. "No, I mean *action*, you know— smack, Mary Jane, reefers?"

I look at Bugs, my face a question mark.

"Oh, you mean drugs?" Bugs, tentatively.

"Well, duh!"

"No, we don't have any of that around here. You can probably find some alcohol in the trash bins of the English country club, but that's about it."

Chad stares even more disbelievingly. "Don't worry, I won't snitch. I'm not a stooge! I just want to hook up."

"Hook up? Like with a girl?"

"Oh, you guys are so dense! You gotta get with it, man."

"With what?" My temperature is rising; this conversation has turned into gibberish.

"All right, let's cool this jive. I'm too wasted to keep playing this record. Let's pick it up later."

Bugs and I leave, scratching our heads.

"What's with that mop-head?" Bugs queries. "Beatle haircut must have scrambled his brains."

"Yeah, saw a shirt like that in *Time* magazine. Lots of prissy flowers all over it. And his hair! What a stench. Does he ever bathe? We should send him down to Phelps and let the *ayahs* get at him."

That night, as I review the events of the day, I realize this is the first time I've encountered someone who has used illegal drugs. I've read about this epidemic spreading around the States, but it has never crossed our paths in South India. I decide I'll avoid that side of Chad.

Much to my relief, Chad doesn't show up to the Wednesday night canteen dance. I arrive with BB just as the slow dances are about to begin, and I really don't want any other distractions. The music begins with one of my favorites, a Brothers Four folk ballad, and I sweep BB out onto the dance floor. I am already floating when BB looks up at me.

"You know, I broke up with my boyfriend so that I could date you," she whispers. I almost miss a step as my knees grow weak. My hands begin to sweat.

"I didn't know that. Thank you."

Thank you? What's the matter with me? This isn't a birthday present she's given me.

"BB, you know how much I care for you," I stumble, trying to retake command of the conversation. She just floats along in my arms, her head tilted gracefully as she buries herself in my eyes. "Would you, uh, would you like to go steady?"

To my utter amazement, she breaks out in a hearty laugh. And then squeezes me tightly, reassuringly.

"You Doofus! We've been going steady for the last month. Where have you been?"

I had figured we were going from one date to the next–until she grew tired of me and moved on. But this is something totally different; this beautiful angel, always impeccably turned out and always so poised, thinks we are already going steady.

"Of course," I stammer. "I just wasn't sure that *you* knew it."

The merry twinkle in her eyes tells me she doesn't believe that for a second. She knows me so well that it almost hurts. I love this girl.

At that moment there is a stir at the door to the gym. A bunch of my friends have just entered, jabbering loudly. In the middle of them is BB's classmate, Gwen. Even in the dim light of the dance hall, I can see that she is wearing the shortest dress I have ever seen. I can't help steering BB away from the door so that she can't see Gwen and her coterie of admirers. But the music suddenly stops, and in the unexpected silence everyone hears Mr. Root, the principal.

"You've got to be kidding me!" he groans aloud. His face is contorted in anger, his eyes wide and his jaw set. "Gwen, go back to your dorm right now and put on some real clothes."

There is an audible moan as twenty guys protest this edict. A rumble of laughter sweeps the room. Gwen, not even blushing, turns on her heels, waves over her shoulder, and walks out the door. In five seconds, she returns, wearing the same dress, but now it is five inches longer.

"Is this one okay, Mr. Root?" she simpers, blinking coquettishly.

He knows it's the same dress, but miraculously it has grown in length. "Kneel down," he commands. By now everyone—including BB—is focused on Gwen and Mr. Root and this legend in the making. I'm already sketching out the plot for retelling to those who are not here.

Gwen obediently kneels down, and Miss Slifer comes over to check the gap between her skirt and the ground. "It's less than two inches from the floor, Mr. Root. It meets our regulations."

"Okay, Gwen. Watch your step. You can stay." Mr. Root winces.

Gwen, triumphant, stands up and smooths her dress. I almost expect to hear clapping; this has been a brilliant victory of courageous youth over prudish age. As Gwen melts into the crowd, I sense BB's eyes boring into the side of my head.

"Do you think *my* skirt is too short?"

Honestly, I don't know how to reply. Is she asking for my opinion on the seductiveness of her hem, or is she asking if I think her skirt would meet the school's two-inch code? I think that, no matter how I answer, it won't be the right answer. "It's fine," I mumble. Our gazes are locked, and before I look away I see the twinkle return to BB's eyes. Whew, I survived that minefield! I'm going to have to pay closer attention to BB's attire in the future. Clearly, she sees clothing as more important than I ever have. I'm not even sure my pants have been washed in the last two weeks, much less ironed since I left the States.

As we continue to sweep across the dance floor, we pass Gwen dancing with Jake. Somehow, her dress has shrunk back five inches. Clearly this is a magical piece of wardrobe.

That night, as I walk BB back to Easthouse, we detour through Coakers Walk. I tell BB that long ago I walked this same romantic path with Dave and his girlfriend, Peggy. Now I'm a senior, and it is my arm that encircles a beautiful girl. The sun has faded, but a glow remains, allowing us to see the hills beyond, with Mount Perumal prominent in the distance. Below us, flickering lights come on and announce that families are gathering for supper in homes down the mountainsides and into the faraway plains thousands of feet below. Dave used to call this view at this time of the night "a jewel box." It's a magical time, so BB and I pause to take it all in.

After the bustle of the crowd at the dance, the solitude is warmly enveloping. We amble into the garden of the nearby Anglican Church and sit on a bench. In the silence, I turn to kiss BB. She yields, and we are soon lost in each other's arms. There are no services on Wednesday evenings, so we stay in the garden, looking down on the distant landscapes and relishing our happiness together. Life is good. Again.

When it comes time to take her back to Easthouse, I throw out a crazy idea.

"How about returning to Coakers after lights out?"

"When? Tonight?"

"Yeah. You could go in, and when everyone is asleep, you could climb out the window and join me. I'll wait in the bushes and whistle so you can find me. That way, we can spend some more time together. What do you think?"

"Okay." Eagerly, tentatively.

So we walk back to Easthouse and kiss good-night under the watchful, approving eye of Mrs. Shackleton.

An hour later, after the house lights have all been turned off, I hear a rustling from the side of the house. In the silver moonlight, I see BB wiggle out of her first-floor bedroom and land lightly on the ground. We run to meet each other and embrace.

"You won't believe what happened this morning!" BB wails when we meet the next day at noon. I'd grabbed a sandwich, and we're about to enter the library. "I've been banished to Kennedy!"

"What? You're back on campus?"

"Yeah. Mrs. Shackleton was watering her plants this morning and found footprints in the garden under my window. She asked if they were mine, and I couldn't lie to her. So she told me to pack my bags because she is sending me back to Kennedy where I could be "properly watched." There goes our excuse for long walks along Coakers's magical pathway.

Two weeks after BB returns to Kennedy, my friends Peck, Fletch, and Zorn go in search of elephants with me, with Mr. Reimer as our chaperone. Although we don't see any elephants during our camping trip, we do find evidence of their presence. The clearest sign that they're in the area is the spoor we find in abundance. It has dried and hardened into straw-filled balls. Fletch thinks it would be fun to play with these balls, so he and Peck launch into an impromptu game of "elephant baseball." Here we are, a pack of American teenagers, romping through an elephant-infested valley in South India, and we dream up a novel game true to our unique selves. No sane American would consider using elephant dung to play the national pastime; and no self-respecting Indian would play baseball, the ultimate trivialization of cricket. Yet, here we were, Americans in India, happily making do.

Falling asleep in the shade that afternoon, I wake to find myself baking in the sun. My feet are thoroughly scorched, and the trek back out of the valley doesn't make them feel any better. When we finally arrive on campus, the nurse orders me to bed for two days. Despite my sore back and pain-wracked feet, I conclude that the "hunt" has been a blast.

BB gets permission to visit me in my dorm room. When I tell her the story of elephant baseball, she laughs uproariously. If anything, I think my stupidity makes her like me even more. Her laughter is infectious, and I join in, laughing at myself for the first time in months. Her light-hearted response to the ridiculousness of my burned feet further endears her to me.

Wonders never cease in Kodai. On Saturday, once I regain my ability to walk, I join a group of classmates on an investigative adventure. They have heard about an itinerant holy man who recently arrived in Kodai and who will perform a public miracle down by the lake.

The crowds are noisy and tightly packed along the lakeshore by the time we arrive, and the buzzing is playful and lighthearted. Although I don't comprehend all that I hear, my friends and I get good spots on the campus wall so that I can see what's going on.

At the end of one of the long piers is a cluster of holy men. They're all dressed in ragged, dusty, orange robes and loin cloths. In their midst is a very elderly man who is clad in white. The others are obviously deferential to the old man, bowing and touching their foreheads in signs of veneration.

"He's going to walk on water," says an Indian man standing below us on the ground. He motions with his hands to indicate that the walk will be on top of the water. He's dressed in the Western clothes of a government agent or a teacher and figures, correctly, that we can't understand a thing that's being said. "He wants to show his disciples how much he has grown in his spiritual being." Hands together, and then swept skyward.

Walk on water? Not since Jesus, I figure. I can't help but think that this kind of religious stunt would be laughed out of town in America, but here it is one of the many ways that holy men show the depths of their faith. Crowds like this one treat these events as public theater, and that is probably what they are.

Now the elderly *sadhu* briskly waves his disciples away, turns, and marches to the end of the pier, where he pauses for a moment. The crowd grows so silent that I can hear the branches of the eucy trees waving in the wind overhead. A pie-dog barks, and a baby lets out a stifled wail. As he approaches the end of the pier, the *sadhu's* disciples begin a low chant. I hold my breath when he steps off the end of the pier and disappears into the lake.

One one-thousand, two one-thousand, three one-thousand, I tick off in my head. No one has stirred. The ripples fade from the surface of the water, and time ominously ticks by. Suddenly, three orange-clad disciples strip to their loin cloths and jump into the water.

Sputtering and protesting, the *sadhu* is dragged from the depths and hoisted onto the pier, where he rolls around. Mesmerized, the throng stands stationary, unable to wrench themselves from the power of the scene unfolding before them. After a couple of moments, the old man struggles to his feet, pushing away those who would hold him up. He launches into a raspy speech, which is met with nods and murmurs of assent and then louder affirmations of praise and support.

Our interpreter turns to us with a wry grin. "Amazing! He says that he failed because he was unable to create the necessary vacuum in his large intestine."

Though the stunt failed in a nearly comical manner, even in the laughter I sense that something hard to comprehend, yet spiritual, transpired here.

Before I can follow up that extraordinary explanation with a question, a disciple from the orange brigade begins to shout from the pier. Our translator turns his attention in that direction. When the shouting is done, he swivels back to us in disgust. "He says that he saw the *sadhu* sink much slower than normal men, so that is almost as good as walking on water." I don't know whether to laugh or to cry.

In late April I have a silver ring made for BB. Our names are inscribed inside. When I give it to her, there is a sparkle in her eyes before they fill with tears.

"Why didn't you give this to me earlier?" She asks sadly. "Our time in Kodai is going by too fast!" I don't have an answer for that. I'm only too aware that my time in Kodai is racing to a close.

Commencement and graduation crash around me in mid-June. Teddy, Bugs, and I take a quick, post-commencement trip around South India, to Madras, to Goa, and to Bangalore. But my heart isn't fully in the excursion. I can't wait to get back to Kodai and see BB.

However, when we finally return a week later, I discover that she has already returned to Thailand. I never had the chance to bid her a proper good-bye. I never had the chance to thank her for helping me return to the land of the living. I never had the chance to tell her how much I cared for her. I hope she knows, and I wonder if I'll ever see her again.

Leaving Kodai is even more difficult than missing BB. Riding down the *Ghat* for the last time, I am aware that I am leaving my accustomed way of life behind, and there is no going back. The world I knew would be a thing of the past, slipping from my grasp. It was a good world I'd grown up in, overflowing with fond memories and favored friends. I have loved its exotic ambiance, its piquant food, its diverse people, its fickle weather, its multihued cultures, and its compelling sights, smells, and sounds. Indelibly, elephant baseball and all these vivid images have become part of me, a lasting legacy to cherish and a firm foundation on which to build a life.

Typical roadside store

Epilogue

In retrospect, I suppose, one could ascribe the thread of events that formed my adult life to simple coincidence. But I can't. I'm convinced that there was a guiding hand weaving these threads together into a unique tapestry. This is especially true for a chain of events that took place during my time in the Navy.

After graduating from Kodai School in 1968, my mother and I left India and moved to Holland, Michigan, where she rented an apartment and I moved onto Hope College's campus to start my freshman year.

Initially, it was difficult adjusting to American life. But after a few months, I joined the Cosmopolitan Fraternity, became a "frat brother," and enjoyed the camaraderie and silly antics membership afforded. I began to settle into life in the American Midwest.

For two years after joining the fraternity, I never mentioned to anyone that I had grown up overseas. In retrospect, it's amazing that I could cover up my past so well. I still marvel at how I was able to function as a person without a past. By doing so, I was following the example my mother and older brothers had set. They behaved and talked as if we had never lived overseas. They never brought up the subject of our youthful capers, and they never talked in my presence about my father. In my mind, my early life took on the shades of myth rather than reality. Even my father's presence seemed to fade into the background. I occasionally tried talking with my family about those earlier days in India and the Persian Gulf, but my attempts at such conversations were rebuffed. Being far too young to have an inkling of what was going on in my mother and brothers' minds, I soon sensed that delving into our past was something I just shouldn't do. It began to seem like there was something wrong with recalling those times and those places and those people.

So, with unbridled gusto, I participated in the crazy, immature shenanigans that fraternity boys are renowned for. I was fully accepted as one of the guys. My frat brothers treated me like just another average, good-ol'-boy from West Michigan— and that's what I longed to be. So fully did I immerse myself in the college scene that, much to my amazement, in my senior year, I was elected president of the Cosmos. I felt the honor was the final, official seal that I was now truly an American kid. I had successfully navigated the trek from the world of mish kid to that of "average" American. Somehow, I sensed that I had arrived.

Even the downside of frat life seemed to affirm my normality. The fraternity was often in trouble with the college administration for our hijinks. On numerous occasions, in my role as president,

I would sit in front of the expansive desk of the dean of men and take the full brunt of his fury. But I took it for my "brothers."

Finally, I was called in for a meeting about myself; it turned out to be a meeting of reckoning to put me back on the straight path. I couldn't help but recall a similar episode in Kodai, when the principal called me in about a boat being vandalized. That hadn't gone well, either.

"Young man, your academic record is not what it should be," began the dean, "and you seem to be heading into troubled waters. The fraternity life has not been good for you. You need to decide now between academics and your fraternity; you need to decide which will govern your life. So, what will it be?" I was asked in a tone that left little doubt as to what my answer should be.

As I sat in his office, I knit my brow and carefully grappled with the question. I remained appropriately thoughtful, knowing that I should take a little time to answer such an important question.

"The fraternity," I said at last.

The dean's jaw dropped. He was speechless and simply pointed to the door, indicating that I should leave.

I felt no remorse for what I had said. What the dean couldn't comprehend was how important it was for me to be one of the guys and to fully immerse myself in their world. Now that I was accepted as a full member of American student life, I wasn't going to risk that for something as trivial as a better grade or two.

Moreover, after fully embracing this new life and new self, I rarely looked back on the first eighteen years of my life. It was too long ago and far away, too unlike the life I now had that I didn't want to jeopardize. I had no intention of turning back to my earlier existence or to the lands where I grew up. I thought I had flushed them from my identity.

During my last semester at Hope College, a Navy recruiter visited the campus, setting up a booth in the student center. He was intent on recruiting Hope students, a particularly daunting endeavor at the time. It was the height of the Viet Nam War, and due to the strongly antiwar sentiment among students, his presence was not appreciated. In protest, one of the students grabbed his display table and turned it over, scattering his material and leaflets all over the floor.

For some reason I felt sorry for the recruiter, dressed in his sharp uniform, as he tried to maintain his dignity while picking up the material and once again setting up his display. I think I felt that way, in part, because my dad had served in World War II and had always been proud of his military service. In any case, I reasoned that the sailor had been unfairly treated merely for doing his patriotic duty.

One of the recruiter's pamphlets caught my eye. It was a slick brochure showing a Navy jet taking off from an aircraft carrier, and I picked up a copy. Over the following days, I studied it with great interest, lost in the adventure of flying which the image evoked. I remembered the countless times—too few, in the end—when Dad and I had visited the airport in Manama or had flown kites in the desert.

With graduation approaching, I finally had to admit to myself that mediocre grades in my pre-med classes would not get me into medical school. So I explored other options. Flying had always sparked the sense of adventure in me, so I signed up for flight lessons at Holland's Tulip City Airport. After eight training flight-hours with an instructor, I was flying solo over Michigan's vast rural landscape—a patchwork of small farms and forests—and even near to the shore of Lake Michigan. The sensation of floating alone in space, viewing Earth from God's vantage point, seeing Lake Michigan's deep blue waters stretch to the horizon's edge, and maneuvering between majestic cloud formations was intoxicating. I was enthralled; I wanted more!

At night, lying in bed, I would page through the stack of airplane magazines I had collected, wondering what it would be like to land a jet on a swaying carrier deck. The Navy aviation pamphlet kept beckoning me. Finally, I decided to take the test to become a naval aviator, and—thanks to the knowledge gained in my math and premed classes—I passed. By the fall of 1974, I was in Pensacola, Florida, in naval flight school, and soon thereafter I was commissioned as an ensign and naval aviator.

Life as a Navy officer suited me. I liked the camaraderie, excitement, sea stories, endless jokes, career challenges, strong nationalistic sentiments, and crazy antics sailors are known for. It was like a huge fraternity—with uniforms—and, as before, it was great just being one of the guys. I reveled in the lifestyle; all my housing and food and medical needs were taken care of. I lived day by day with no plan other than making a career in the Navy.

Unfortunately, and much to my surprise, what didn't suit me was naval aviation. It was the flying—doing all manner of aerial acrobatics in a powerful jet aircraft that one moment shoved me back in my seat with breathtaking force and the next moment had me hanging upside down with my harness straps digging into the flesh of my chest and groin, and the next minute slapping me against the sides of the cockpit—that didn't agree with me. I was puking constantly, and when I had nothing left to upchuck, the urge didn't go away. Within a year I "turned in my wings," which meant I took off the gold winged badge I had proudly worn on my chest. With real disappointment, I put the emblem on the desk of my superior officer and told him I no longer wanted to fly.

The Navy had invested a lot of money in training me and reluctantly accepted my decision. My commanding officer understood that I had tried my best and was strongly motivated, but I just wasn't aviator material. The puke told it all. With that avenue behind me, I was given a new job. I would be sent to sea to serve on ships.

In order to prepare me for this new assignment, I was asked if I'd like to go to language school and become an international expert of sorts. I couldn't have been happier with the offer, and I fervently requested language training in German, French, or Russian. I made it clear that the one language I didn't want was Arabic. I never wanted to return to Arabia.

However, when I reported to the Defense Language Institute in Monterey, California, I was put in an Arabic class–in direct disregard of my desires and expectations. I fumed with the decision, but couldn't do anything about it. Like it or not, I was going to learn Arabic.

Although I wasn't aware of it at the time, this was the first thread in the series of events that would alter my life in profound ways.

The year in Monterey was wonderful! Having spoken Arabic fluently in my youth, I quickly rose to the top of the class. The sounds of Arabic came back to me quickly, and I was soon able to put sounds to letters and words.

To cap my time in Monterey, I met a beautiful and charming young woman who was in German language training. We often saw each other in the cafeteria, then started dating, and after a few months I proposed to her. Thankfully, she said yes. We were married in January 1977, at her family's home in Vermont.

Following a year of intensive Arabic classes, I received orders to join a Sixth Fleet airwing in Athens, Greece. That was to serve as my home base as I traveled around the Mediterranean. Surprisingly, just as I was about to leave Monterey, those orders were cancelled. I was ordered to Rota, Spain, where the naval base provided support to Sixth Fleet ships in the Mediterranean and occasionally to the small, three-ship contingent of the Navy's Middle East Force in the Indian Ocean. The change in orders was the next unexpected thread to be woven into my life's tapestry. Had my initial assignment to Athens remained operative, much of what subsequently transpired would never have come about.

Spain, October 1978

"The Captain wants to see you," Petty Officer Rita informed me as he passed the command duty officer's desk. I was cleaning up the duty desk as I wrapped up my stint as the midnight duty officer, preparing to turn over the desk's responsibilities to the next junior officer who was due to arrive for the day shift.

"No way! Why would the captain want to see me? I've done nothing he'd want to talk to me about, and I'm just coming just off the night shift and heading home," I replied defensively. It had been a long shift, and I was exhausted.

"Look, Heusinkveld, you got an oh-nine-hundred with Captain Pearce and you better get your rear end over to the command building now!"

Despondently I walked out of the operations building, taking advantage of dawn's dim half-light to carefully maneuver around numerous puddles that had formed from the night's storm. I had to hold on to my hat to keep it from getting blown into a wet patch. I couldn't help feeling quite apprehensive, although I had no reason to be so.

My mind was reeling as I tried to imagine why the commanding officer had ordered me, personally, to come to his office. Officers at my level only saw the captain for very good news—or very bad news. My mind played with the latter option. The "Old Man" had eight hundred sailors and fifteen hundred family members to think about; why would he want to see me?

My life was about to take another major transformation, but I didn't see it coming.

The captain greeted me and instructed me to sit down.

"There's a grave state of affairs developing in the Red Sea," he began. "Strategic sea lanes are under threat due to a prolonged war between Somalia and Ethiopia. The two countries border the narrow straits connecting the Indian Ocean to the Red Sea, known as the 'Bab-el-Mandeb.' A large portion of the world's oil and commerce passes through those straits. We are particularly concerned because the Soviet Union, using their Cuban surrogates, is involved in the fighting. The Soviets and Cubans are supporting Somalia, which is fighting our ally, Ethiopia. Today, Washington tasked the *USS Davis* to monitor the situation and ordered our command to provide support for that ship."

His voice became slow, commanding: "I'd like you to volunteer to lead a team of eight men on a mission aboard the *USS Davis*, cruising off the coast of Ethiopia for three months." He didn't elaborate on the mission.

After his speech was over, I paused briefly to think it over.

"Yes," I replied, since that was clearly expected of me. As a young officer trying to make my mark, I really had no choice but to "volunteer." Having accepted the assignment, I was expected to make a hasty exit.

"But..." I continued, being bold—or stupid—enough to add a condition to my volunteering. The captain's eyes widened in surprise, as if his well-orchestrated day was about to be severely disrupted.

"I request that if the ship were to go to Oman, I would be pulled off of it."

The captain, taken aback by my impertinence, looked perturbed and puzzled.

I quickly explained that as a child I had lived in Oman, and although I had loved the country, my family had suffered a tragedy there, and I had vowed never to return. I added that there was substantial reason for me to feel a certain amount of physical threat were I to return. I didn't go into greater detail.

He contemplated my unusual request and finally agreed. He then shook my hand, wished me well, and indicated that it was time for me to leave his office.

After a week of hasty and intense preparations, I boarded the *USS Davis* with my team of sailors. We made our way through the Mediterranean, the Suez Canal, and the Red Sea, and eventually swept into the Indian Ocean.

The heat, humidity and languid boredom of the Red Sea and Indian Ocean were overpowering. For two months we saw no ports of call, except for a dozen brief refueling stops in the abject and lonely port of Djibouti. While docked there, no one was allowed to go ashore. The crew was restless. In response, the command officer, Captain Flanagan, decided we needed some rest and relaxation, so he arranged for a late-December visit to a port with a well-deserved reputation for fun. Accordingly, we set course for Mombasa, Kenya, for a two-week stay.

The fleet admiral flew into town to participate in the port visit and, unexpectedly, he decided to board our ship and sail with us for a few weeks. Having an admiral on a relatively small ship—our crew consisted of just 170 sailors—put everyone on edge as we did our best to accommodate him.

When the ship was departing Mombasa in early January, Captain Flanagan received an urgent message from headquarters directing the ship to change its scheduled course and proceed immediately to Muscat, Oman.

Dumbstruck, angry, and frightened, I dispatched a person-to-person message to Captain Pearce in Rota reminding him of his promise that I would not have to go to Oman. He responded acknowledging his promise but, stating his regrets, said he could think of no way to get me off the ship since we had no more port visits.

Frustrated, I requested a formal meeting with Captain Flanagan, which took place in his stateroom. Such a meeting was unusual, and when he saw me in my best uniform, he must have wondered what in the world was going on.

Captain Flanagan listened patiently as I retold the story I had told Captain Pearce and related Pearce's promise. After some thought he said, "You must realize that when Captain Pearce made his promise, no one could have foreseen this change in plans coming from our superiors."

I stared at him.

"You must realize there isn't another Navy ship within a thousand miles, so I can't have you transferred to another ship."

"Could you arrange for the ship to stop at some port along the way?" I asked in desperation.

"There is simply no way to get you off this ship; you're going to Oman. You need to understand that I now have an admiral aboard, and that's a lot of extra pressure. I need every ship's hand possible. Paul, you need to grow up!" he stated with stern finality. And that was that. Willy-nilly, I was going to Oman.

Of course, as I thought about it, I realized that he was right on both counts: unloading me was an impossibility, and I needed to face my demons like an adult. As circumstances demanded, I did as he requested.

As our ship cruised north toward Muscat, I had no idea that the threads of my life were converging. In hindsight, I should have noted the pattern of events that was building, but at the time I couldn't see it.

By the time Oman's jagged shoreline rose above the ocean's horizon, my anxiety had built to a fever pitch. Reminiscences and long-suppressed emotions flooded into my mind, and I was nearly overcome by their intensity. I had buried so much in my memory that it felt like a scab being pulled off an almost-healed wound.

Muscat's all-too familiar harbor, bordered by steep stone mountains on either side of its narrow entrance, added to the sense that something dramatic was taking place. Two ancient forts, built in the 1500s by Portuguese seafarers, stood atop the crags on each side of the bay. In honor of the admiral aboard our ship, salutatory cannon blasts thundered from the fort's crenelated ramparts as we glided into the harbor and dropped anchor.

On our second night in the port of Muscat, the admiral hosted a gala reception aboard the ship's afterdeck. Local dignitaries—government officials, businessmen, community elders—were invited. The ship's crew was all dressed in fancy white uniforms for the momentous event. The vessel was on show, representing the power and dignity of the United States of America.

Navy tradition was evident as each new arriving dignitary was announced over the ship's public address system and escorted aboard with military decorum. As an officer I was one of the greeters, and it was my job to mingle with the dignitaries, make small talk, and ensure that they felt welcome and had a memorable evening with a positive view of America.

As the evening wore on, I was surprised to see the Reverend Jay Kapenga come aboard. He was a missionary with the Arabian

Mission in Muscat and an old family friend who had been a close colleague of my parents. In fact, he and his wife, Midge, were with my father and mother the night Dad died. I had not seen him since.

I talked to Jay for some time, catching up on the mission's news. I made sure that the conversation was casual, almost aloof. We talked about his children and my brothers and how they had all found a way in the world. It had been years since we had seen each other, and I was just passing through. I didn't want to dredge up unpleasant memories, so I steered the conversation into safe harbors.

Later, surprisingly, I spotted Jay talking to Captain Flanagan.

After the party was over Captain Flanagan took me aside.

"I met a certain Jay Kapenga tonight," he related, "an interesting character. He told me about your father and asked if he could take you to your father's grave." I was stunned, unable to protest. This conversation was not going well, and I didn't know how to stop it. "Jay said the only way to get to the cove which shelters the 'foreigners' cemetery is by sea. I've arranged for you to meet him on the after-deck at seven tomorrow morning, and I'll have my captain's gig ready and waiting to take you both to the cove." It was an order, not an invitation. My worst nightmare was playing out, right in front of me, and I couldn't wake up.

By the time Jay arrived on board the following morning, a crew of four sailors had already lowered the captain's gig into the water and was waiting for us to join them. I felt self-conscious and embarrassed that these sailors had "voluntarily" given up a day of liberty to take me to Cemetery Cove. Especially since it was against my will and better judgment.

The ocean was completely flat, the light breeze not strong enough to build up any waves as we set off. No one spoke.

Hugging the shoreline, the water was so flat and clear that the rocky bottom was brilliantly visible and we could see fish, including sharks, cruising lazily in the depths below. After half an hour of silent sailing, we came to the bay's entrance. It was surrounded by mountains so steep that the only access to the inlet was by sea. Halfway into the cove, the boat jerked to a lurching halt. The propeller had become entangled in some old fishing nets and ropes which floated beneath the water's surface. The crew struggled successfully to free the boat, but fearing further entanglement, they told me the gig could go no further. Their decision was reasonable, but by now I was distraught at having gotten so close to the small beach where the cemetery lay. I could just see a score of stark, white gravestones on the distant shore. One was my father's.

"We're going to swim in," Jay announced in a decisive manner, countenancing no objection. "You've come half way around the world to do this, we're not giving up now!" He made this pronouncement as if I had intended, all along, to join the Navy and sail the world, take Arabic language training, shift my orders from the Sixth Fleet to the Middle East Force Fleet, take on a boring tour of duty off Somalia, invite an admiral to join our ship, dock in Muscat, invite Jay Kapenga aboard, commandeer the captain's gig, and float out to this desolate cove just to see my father's grave.

Reluctantly, I stripped to my underwear. Jay was already ahead of me as we splashed into the bitter, cold water. The gentle winter breeze made our swim especialy frigid. Thirty feet beneath us, we could clearly see the sharp edges of the rock-strewn bottom. Fish, both large and small, swam back and forth eyeing these aliens in their midst. Sharks circled ominously.

At last we arrived on shore, shivering from the cold. Barefoot, hugging myself to warm up, I staggered around the graveyard until I found my father's grave marker. Silently, I stood over it, reading his name on the plaque, dumbfounded by its simple reality. This was his last resting place. This was it. I had never seen his grave, never returned to Oman after his death. For the last decade, my family had intentionally avoided mentioning his name, his death, his life, our life together with him. What had become a vanishing myth, now lay before me in stark reality.

The reality of seeing Dad's grave broke my heart. For half an hour I gave in to the long-suppressed sorrow, releasing pent-up feelings that had had nowhere to go for ten years. I had left all of my life with him behind and had constructed a new life without him. My remorse was irrepressible.

Yet, unexpectedly, those short moments witnessed the birth of a new self in me. In a matter of thirty cleansing minutes I was able to integrate my past and present selves. I felt whole, alive, with incredible clarity of mind. Physically, it felt like a huge weight had been lifted off of my shoulders.

The same dreams and ideals that had carried my father from Minnesota farm boy to missionary doctor now filled me. Somewhat oddly—considering where I stood—I felt a sense of joy, a vital connection to my father, to something important. I felt a sense of mission.

I knew I had to return to Arabia in the near future—it was a clear calling, one which echoed my dad's clarity so many years ago.

The new vision of myself and what I was to do with my life did not fade with time. If anything, it became clearer. I applied to take the Foreign Service examination with the goal of entering the State Department and using my experience in Arabia and my Arabic language skills to return to the Middle East. I did return— for three decades—serving in diplomatic posts in Kuwait, Saudi Arabia, Israel, Syria, and Bahrain.

The intertwining threads of my life have come together in an intricate tapestry. Growing up as an Arabic-speaking missionary kid, finding ways to live comfortably in several cultures at once, flying kites with my father in the arid deserts of Arabia, taking long walks with him while sharing life's imponderables, playing elephant baseball with boarding school buddies in the teeming jungle of South India, and serving with pride my native country have all set their marks on my life's path. The resulting tapestry has guided me since that fateful day on the banks of a frigid Indian Ocean cove where I stood next to a white tombstone with my father's name etched deeply on its face.

Index